Strange Felicity

Strange Felicity

Eudora Welty's Subtexts on Fiction and Society

Naoko Fuwa Thornton

PRAEGER

Westport, Connecticut
London

Library of Congress Cataloging-in-Publication Data

Thornton, Naoko Fuwa, 1943–
     Strange felicity : Eudora Welty's subtexts on fiction and society / Naoko Fuwa Thornton.
     p. cm.
     ISBN 0–275–98048–0 (alk. paper)
     1. Welty, Eudora, 1909– —Political and social views.   2. Literature and society—
United States—History—20th century.   3. Welty, Eudora, 1909–   —Technique.
4. Social problems in literature.   5. Narration (Rhetoric).   I. Title.
     PS3545.E6Z88   2003
     813′.52—dc21   2003042081

British Library Cataloguing in Publication Data is available.

Library of Congress Catalog Card Number: 2003042081
ISBN: 0–275–98048–0

First published in 2003

Praeger Publishers, 88 Post Road West, Westport, CT 06881
An imprint of Greenwood Publishing Group, Inc.
www.praeger.com

Printed in the United States of America

The paper used in this book complies with the
Permanent Paper Standard issued by the National
Information Standards Organization (Z39.48–1984).

10 9 8 7 6 5 4 3 2 1

Acknowledgment is made to Russell & Volkening, Inc., literary representatives, for permission to quote from the copyrighted works of Eudora Welty.

The Collected Stories of Eudora Welty: Reprinted by the permission of Russell & Volkening as agents for the author. Copyright © 1941 by Eudora Welty, renewed 1969 by Eudora Welty.

The Robber Bridegroom: Reprinted by the permission of Russell & Volkening as agents for the author. Copyright © 1942 by Eudora Welty, renewed 1970 by Eudora Welty.

Delta Wedding: Reprinted by the permission of Russell & Volkening as agents for the author. Copyright © 1945, 46 by Eudora Welty, renewed 1973, 74 by Eudora Welty.

The Golden Apples: Reprinted by the permission of Russell & Volkening as agents for the author. Copyright © 1947 by Eudora Welty, renewed 1975 by Eudora Welty.

The Ponder Heart: Reprinted by the permission of Russell & Volkening as agents for the author. Copyright © 1954 by Eudora Welty, renewed 1982 by Eudora Welty.

The Bride of the Innisfallen and Other Stories: Reprinted by the permission of Russell & Volkening as agents for the author. Copyright © 1955 by Eudora Welty, renewed 1983 by Eudora Welty.

Losing Battles: Reprinted by the permission of Russell & Volkening as agents for the author. Copyright © 1970 by Eudora Welty, renewed 1988 by Eudora Welty.

The Optimist's Daughter: Reprinted by the permission of Russell & Volkening as agents for the author. Copyright © 1972 by Eudora Welty.

The Eye of the Story: Selected Essays and Reviews: Reprinted by the permission of Russell & Volkening as agents for the author. Copyright © 1979 by Eudora Welty.

I wish to acknowledge permission from the following journals to reproduce, with some changes, materials previously published: chapter 5 (under the title "A Hilarious Destruction: *The Ponder Heart* as a Metanarrative"), *Southern Quarterly* 36, no. 1 (Fall 1997); chapter 6, *Japan Women's University Studies in English and American Literature* 34 (March 1999); chapter 7, *Nihon Joshidaigaku Kiyo: Bungakubu,* no. 50 (March 2001); chapter 8, *Studies in American Literature* 33 (March 1997), American Literature Society of Japan; chapter 9, *Studies in English Literature* (English no. 1998), English Literary Society of Japan.

We were a rim of fire, a ring on the sea. His ship was a moment's gleam on a wave. The little son, I knew, was to follow—follow and slay him. That was the story. For whom is a story enough? For the wanderers who will tell it—it's where they must find their strange felicity.

—Eudora Welty, "Circe"

The text also points obliquely to literature, speaking of itself as a literary effect—and thereby exceeding the literature of which it speaks. But is it not necessary for all literature to exceed literature? What would be a literature that would be only what it is, literature? It would no longer be itself if it were itself. This is also part of the ellipsis of "Before the Law." Surely one could not speak of "literariness" as a *belonging to* literature, as of the inclusion of a phenomenon or object, even a work, within a field, a domain, a region whose frontiers would be pure and whose titles indivisible. The work, the opus, does not belong to the field, it is the transformer of the field.

—Jacques Derrida, "Before the Law"

For Ron

Contents

Acknowledgments

This book would not have come into being without the help and encouragement of a number of people and institutions. Among them I especially wish to thank Rikutaro Fukuda, professor emeritus of the Tokyo University of Education, who encouraged me to pursue an academic career when I was still an undergraduate at Japan Women's University and who all these years has been my mentor in literary scholarship and has provided valuable advice and encouragement. Thanks are also due to Tomohisa Shimizu, my former senior colleague at Japan Women's University, who has given me continuous moral support for my academic projects, even since his retirement. I am grateful also to my colleagues in the English Department of Japan Women's University for their understanding and encouragement, and to Japan Women's University itself for granting me a year's leave in 1998–99, during which time I was able to do the major part of the research for this book.

My thanks are also due to Professor Noel Polk at the University of Southern Mississippi and Professor Peggy Whitman Prenshaw at Louisiana State University, both of whom read the manuscript at its earliest stage and encouraged me to seek publication, and to Barry Blose and Jan Nordby Gretlund, who gave me valuable practical advice while I was seeking publication. I also wish to thank deeply Suzanne I. Staszak-Silva, acquisitions editor at Greenwood Publishing Group, and the anonymous reviewers for Greenwood, whose kind efforts have led to the publication of the book in this final form.

My heartfelt gratitude is due to my husband, Ronald Thornton, who gave me constant moral support and contributed many hours checking my manuscript, and to our two sons, Takeshi Arthur and Peter Guy, whose unreserved criticism also improved my manuscript.

Yet my strongest expression of gratitude must go to the late Miss Welty, for her remarkable stories and novels, which have proven to me how literary art like hers can transcend cultures and become an enduring source of personal enrichment and scholarly inspiration. The depth of emotion her works inspire in me and the memory of a delightful visit my family and I had with her at her Jackson home on a bright June afternoon in 1989 are treasures I will always hold dear.

Introduction

One of the assumptions of the various narrative theories proposed by such scholars as Todorov, the early Barthes, Greimas, Doležel, and Iser is that a narrative is a complex construction loaded with meanings rising from multilayered semantic structures. Indeed, from their viewpoints, it is due to this depth of layered meanings that readers and students of literature find pleasure and worth in time spent on novels and stories. The idea of layered structures implies that even if we do not suppose any stratified order among the structures, there should be the "surface" structure, under which other various structures exist. For those who have been baptized in so-called poststructuralism and postmodernism, however, the "surface" structure is a vulnerable concept, since what one calls the "surface" story of a text is based solely on one's interpretive act; another reader, or the same reader at another moment, may identify a story on another level of structures to be the "surface" story.

The supposition that there may be an indefinite number of "surface" stories, however, does not nullify the concept of the "surface" story itself. Rather, it confirms that any act of interpretation assumes the existence of a "surface" story, beyond which one seeks further meaning. The present book supposes that a text is a semantic amalgamation of an indefinite number of "subtexts," which have nebulous boundaries but can be distinctly recognized by the reader's interpretive act. The "surface" story is, as this book also supposes, one of the "subtexts" the semantic details of which the reader interprets as most generally given by the text and *beyond* which his or her further

analytical and interpretive efforts are to be projected. It does not suggest by any means that there should be any single "surface" story of
a text that can be objectively recognized, for any "surface" story is
also a product of subjective interpretation. With this understanding,
this book explores two specific kinds of subtext in Eudora Welty's
prose fictions, namely, the subtexts on fiction and the subtexts on
society.

Welty's fictions quite frequently create an impression that they are
telling us, among other things, something about themselves as fictions.
In such fictions one recognizes under what can be considered the
surface story the power of that particular form of fiction she has chosen
by which to achieve whatever result she desires, or, more broadly, one
discovers her ideas about such general issues as the power of fiction
or the role of fiction for the reader as well as the author.

When Welty was writing, the terms "metafiction" or "self-reflexive
fiction," now used almost synonymously, had not yet been born.[1] Nor
can Welty's fictions that reveal authorial ideas about fiction be necessarily categorized as "metafiction," which, as defined by Patricia
Waugh (to take one example), is "fictional writing which self-
consciously and systematically draws attention to its status as an arte-
fact in order to pose questions about the relationship between fiction
and reality" (2). Yet in the theoretical analysis of this subgenre, which
Waugh recognizes as constituting one kind of "postmodernist" fictions, she makes an ahistorical reference: "Metafiction is a tendency
or function inherent in *all* novels" (3). In a similar purport, Raymond
Federman argues in his essay "Self-Reflexive Fiction":

> Certainly self-reflexiveness and self-consciousness are not new in the
> novel. They are not inventions of the 1960s and 1970s. In fact, all works
> of fiction are ultimately about themselves, about their process of com-
> ing into being and maintaining existence. That much any careful reader
> of fiction knows. Whether self-reflecting or simply reflecting, a work of
> fiction continually turns back on itself and draws the reader into itself
> as a text, as an ongoing narration, and before the reader knows what is
> happening, the text is telling him about itself. That is the fundamental
> truth of all fictions: it is always *implicitly* reflexive. (1142–43)

These sweeping statements neatly characterize what I will refer to as
Welty's metafictional, or self-reflexive, fictions, fictions constituting just
such instances in which this quality particularly stands out.

Despite the fact that all of Welty's fictional writings available so far
date from before William H. Gass's coinage of "metafiction" in 1970,[2]

Welty's critics have discerned in her fictions a concern for and interest in the role and status of fiction and fiction writing, especially since
poststructuralist and postmodernist theories incited the self-exploratory reviewing of social and cultural activities. Among such criticisms,
Danièle Pitavy-Souque's classic essay "Technique as Myth: The Structure of *The Golden Apples*" (1979), drawing on Jean Ricardou's remark on the *nouveau roman* that "great narratives can be recognized
in that the story they tell is nothing but the dramatization of their own
functioning" (267), considers *The Golden Apples* (1949) as consisting
of narratives that are "dramatizations of the functioning of the myth
of Perseus—the essential theme of the book" (267). Noel Polk, in his
"Welty, Hawthorne, and Poe: Men of the Crowd and the Landscape
of Alienation" (1996), views Welty's "Old Mr. Marblehall" (1941) as
an example of that modernist fiction in which the alienated modern
man's identity as a character is constructed solely out of language,
testifying to the process of modernist fiction that "feeds upon but is
not by any means tied to the real" (262). Michael Kreyling in his
"Eudora Welty as Novelist: A Historical Approach" (1998) parallels
Welty's process of forming her first novel *Delta Wedding* (1946), with
its main characters' personal development and states: "Welty cleverly
pushes empirical and self-reflexive registers upon each other; *Delta
Wedding* is, therefore, both a novel and a novel about 'the novel'"
(16). Richard Gray's "Needing to Talk: Language and Being in *Losing Battles*" (1998) relates what the characters achieve through talking to the author's use of words in the novel, and ultimately to what
the use of words might mean.

Waugh's and Federman's idea that all literary texts are inherently
self-reflexive derives from the assumptions that a text contains various
buried subtexts and that through one of those subtexts, or multiple
subtexts, the text is speaking on behalf of the author about itself, or
about the fiction or literature of which it is an example. This book
identifies in Welty's fictions the kind of subtext that deals with such
intrinsically literary issues as language, fiction, readership, and authorship as they are embodied in the particular fiction. My selections from
Welty's fictions for this kind of subtext include some of which the
metafictional aspects have already received extensive critical attention,
such as the criticisms cited above, but on which I hope my argument
will shed a somewhat different light.

There is, moreover, in Welty's fictions yet another kind of subtext,
one that brings to light the social situation in which the particular text
has come into being. This kind of subtext may be called the social

subtext, to be distinguished from the first kind, which I would call the literary subtext. This second kind of subtext carries a social message or offers a social observation that the author for some reason or other has chosen not to express outright but rather to bury under the surface to be excavated by the reader. This kind of subtext testifies to one role of fiction, the provision of a space to accommodate the author's motivation for expressing ideas that might unnecessarily make wary or turn away the reader were they not offered under the camouflage of the surface story—ideas that become more amenable to the reader's attention if they are excavated as part of the natural process of unguarded reading. This device is particularly well exploited by Welty when her ultimate purpose is a critical exposé of contemporary social realities, the kind of theme in her fictions that I believe many of her readers, blinded by her ostensibly nontendentious surface stories, have tended to belittle, or even overlook. When we consider the period of Southern history in which Welty lived and the kind of censures she faced as a writer, we recognize that the social subtexts demonstrate a particularly important role of fiction for her. In this sense, although I distinguish between the literary and the social subtexts, what I call the social subtext may well be identified as just another aspect of the "implicitly reflexive" quality of fiction, as Federman describes it above.

Preliminary to the discussions on Welty's literary and social subtexts, one may ask why the fiction genre inherently invites such self-exploratory issues concerning its own role and status. Within the scope of an introduction, I allow myself two points in response, points that are closely related to the forthcoming discussions on Welty's fictions.

The first derives from fiction's lack of a stable generic canon. This lack should not be considered negative. It was in this lack that Virginia Woolf saw a fertile virgin land for women writers. Advocating a kind of women's writing that would be different from men's, Woolf insists, in *A Room of One's Own* (1929), that "all the older forms of literature were hardened and set by the time she became a writer. The novel alone was young enough to be soft in her hands—another reason, perhaps, why she wrote novels. Yet who shall say that even now 'the novel' (I give it inverted commas to mark my sense of the words' inadequacy), who shall say that even this most pliable of all forms is rightly shaped for her use?" (116).

Around the same time in the Soviet Union, Mikhail Bakhtin, constructing his ideas about the novel, found the same aspect of the status of the novel to be valid and fertile for male writers as well. Bakhtin argues that the most prominent uniqueness of the novel genre is its being still "uncompleted":

> Of all the major genres only the novel is younger than writing and the book: it alone is organically receptive to new forms of mute perception, that is, to reading. But of critical importance here is the fact that the novel has no canon of its own, as do other genres, *only individual examples of the novel are historically active*, not a generic canon as such. Studying other genres is analogous to studying dead languages; studying the novel, on the other hand, is like studying languages that are not only alive, but still young. ("Epic," 3, emphasis added)

In this sense, each prose fiction, or in Bakhtin's terminology, "novel," embodies an effort to justify its existence as representing and contributing to the genre. At the same time it repudiates for itself the possibility of any exclusive representation and contribution, admitting all other fictions as representing and contributing to the genre as well. This "democratic" nature is the core of the genre. Just as democracy rejects any monolithic ideology to control the state except democracy itself—democracy being theoretically nothing but an ideology simply to ensure a process by which all current ideologies can be heard—the fiction genre only ensures a space that can accommodate any literary product of the creative imagination, free from constraints of pre-existing literary canons. Democracy does not envision any ultimate political destination but rather lets itself pursue a voyaging without destination, selecting only what suits the current desires of the passengers most effectively. Bakhtin's observation about the novel's mode of existence, if you will, parallels that of this political system: "It is a genre that is ever questing, ever examining itself and subjecting its established forms to review" ("Epic," 39). This inherent contradiction within the fiction genre, namely, its perpetual questioning of the validity of what it has achieved and of what it is attempting, is one of the sources of the genre's youthfulness. Each production of fiction is the writer's individual response to this contradiction, destined to be perceived by the receptive reader.

The second point concerns fiction's relation to reality. Although we may accept that fiction inherently possesses no canon of its own, there is one quality essential to the genre, namely, that of its being a lie: a fiction constructs with words an unreality, an illusion. Yet at the same time, a fiction ostensibly attempts to "sound like the real." Even if the setting and the course of events are too outrageous to be true, the fiction writer expects some components, if not all, in the fiction to be taken by the reader as truthful—such as a character's interiority, if not his or her speech and actions; an archetypal human relationship, if not an actual relationship; an inevitable historical development to come, if not one having already happened; and so on. If reality is truth and unreality is untruth, how should we accept the fiction writer's success in creating a certain truth? Perhaps we never actually do. Perhaps we know that any truth a fiction seems to present is after all an illusion, but again, perhaps it is something that does not matter to us very much. Writing and reading a fiction must absorb this contradiction of creating an unreality as if it were a reality, and of reading it with the full knowledge of its being unreal.

So far, I have been using the word "reality" quite loosely, as if to say there is such an autonomous state called "reality," a state that possesses its own substance and order, and that, more importantly, "preexists" fiction. No one doubts there is a material world existing beyond fiction, but the question is how one can conceive of it. For instance, Harold Bloom in his *Shakespeare: The Invention of the Human* (1998) takes an extreme position: "Shakespeare will go on explaining us, in part because he invented us. . . . The dominant Shakespearean characters—Falstaff, Hamlet, Rosalind, Iago, Lear, Macbeth, Cleopatra among them—are extraordinary instances not only of how meaning gets started, rather than repeated, but also of how new modes of consciousness come into being" (xviii). In other words, Bloom's contention is that most human emotions were defined and exemplified by the Bard for generations of writers to come, in effect suggesting that since he showed us in his plays and poems what love is, we have come to know when we are in love. Or, when one says, "My life has been happy," the temporal and spatial expanses encompassed by "my life" and the kind and the degree of the feeling to which the word "happy" corresponds may have derived most readily from the fictions one has read. This is true even in the case of much more concrete occurrences in the material world. An automobile accident one comes upon, for instance, is an occurrence that one constructs by selecting certain items from a mass of items existing at a certain time and place, and the conditions for selecting these and discarding the rest are based on some preexisting set of items called "an auto accident." From this viewpoint we can even say that through preexisting fiction we conceive of reality.

This hierarchical confusion between reality and fiction leads to the recognition of fiction's capacity to affect reality, namely, that fiction can influence our way of conceiving of reality and of understanding the society and the world we live in. This may be the reason why dictators and totalitarian governments in history have feared and hence persecuted certain fiction writers, whose achievements have been nothing but compositions of unreal, imaginary stories and novels, sometimes about situations quite remote from their societies. Thus persistent concerns of metafictional writing include the meaning of reality and its relation to fiction, and the role of fiction in social realities. Welty's fictions taken up in this book reveal the author's ideas about these subjects. Sometimes the main theme of the fiction can be interpreted as one of the subjects indicated above, and sometimes two or three seriously literary and social questions are interwoven under an ostensibly carefree story.

As the following chapters will demonstrate, the two kinds of Welty's subtext I am identifying in this book—the literary and the social—are not incompatible one with the other and in fact quite often intermingle to constitute a single subtext. This book does not attempt a comprehensive review of Welty's oeuvre but selects works pertinent to my theme. Nor does it include Welty's nonfictional writings such as her essays, reviews and autobiographical essays, save when I consult them in connection with the fictions I am considering. The arrangement of my discussions is based not on the order of publication of the works but on the direction in which each fiction's literary/social concern takes it. Yet by devoting attention to these particular aspects of the fictions selected from different stages of Welty's literary career, I also hope to bring out what has undergone change and what has remained constant through the years in Welty's ideas about what she is doing as a fiction writer. These fictions do not offer any systematic theoretical argument about fiction, but I believe they embody a kind of convincing testimonies about the felicity of writing and reading fiction that none of the theories I refer to in this book can provide.

PART I

Speaking For: Race

CHAPTER 1

❦

The Smoke and
Safety-Valve of "Powerhouse"

The first paragraph of Welty's story "Powerhouse" (1941) consists of this one sentence: "Powerhouse is playing!" (131). What Powerhouse plays is not specified. The second paragraph tells us that Powerhouse is playing, for one thing, the piano. Yet this paragraph and all those that follow point to various other things that Powerhouse is "playing" and suggest the weight of the first sentence–paragraph upon the whole of the story. Apart from simply performing music, Powerhouse's "playing" refers to the word's most basic meaning—that is, being engaged in having fun, and in this case the fun is his improvisation as he performs jazz. To play can also mean to make use of double entendres or of the similarity in sound of two words for humorous or satirical effect, and Powerhouse certainly does this too. He also "plays" roles, as in dramatic productions, and he feigns and lies. Finally Powerhouse's "playing" signifies "contending," as in a game, with overtones of "fighting." All these meanings of "playing" share one commonality: they imply deflection from or opposition to reality. Ultimately, they challenge reality with a full awareness of the irrationality of such acts, an awareness that I believe constitutes this story's self-reflexivity.

"Powerhouse" is one of the first three of Welty's stories to be published in a major, prestigious magazine of national readership. Since 1937 her stories had been appearing in such local, though also prestigious, journals as *Southern Review* and *Prairie Schooner*, but the acceptance by the *Atlantic Monthly* of "A Worn Path" and "Powerhouse," for its February and June 1941 numbers respectively, and then of "Why I Live at the P.O." for publication in the intervening April number, seemed to mark Welty's truly national debut. Welty must have been delighted by the prospect of seeing three stories published in five months in the *Atlantic*, but she was particularly pleased that it accepted "Powerhouse," which had been rejected by the *New Yorker, Collier's, Harper's Bazaar, Good Housekeeping, Mademoiselle,* and *Harper's,* even by *Southern Review* (Kreyling 1991, 39–40). She wrote to her literary agent Diarmuid Russell: "And to think that THAT magazine is going to print THAT story. You ought to be congratulated twice as hard as I think—at Bead Loaf the unanimous opinion was that NOBODY would EVER buy 'Powerhouse'" (Kreyling 1991, 54). The author had been well aware that "Powerhouse" contained elements and innuendoes that the publishing establishment would likely shun, very much in contrast to the wholesome content of "A Worn Path," although both stories were about "Negroes" and their interactions with local whites.

What had turned the editors against "Powerhouse"? What occurs most readily to our mind is the story's explicit and implicit obscenity. It is well known that the *Atlantic* accepted the story on condition that the last song Powerhouse plays be changed from Welty's original choice, "Hold Tight, I Want Some Seafood, Mama," to "Somebody Loves Me, I Wonder Who!" a substitution that the author in a 1977 interview only half-jokingly termed the *Atlantic*'s "censorship" (Prenshaw 1984, 209). (In this interview Welty calls the song "Somebody Loves *You* . . . ," probably a slip of the tongue.) Alan M. Cohn, reminding the reader of the more explicit lines in the earlier song ("When I come home from work at night, I get my favorite dish—FISH!"), reports that *Time* in April 1939 had decoded the lyrics as "piscivorous allusions to the *pudendum mulierbre*" and notes that "the white establishment had made a hit out of the song while 'Harlemites chuckled,' like tricksters in a folk tale, at the uncomprehending *ofays* [white people]" (75). Even without the final song, the sexual innuendoes of which were already familiar to the white editors when they read Welty's manuscript, "improper" allusions to sexuality and the body, sometimes outright, abound in the story, and it is likely that the editors considered much of such Harlem lingo unfit for their magazines. Yet it is noteworthy that since the story began attracting critical attention in the mid-sixties, most critics have more or less dismissed Welty's pointed emphasis on the uniqueness of African American language and manner and have adopted a "humanistic" view that considers Powerhouse as the universal image of the artist, or everyman, and the story's theme as what art is, or what life is. Alfred Appel, Jr., for example, argues that in "Powerhouse" "one may see [that] a story that is explicitly about one racial group is implicitly about all of us" (221) and that "Powerhouse's attempt to communicate is a paradigm of *all* human isolation" (234). Some critics relate this "universality" to Welty's own stance on art and struggle as an artist, while others extend their scope in varied degrees from the state of the storyteller to the mythological, archetypal image of the artist.[1]

In contrast to those critics, Timothy Dow Adams and Richard N. Albert in separate articles pay special attention to the story's African American elements and see in it the black-white rivalry that existed among jazz musicians in the 1930s. Albert's "Eudora Welty's Fats Waller: 'Powerhouse'" (1987) maintains that articles such as Appel's, pointing out Powerhouse's universality, "gloss over the obvious to seek more deeply implicit ideas" (63). Adams's "A Curtain of Black: White and Black Jazz Styles in 'Powerhouse'" (1977) points out specific instances in this story of the African American jazz musicians' euphemistic expression of resentment of white musicians. Adams equates the fictitious Uranus Knockwood—of whom the blacks in the story say, "He come in when we goes out!"—with real-life white jazzmen such as Benny Goodman, whose "Who Walks In When I Walk Out" had been a hit, and argues that the black-white rivalry in the U.S. jazz scene is reflected in "Powerhouse." Further attention to this context of racial rivalry in the story will reveal, as I intend to show, the kind of self-reflexive quality that this story demonstrates. In this story the literary and the social subtexts are in effect organically fused.

The narrator of "Powerhouse" is not a rigorously Jamesian narrator sustaining a consistent point of view but one who freely crosses the racial divide in the town of Alligator, Mississippi, to follow Powerhouse—an implausible liberty neither a white nor an African American person was likely to enjoy in the Mississippi of the 1930s or 1940s. If this narrator is to be considered omniscient, he or she certainly lacks the kind of dignity that an omniscient narrator is expected to have; the narrator becomes, however omniscient, an excited, ardent fan of Powerhouse, very much like Welty herself admiring Fats Waller at a concert and dance in Jackson. The legendary origin of "Powerhouse"—written, Welty claimed, in one sitting after coming back from the Fats Waller performance—is confirmed in several Welty interviews, but one with John Griffin Jones on 13 May 1981 offers an instructive parallel between this unusual narrator and the enraptured author:

> I loved the music of Fats Waller and had all his records. He played here in Jackson at a program sort of like the one, well just like the one I described. I went and watched him, and I was just captivated by his presence, in addition to the music, which I already knew and was familiar with. . . . Oh, I was listening to them. I was one of those people who were just hanging around listening. . . . I had no idea what they did at intermission. Everything

I wrote is made up except the program itself and the impression it made
on me, both hearing and seeing it. (see Prenshaw 1984, 327–28)

Just like the dazzled Welty, the narrator watches Powerhouse and his men
with amazement and wonder and, when the musicians disappear from the
stage for intermission, follows them—as the author was to do in her fantasy—to the "Negrotown" restaurant, as unfettered as her imagination
allows. Pedantic rules of point of view disappear at this point.

Welty testifies in interviews that she wanted to express how Powerhouse's improvisation works (Prenshaw 1984, 266, 328); so also is the
narrator captivated by the ingenuity of the musician's various improvisa-
tions. Even his physical appearance on first sight seems improvisatorial:
"'Negro man'?—he looks more Asiatic, monkey, Jewish, Babylonian,
Peruvian, fanatic, devil. . . . [L]ooks like a preacher when his mouth is
shut, but then it opens—vast and obscene." He even calls his band members "Tasmanians" (131). Besides all this, of course, he is constantly improvising in his performance.

Improvisation is what lends jazz one of its most unique and basic qualities. It is a paradoxical composite of the individual and the communal:
while it originates from the individual freedom of the respective players,
it has to match and be backed by the playing of the other band members. The narrator observes how Powerhouse and his men deal with this
paradox and cautions him/herself, or the reader, not to miss this process:
"Watch them carefully, hear the least word, especially what they say to
one another, in another language—don't let them escape you" (132). At
the whites' dance, for which they are playing, "Powerhouse and His
Tasmanians" are literally foreigners or strange beings who are kept apart,
living only on an island—the stage—and speaking among themselves in
a strange language, the language that in turn isolates their individuality
and communality from the white audience. They have fun playing with
their code words, whose true meanings the white audience does not suspect. Through the narrator's cautioning, Welty is suggesting that the
whole story is being told in "another language" so that the reader may
become alert to the subtext of codes and double meanings.

Even Powerhouse's choices of tunes from among the audience's requests are relayed to the band members not by their titles but by codes—
numbers or combinations of figures; actually, the audience does not know
whether Powerhouse is truly complying with any of their written requests,
since he is the only one to read them. When the band plays "Pagan Love
Song" as "the only waltz they will ever consent to play" (133),
Powerhouse's excessive demonstration of sadness appears to the careful
reader all the more deceptive and derisive. "Pagan Love Song," popular-

ized by Hollywood in the movie *The Pagan* and the musical film *Pagan Love Song*, became a hit in 1929; its lyrics were written by Arthur Freed and its music by Nacio Herb Brown, a partnership that also produced the memorable "Singin' in the Rain" in the same year. Though feigning sorrow to a preposterous degree—he is *playing*—Powerhouse nevertheless cannot endure the overly sentimental "white" love song and starts improvising on it with genuine African American musicology. He abruptly says: "'I got a telegram my wife is dead.' . . . 'Telegram say—here the words: Your wife is dead.' He puts 4/4 over the 3/4" (133). Powerhouse thus changes the sentimentally sweet lyrics of "Pagan Love Song" to shockingly spare words of catastrophe: over the 3/4 waltz beat, which would correspond to the telegraphic style of "Your wife dead," he chooses the 4/4 blues beat of "Your wife is dead." As Appel suggests, Powerhouse's telegram echoes an old African American work song, "Death Letter Blues," one version of which goes: "Got me a letter, / What you think it read: / 'Come home, come home, / Yo' mammy's dead'" (226).

Powerhouse even discloses who had signed the telegram—a certain Uranus Knockwood. His sidemen playing close to him have quickly caught on to Powerhouse's *playing*, and a lively exchange follows:

> "Say it agin."
> "Uranus Knockwood."
> "That ain't Lenox Avenue."
> "It ain't Broadway."
> "Ain't ever seen it wrote out in any print, even for horse racing."
> "Hell, that's on a star, boy, ain't it?" Crash of the cymbals. (134)

The musicians pretty well run down Uranus Knockwood for not belonging to their celebrated Harlem establishments, such as the Cotton Club, the Lenox Club, Dicky Wells's, or Small's Paradise, to name a few, or to such Broadway clubs as the Roseland Ballroom or the Club Alabam, not even on the horse-race sheets. He belongs to a place somewhere far out in the universe—nowhere. Yet their condemnation of this nosy outsider is to be amplified as the words of the telegram are repeatedly called out through the story; this is an important motif to which I will return later.

Powerhouse's improvisational change from waltz to blues is not limited to changes in the content and beat of the band's music. Welty in effect, though loosely, has Powerhouse and his sidemen demonstrate in their action the classic stanzaic structure of the blues form and its accompanying patterns. Marshall Stearns summarizes the peculiarities of the three-line stanzaic structure of the blues form:

Roughly speaking, the time taken in singing the words of each line is a little more than one half of each of the three equal (musical) parts, which leaves considerable room for an instrumental response after each line. Here is the call-and-response pattern. . . .

The unusual fact about this blues form is that it consists of three parts, instead of two or four. This stanza form is quite rare in English literature and may have originated with the American Negro. Like the ballad stanza, it furnishes a good vehicle for a narrative of any length. At the same time, it is more dramatic: the first two lines set the stage clearly by repetition and the third line delivers the punch. (78–79)

What Powerhouse and his sidemen utter and perform echoes these characteristics: the call-and-response pattern with improvisational additions and the narrative development through repetition and the "punch"—the AAB, CCD, etc., pattern. If we consider the part with Powerhouse's first mention of his wife's death as A, the one with his second mention also as A, and the Uranus Knockwood topic, composed of the band members' communal effort, as B, we see that the same pattern repeats itself through the story as in the blues, each time shifting the emphasis and viewpoint, yet increasingly delving into the core of the bad news. The core revealed by the elaborations is ultimately racial pride.

Powerhouse's first repeated elaboration, incited by his sideman Valentine's remark—"You say you got a telegram"—concerns African American musicians' social status: "Yas, the time I go out, go way downstairs along a long cor-ri-dor to where they puts us: coming back along the cor-ri-dor: steps out and hands me a telegram: Your wife is dead" (134). The point of the elaboration is not really when and where Powerhouse received the telegram but the fact that, offstage, he and his band members are put in some back quarter downstairs, separated from the white audience and the white staff. In the intermission that follows they are not allowed to eat and drink in the hall where they play but are obliged to go out to a Negro restaurant. Powerhouse and his sidemen walk to "Negrotown" in a downpour. One cannot but recall "Singin' in the Rain," the work of Freed and Brown, who collaborated on "Pagan Love Song," the tune hated and ridiculed by Powerhouse earlier. Nor can one fail to notice that Powerhouse and his sidemen's miserable walk in the drenching rain makes a striking contrast with the carefree mood of Freed and Brown's song. The racial discrimination is not limited to these musicians but extends, of course, to all the African American inhabitants of the town of Alligator, Mississippi. The narrator reports that when the musicians start walking, "a hundred dark, ragged, silent, delighted Negroes have come around from under the eaves of the hall, and follow wherever they go" (135). One is reminded that these people could not enter the whites' dance hall to hear their own ethnic music but were forced to stand outside, under the eaves, barely out of the driving rain.

The Negrotown joint they enter is the World Café, Alligator's version of the New Orleans French Quarter landmark the Café du Monde; this is apparently Welty's hint of a tribute to the African American origin of New Orleans Dixieland jazz. In this café, what we can consider the third stanza of Powerhouse's "Death Letter Blues" is *played*. As Adams points out, the selection of the records in the café's nickelodeon disappoints Powerhouse—it offers only songs of white musicians. Actually, these songs are "swing" selections, the kind of white jazz pieces composed and arranged for the "big band" form. These pieces were composed and arranged in compliance with the increasing demand of recording and broadcasting studios for strict observance of performance-time limits, thus allowing considerably less room for improvisation than in the performance of Dixieland, the more nearly original form of jazz. Ironically, those who enjoyed financial success through recording, radio, and film were in reality white performers of this standardized form of jazz, such as Paul Whiteman, Benny Goodman, and Glenn Miller, musicians who imitated African American rhythms but not so much their liberating style of improvisation. When Powerhouse is told that "Tuxedo Junction" on the café's nickelodeon is "You know whose" (136)—that is, Glenn Miller's—his contempt for such music is reflected in his request "to play 'Empty Bed Blues' and let Bessie Smith sing" (136), a request made in vain. Alligator's Café du Monde no longer plays the old Dixieland jazz but at best only such swing pieces as "Sent for You Yesterday and Here You Come Today," probably by Count Basie, the African American swing musician who had been in real life Fats Waller's piano disciple at one time but later became Benny Goodman's right-hand man.

Yet Powerhouse's blues improvisation is again inspired, this time by the café's vivacious African American waitress. Asked by the waitress who they are, Powerhouse responds, "Boogers," and the girl sensibly reacts with a delicate scream of "pleasure": "O Lord, she likes talk and scares" (136), the narrator reports. The third stanza, *played* in the World Café before "the humble beautiful waitress waiting on them" and "all the watching Negroes [who have pressed] in gently and bright-eyed through the door, as many as can get in" (137), is truly African American in narrative style and sense of racial communality.

In the first line of this "stanza," if one may so describe it, Powerhouse depicts, as if he could see the scene in front of him, his wife, Gypsy, becoming so distraught at his absence that she jumps out of the window to the street below to "bust her brains all over the world." Valentine seconds him: "That's it. . . . You gets a telegram" (137). Powerhouse then, as his second line, repeats the suicide scene and elaborates on it—Gypsy shaking all over, listening for her husband's footsteps in vain, getting on her nightgown he knows well, and jumping out the window—and again his sideman ecstatically responds: "Brains and insides everywhere, Lord, Lord" (137). The intense delight in this grotesquerie intoxicates all the local African American spectators, as well as, apparently, the narrator. It is a communal catharsis that overwhelms the mundane sorrows and hardships of African American lives in a Mississippi town.

The "punch" for the third line is Powerhouse's subsequent cry:

> "I even know who finds her," cries Powerhouse. "That no-good pussy-footed crooning creeper, that creeper that follow around after me, coming up like weeds behind me, following around after me everything I do and messing around on the trail I leave. Bets my numbers, sings my songs, gets close to my agent like a Betsy-bug; when I going out he just coming in. I got him now! I got my eye on him."
> "Know who he is?"
> "Why, it's that old Uranus Knockwood!"
> "Ya! Ha!" (137–38)

Adams maintains, as noted earlier, that "Uranus Knockwood" is "intended to stand for all of the white jazzmen who have used African American jazz material for their own gain, coming after the African American jazz creators and following their musical trail" (60). He identifies the "crooning creeper" with Bing Crosby and points out that "Who Walks In When I Walk Out" was Benny Goodman's hit. Adams's claim is well taken; it is certainly in "another language" that Powerhouse communicates with his sidemen and his African American audience.

Although Adams does not go farther into what exactly Powerhouse communicates, decoding the blacks' secret language at this point reveals one of the main themes of the story. Powerhouse's identification of Uranus Knockwood with a song stealer as well as a wife stealer—"'He takes our wives when we gone!'" (138)—indicates that Gypsy is not merely Powerhouse's wife. Rather, Gypsy symbolizes his music—or, more exactly, African Americans' hard-won, beloved treasure, jazz. But this treasure cannot be usurped from them so easily, because, before he carries away Gypsy's lifeless body, Uranus Knockwood has to step into the awful mess of "her insides and brains" (138). He cries out, with Powerhouse mocking him: "Jesus! . . . Look here what I'm walking round in!" (138). To this, the musicians and the audience all burst into wild laughter and a series of hilarious calls and responses starts, both sides knocking the clueless Uranus Knockwood. At the end of this ecstatic chorus, a symbolic Mass is celebrated: "Everybody in the room moans with pleasure.

The little boy in the fine silver hat opens a paper and divides out a jelly roll among his followers" (138). The "jelly roll" is without doubt a tribute to Jelly Roll Morton (1885–1941), the Mississippi-born ragtime and blues pianist of New Orleans who claimed to have invented Dixieland jazz. Sharing a jelly roll is their Holy Communion.

What Welty describes as taking place at the World Café corresponds to some major aspects of what Mikhail Bakhtin calls "carnival." Since the late 1930s Bakhtin had been discussing the ideas that were to mature as the concept of "carnival,"[2] but I am here especially drawing on his two books *Rabelais and His World* and *Problems of Dostoevsky's Poetics*, which expound his theory of carnival and carnivalized writing, namely, that which has in modern society developed into novelistic prose. Yet since what Bakhtin calls "carnival" considerably differs in spirit even between those two books,[3] my references will indicate the specific source whenever necessary. In *Dostoevsky* Bakhtin sums up the basis of his argument:

A person of the Middle Ages lived, as it were, *two lives*: one was the *official* life, monolithically serious and gloomy, subjugated to a strict hierarchical order, full of terror, dogmatism, reverence, and piety; the other was the *life of the carnival square*, free and unrestricted, full of ambivalent laughter, blasphemy, the profanation of everything sacred, full of debasing and obscenities, familiar contact with everyone and everything. Both these lives were legitimate, but separated by strict temporal boundaries. (129–30)

Among the various aspects of carnival that Bakhtin identifies, the World Café scene demonstrates, first of all, the suspension of hierarchical order— that is, "everything resulting from sociohierarchical inequality or any other form of inequality among people (including age)" (Bakhtin, *Dostoevsky,* 123). Everyone is admitted into the World Café, as its name suggests, and can enjoy eating and drinking. If the music the café's nickelodeon can play is limited by racial and social factors, Powerhouse and his sidemen can simply reject it and play their own. The suspension of hierarchical order leads to what Bakhtin calls *"carnivalistic mésalliances,"* or combinations of the sacred with the profane, the lofty with the low, the wise with the stupid. Thus the self-important Uranus Knockwood is laughed at as stupid enough to step into the crushed brains and bowels, like stepping into a pile of dog's dung. Yet the opposite case is also seen as a form of *"parodia sacra"* (Bakhtin, *Rabelais,* 14 and passim), when Jelly Roll Morton (as the self-proclaimed originator of jazz) is compared to Jesus Christ, and the act of dividing out a jelly roll to Holy Communion, with the celebrant of the Mass being merely a boy wearing a "fine silver hat" to signify holy orders.

Another important aspect of the Bakhtinian carnival witnessed in the World Café scene is that of communal performance. As Bakhtin states that "in carnival everyone is an active participant, everyone communes in the carnival act" (Bakhtin, *Dostoevsky,* 122), the action in the café proceeds out of the voluntary participation of the people present. The lively exchanges between the waitress and Powerhouse and then with his sidemen induce Powerhouse's elaboration of Gypsy's suicide, at which "all the watching Negroes stir in their delight" (139). Then follows Welty's masterful reproduction of a spirited call-and-response between Powerhouse and his sidemen concerning Uranus Knockwood:

"Why, he picks her up and carries her off!" he says.
"Ya! Ha!"
"Oh, Powerhouse!"
"You know him."
"Uranus Knockwood!"
"Yeahhh!"
"He takes our wives when we gone!"
"He come in when we goes out!"
"Uh-huh!"
"He go out when we comes in!"
"Yeahhh!"
"He standing behind the door!"
"Old Uranus Knockwood."
"You know him."
"Middle-size man."
"Wears a hat."
"That's him." (138)

Animated by this communal performance, the surrounding audience also joins the animated glorification of their racial pride by acting out the Mass with a jelly roll, as we have seen. The liberated audience is now *playing* their own blues improvisation.

As if in a miracle wrought through the act of sacramentally consuming the body of Jelly Roll Morton, the African American inhabitants of Alligator who have gathered in the World Café exhibit signs of new life. Earlier the deprivation of their racial pride had been suggested by the reality that they cannot enter the hall where their ethnic music is performed and that even in Negrotown the jukebox plays recordings of white performers, some who in effect had stolen the black musicians' hard-won ethnic music. But now one man presents to Powerhouse his half-brother as a "hero" of their local community. Sugar-Stick Thompson—with a sobriquet similar to Jelly Roll Morton's—has saved from drowning fourteen white people who fell out of a boat, just by holding his breath, since he could not swim. Surely this fantastic feat should contain a seed of sub-version of the official racial hierarchy that the African American inhabit-ants of Alligator would proudly embrace and elaborate on. Yet it does not turn out so. Sugar-Stick, being "their instrument" (139), cannot speak. Despite his half-brother's seconding, the story does not trigger any ex-citement, and Sugar-Stick and his half-brother simply step back.

This strange interlude has a significance that should not be overlooked. Its significance derives from the difference between the purported truth-fulness of Sugar-Stick's story and the nontruthfulness of Powerhouse's Gypsy story. Immediately after the interlude, when Powerhouse again starts his Gypsy story, he is questioned by the waitress whether the story is true. Against her wishful expectation, Powerhouse bluntly answers: "No, babe, it ain't the truth" (139). Here Welty suggests one of the themes of "Powerhouse." The author exposes the power of fiction, which is, in this and many other cases, stronger than reality in affecting the human mind. The power of Powerhouse's story is generated by his real anger and sorrow about the situation of one who has been robbed of his *raison d'être*—music—and yet is socially placed lower than the robber. His ge-nius is to use his power of anger and sorrow to create an outrageous fic-tion of vivid characterization and sensual depiction, through which he derides his enemy and involves his fellows in merriment. In contrast, Sugar-Stick's feat is said to be true. Yet Sugar-Stick cannot affect people with what he did, because he is like a musical "instrument," which does not have the power to *play* by itself. To produce an effect an instrument needs a musician who *plays* it.

Powerhouse's next remark concerning the possibility of something worse to come remains a mystery for the time being, and the musicians leave the café when the intermission is over. On their way back to the dance hall, another series of calls and responses starts. Told by Power-house to spell "Uranus Knockwood," the narrator reports that "[his sidemen] spell it all the ways it could be spelled. It puts them in a wonderful humor" (140). Smith Kirkpatrick considers this scene an ex-pression of the creativity of Powerhouse and his group, who "are not con-cerned with arbitrary absolutes of man-made dictionaries" (102). This is not only an expression of their creativity but of the carnival spirit of *deg-radation*—that is, "the lowering of all that is high, spiritual, ideal, abstract; it is a transfer to the material level, to the sphere of earth and body in their indissoluble unity" (Bakhtin, *Rabelais*, 19–20). The narrator leaves the specific spellings of "Uranus" to our imagination. How about "urin-ous," "your anus," "ewe anus," or "you're an ass"? With such puns on the first name in mind, we might even venture to play with "Knockwood," not in the sense of fear of Nemesis's vengeance—"Knock on wood"—

but rather of anal sex, with one's "wood" knocking at another's "back door." Powerhouse's men are *playing* on the sound of the words in their lingo.

Powerhouse's telegraphed answer to the physically malodorous and blockheaded pervert Uranus is also cast in the musician's secret language: "I gotcha" (140) does not mean that Powerhouse has understood and accepted the news of his wife's death but rather that he has fooled Uranus, has got him trapped. He even foretells, again in the African American musicians' cryptic language, that the answer will "reach him and come out the other side" (140). One may assume from Powerhouse's "look of hopeful desire" (140) that this is the thing he earlier described as "something worse to come," although Little Brother has not quite understood the scope of Powerhouse's *play*.

Then, what *is* the "something worse" that might come? What does Powerhouse mean by "come out the other side"? Some critics, including Adams and Albert in their articles mentioned above and William B. Stone in "Eudora Welty's Hydrodynamic 'Powerhouse,'" maintain that Powerhouse is prophesying the victory of the emerging black-controlled "bop," which is technically so demanding that white musicians will not be able to imitate and exploit it very well. Whether or not Welty has intended such a specific meaning, the point remains that Powerhouse is declaring war against the Uranus Knockwoods of the world: he is contending, *he is playing the game.*

The final section of the story shows how Powerhouse plays the game at the white dance hall when he and his musicians return from the intermission. His actions preceding the postintermission performance suggest renewed strategy in every way: the way he tunes up the band, the way he faces the piano—"as if he saw it for the first time in his life" (140)—the way he tests its strength, sound, and even the inside of the piano imply his seriousness in comic disguise. But what he then plays is totally contradictory and illusory:

> He sat down and played it for a few minutes with outrageous force and got it under his power—a bass deep and coarse as a sea net—then produced something glimmering and fragile, and smiled. And who could ever remember any of the things he says? They are just inspired remarks that roll out of his mouth like smoke. (140–41)

The power of Powerhouse as he contends against his adversaries is that of controlling the division between reality and unreality: by erasing this division one can produce glimmerings and fragility out of depth and coarseness. He creates his own world of *carnivalistic mésalliances,* in which the audience, liberated from the divisions and reasonings of daily life, *play* in an illusion. The narrator's observation in the first section of the story that "he sends everybody into oblivion" (132) points to this quality of his performance, and we know now that this is the essence of his power and that he is making full use of it.

As mentioned earlier, the song Powerhouse plays at this final point in the story was not Welty's original choice but the publisher's. Still, Welty has after all used the substituted song of a white musician to great advantage. "Somebody Loves Me, I Wonder Who!" (music by George Gershwin, 1924) was used in three Hollywood musical films—*Rhapsody in Blue, Lullaby of Broadway*, and *Pete Kelly's Blues*—and became a classic of the white entertainment industry. Although the song is at the white audience's request, Powerhouse now strikes back to retrieve his race's music by improvising on it and increasing the voltage of African American musicology: "He's already done twelve or fourteen choruses, piling them up nobody knows how. . . . Now and then he calls and shouts, 'Somebody loves me! Somebody loves me, I wonder who!' His mouth gets to be nothing but a volcano" (141). Here Welty is reproducing Powerhouse's real blues-form singing, with its repetition and last "punch": his last words—"' . . . Maybe it's you!'"—are directed at the white audience, implying they are now entrapped in the rapture of love for his music, just as he had entrapped his African American audience at the World Café in a carnival world of illusion. Finally, these words are the fiction writer's proud words, which, like Powerhouse's, have no real substance but are "like smoke," directed at "you," the reader.

My associating Powerhouse's power of performance over his listeners with what Bakhtin calls the energies of carnival does not mean that my argument totally follows Bakhtin's concept of carnival. While Bakhtin, strongly influenced by historical materialism, emphasizes the materiality and reality of *both* the official and the carnival lives of medieval and Renaissance people, Welty in "Powerhouse" focuses on the unreality of what Bakhtin would call the nonofficial life. For Welty, it is the illusory quality of Powerhouse's creations that liberates the people from the constraints and boundaries of their official lives and cosmic solitude and affirms their communal existence. Yet this difference does not derive from a phenomenal difference but rather from a cognitive one; the Bakhtinian concept of carnival effectively explains an important aspect of Powerhouse's power.

Bakhtin's view of carnival has been one of the most controversial of his contentions. One of the questions related to the point of my argument concerns the function of carnival. Simon Dentith summarizes the dissenting view of carnival as opposed to Bakhtin's concept of it:

But the most common objection to Bakhtin's view of carnival as an antiauthoritarian force that can be mobilized against the official culture of

Church and State, is that on the contrary it is part of that culture; in the typical metaphor of this line of argument, it is best seen as a safety-valve, which in some overall functional way reinforces the bonds of authority by allowing for their temporary suspension. (73)

Historical evidence gathered by modern scholarship and apparently was not available to Bakhtin seems to substantiate, among its other aspects, the safety-valve aspect of carnival (Dentith 74–79, 103). Anatoly V. Lunacharsky, Bakhtin's fellow Russian critic, had expressed a similar view that laughter and comic writing act as safety-valves for social tensions. This apparent lack of recognition of the safety-valve aspect in Bakhtin's concept of carnival, however, does not weaken the grounds for our associating the theme of "Powerhouse" with carnival, for the anti-authoritarian energies that surfaced in the carnival square under the obscure shade of the authorities' calculated toleration are comparable to the play of suppressive-permissive counterforces in the early history of jazz and have also become the ultimate effect of Powerhouse's performance.

To clarify the nature of the safety-valve aspect of Powerhouse's performance, I want to digress briefly and explain the subtle friend/foe relationship between authority and anti-authority seen in the early history of jazz. First of all, Congo Square in New Orleans, probably the most fertile of the birthplaces of American jazz, was nothing but a "carnival" space where that friend/foe opposition operated. One of the results of the Louisiana Purchase of 1803 that affected the lives of the African Americans in New Orleans was the lifting of the colonial French prohibition of the practice of *vodun,* or voodooism. Still, the enormous thriving of *vodun,* which seemed dangerous to the populace at large, had to be checked; in 1817 the Municipal Council legalized Sunday dances for the slaves in Congo Square, a wide-open, dusty place, to keep the slaves contented without their indulging in *vodun* rituals. From the viewpoint of the ruling classes, the dances were a kind of safety valve to release the pent-up discontent and frustration of the African Americans in the city. From the slaves' point of view, seasoned in such racial-cultural heritage as the bamboula, they were a temporary suspension of the daily hardships of enslavement. Yet ironically, those public performances by the African Americans in Congo Square, which lasted into the late nineteenth century, brought the *vodun* elements of their music with its rhythm and rituals out into the open. There it blended with European music, eventually giving birth to the unique musical genre of New Orleans jazz.

Another instance of the friend/foe relationship between authority and anti-authority, not only in the early history of jazz but well into the latter half of the twentieth century, is seen in the role of the African American secret societies in New Orleans. These societies strengthened fraternal bonds for the celebration and enjoyment in order to counter social and personal hardship and misfortune. Each society had its own brass band, reflecting the city's enthusiasm for military bands, a legacy of Napoleonic France. The biggest occasion for such bands was of course the parade at a member's funeral. Trumpeter Bunk Johnson's description of such a parade conveys its rambunctious reveling and the authorities' permissiveness toward it:

> We'd have some immense crowds following. They would follow the funeral up to the cemetery just to get this ragtime music comin' back . . . and follow the band for miles—in the dust, in the dirt, in the street, on the sidewalk, and the Law was trying not to gang the thoroughfare, but just let them have their way. There wouldn't be any fight or anything of that kind; it would just be dancin' in the street. Even police horse—mounted police— their horse would prance. Music done them all the good in the world. That's the class of music we used on funerals. (Stearns 50–51)

The expression of sorrow on the death of a band member was released openly and transformed into something quite agreeable and comforting. Here again one sees the unique mixture of exclusiveness and communality in jazz performance: the music was played by the members of a secret society in its own way, not as an expression of an individual member's emotions but of a broader collective emotion, ultimately involving the whole community. The authorities rather freely allowed the reveling to go on, in order to maintain law and order.

If Congo Square and the secret societies in New Orleans were the urban powerhouses of jazz, there were rural wellsprings of jazz wherever African Americans were put to work—on plantations, on the Mississippi levees, beside the railroad tracks, at turpentine plants. Many of the work songs of African American laborers eventually came to be considered jazz pieces. Work songs were largely functional for both the workers and the supervisor: cotton pickers sang to escape monotony, a chain gang coordinated its movements to the rhythm of the song, and stevedores on docks counted their heavy loads by the song; the slave driver or the gang guard or the foreman did not care what the workers sang as long as the song promoted efficiency. Therefore the lyrics often carried double meanings: a clever work-song leader could feign obedience and loyalty to the white supervisor while amusing the workers with various kinds of improvisation, ranging from innocent humor to camouflaged mockery and masked antagonism toward the supervisor and white society. The work songs in effect functioned as a safety valve to prevent smoldering rebelliousness from bursting into open flame.

The reader of "Powerhouse" realizes that the Bakhtinian release of energy, which in effect works as a safety-valve, is present in Powerhouse's art. His improvisational performance, with its grotesque but hilarious fictions, sends the audience—blacks as well as whites—into an "oblivion" and liberates them in an area beyond the social boundaries of daily life. Yet the illusion he creates is so gratifying to the audience that they are deflected from probing the fundamental social injustice in the real world, the very source of Powerhouse's artistic inspiration. The kind of self-reflexivity the racial subtext of "Powerhouse" reveals is this contradictory value of illusion. The irony of this lone contender is that the greater his genius in *playing*—making fun, creating double meanings (camouflaging), lying (making fictions)—the more strongly it reinforces the status quo that he desires to subvert. Yet this *was* the reality of the late 1930s. One could not know how many years or decades would pass before the injustices could be openly challenged and subverted. Until then Powerhouse would have to be just *playing*.

The future of racial relations must have been no more certain to Welty herself when she penned this story. As she cautions the reader to be aware that Powerhouse and his sidemen are speaking in "another language," so also is the whole story of "Powerhouse" written in a coded language of its own. The alert reader, Welty is suggesting, will decode the story's secret and read in "Powerhouse" the author's poignant social criticism and earnest moral support for the cause of the Powerhouses of the country. It is truly amazing that this story was written by a young Mississippi woman in the late 1930s, and even more so that it could be published in 1941. Although the simplest explanation for the earlier publishers' reluctance must have been, as suggested earlier, the story's obscenity, it seems likely that some of the editors sensed in the story a potential political bomb that would endanger the reputation of the author as well as the publisher.

I believe the reason that the story after all "reached the reading mass and came out the other side" was Welty's skillful camouflaging of its real message. Recalling a similarity of circumstance under which Bakhtin wrote his books on carnival is not out of place. His *Rabelais and His World* is regarded by some critics as a camouflaged polemic against the cultural control of the Stalinist regime. As Dentith points out:

> The whole book is best read as a *coded* attack on the cultural situation of Russia in the 1930s under Stalin—or to use a more Bakhtinian vocabulary, the book is to be read as a hidden polemic against the regime's cultural politics. . . . The regime's grip on cultural policy tightened significantly after 1934 when "socialist realism" was officially promulgated as the only permissible aesthetic for the novel: much of Bakhtin's account of grotesque realism may be seen as an implicit rejoinder to this. (71, emphasis added)

Just as Bakhtin's "historical" discussion on the laughter of the Middle Ages justified folk energy for possible *degradation* of state authority and shielded the author from being terrorized by the Soviet authorities, "Powerhouse" camouflaged Welty's serious social criticism with the ostensibly carefree laughter caused by the outrageous fiction and fun-making and protected the author from possible racist antipathy. Welty seemingly adhered to the New Critics' favorite image of the writer—as an apolitical,[4] delicately individualistic member of a literary élite.

CHAPTER 2

Delta Wedding:
A Celebration of a "Horrible World"

Welty's expansion of the thirty-five-page story "The Delta Cousins" into the novel-length fiction *Delta Wedding* (1946), at the urging of her literary agent to comply with the publisher's requests, is a well-known story. On publication Welty's first full-blown novel was enthusiastically received in her home state (Waldron 162), but elsewhere it attracted some fairly negative criticism, faulting it not only for the lack of a traditional plot but also for the alleged dearth of any moral judgment concerning the racist society she dealt with.[1] In the years since, critics have tended to defend the novel from stylistic and, later, feminist viewpoints. Peggy Whitman Prenshaw's essays[2] especially represent this tendency, identifying Welty's insights into the matriarchal cultural patterns of the Southern plantation from feminist and archetypal approaches. Ironically, however, these fruitful studies, thanks to their solid arguments, have actually produced the effect of diverting attention from the question of the novel's alleged indifference to social injustice. Thus, as far as the question of Welty's social awareness is concerned, the situation has remained more or less the same as in the early sixties, when Ruth Vande Kieft wrote about the novel. Vande Kieft emphasized the significance of the power and turmoil within the hearts of the central characters though the novel had "no serious racial or social disharmony [and] . . . no marked tendency to moral ugliness in any character." Vande Kieft declared, "[*Delta Wedding*] may be rediscovered by readers who have dismissed the novel as a social document" (1987, 86). Yet *Delta Wedding* is as much a social document as a delicate stylistic construct of individual sensitivities, and valuing the novel only for its nonsocial merits actually does injustice to it. In *Delta Wedding*, the story of the hearts of the central characters is part of the *surface* story. Beneath it reside complex subtexts—not one but several—carrying the author's acerbic social criticism, and these have tended to be overlooked, ignored, or belittled. Kreyling convincingly argues that Welty's style of "fragment[ing] the monolithic obligation to form and content, and distribut[ing] it spatially among several characters" (1998, 16) effected its evolution from a story to a self-reflexive novel. I believe the social subtexts, which I will bring to the surface here, constitute yet another element that has contributed to the work's having acquired the substance proper to a novel, both in length and content, and that for this reason points to the metafictional quality of this novel in a sense different from Kreyling's.

In considering the value of Welty's social subtexts for the formation of *Delta Wedding* as a novel, the view of literature of the French Marxists Etienne Balibar and Pierre Macherey provides a helpful perspective. In "On Literature as an Ideological Form" (1974) they maintain that literature is produced "through the effect of one or more ideological contradictions *precisely because these contradictions cannot be solved* within the ideology, i.e., in the last analysis through the effect of contradictory class positions within the ideology, as such irreconcilable" (284, emphasis added). Thus, in their argument, all literary texts, due to their very origin, lack solution and can at best provide only an *imaginary solution* or replace real contradictions with *soluble imaginary contradictions*. Literature, Balibar and Macherey continue, "'begins' with the imaginary solution of implacable ideological contradictions, with the representation of that solution: not in the sense of representing . . . a solution which is really there (to repeat, literature is produced because such a solution is impossible) but in the sense of providing a 'mise en scene,' a *presentation as solution* of the very terms of an insurmountable contradiction, by means of various displacements and substitutions" (284). This is a sweeping Marxist premise, one that Balibar and Macherey believe to be applicable to all literary texts. Whether we accept this premise unquestioningly or not, I find it helpful in assessing what Welty has achieved in *Delta Wedding*. Does in effect *Delta Wedding* follow this Marxist premise? This chapter examines to what extent and in what way *Delta Wedding* owes its status as a novel to the conditions prescribed by this Marxist premise and attempts to clarify the value of its social subtexts.

In an interview in 1972 Reynolds Price said that *Delta Wedding* was "probably the single most illuminating book we [had] about the fantastic complexity of racial relations in the Deep South, how people of enormous culture, kindness, generosity, goodness like the Fairchilds, with great human richness—human in *nature*—were capable of living on a base of virtual slaves" (Humphries 47). Observations as perspicacious as this are rare. Even as recently as 1998, the *New Yorker* carried a long article on Welty's legacy by Claudia Roth Pierpont in which the critic extensively censured *Delta Wedding*:

> This might have been the greatest plantation novel of all had Welty had the courage of Margaret Mitchell's conviction, or the courage to expose the lies and fears that lay beneath them. Instead, she spread fairy dust over the cotton fields and refused to confront, or even explore, any of her pretty characters. As a result, "Delta Wedding" is a tour de force of distraction—food, flowers, dotty old aunts—its focus always shifting around a non-existent core. Perhaps this justly reflects how such a family lived with itself, but the artistic price that Welty paid for so successfully mirroring its self-deception is heavy. Her characters remain blurred, as in a faded photograph—closed off in their delusions, small and indistinct against the beauties of the land that cannot save them or this book from being, finally empty and unfulfilled. (100)

It is simply sad to see such an influential magazine publishing a critic too obtuse to match Welty's literary sophistication in laying down the subtexts of "the lies and fears" of the Deep South for those who would *read* and recognize them. One of the best *readers* in this respect comes from abroad. The Danish scholar Jan Nordby Gretlund identifies the humiliation of the African American servant girl Pinchy, buried in the story of the Fairchilds, in a remarkable and gratifying feat of literary excavation. Gretlund exposes a subtext, "an indictment of the Fairchilds" (115), in Pinchy and the white overseer Troy Flavin's sexual relationship and Flavin's abandonment of her upon his engagement to the planter Battle Fairchild's daughter Dabney, the Fairchilds tacitly condoning the situation (116–19). In the United States, Ann Waldron, in her *Eudora: A Writer's Life* (1998), citing Reynolds Price's remark above, asserts that Welty reveals "such problems of discrimination and economic bondage . . . without editorializing" (164). Actually, what is buried or left "without editorializing" is not only the racial injustice at Shellmound plantation but the author's critical condemnation of the whole Southern pattern of social relations of whites and blacks, haves and have-nots, men and women, husbands and wives, adults and children, the sane and the insane. Welty's condemnation is buried under the surface because the carriers of the points of view all belong to the racial and economic classes vested with power in the society and are understandably calloused to the views of the other side. It is a remarkable way of criticizing the society the author contemporaneously lived in, since by revealing the natural goodness of those characters of the powered classes, she sidesteps possible antipathy in perfunctory readers of those classes in the society, while more perceptive readers are expected to feel the enormity of the injustices and unfairness existing in that society.

Vande Kieft and several critics after her have pointed out the symbolic significance of the porcelain lamp that Dabney is given as a wedding gift. Its cylindrical shade is painted with a scene of a little town, but when the candle is lighted the town appears to be all on fire, "even to the motion of fire, which came from the candle flame drawing" (46). Vande Kieft characterizes this lamp as representing the layers of the external events surrounding the wedding and the inner flames of the central characters (1962, 94). In similar tones later critics generally interpret the lighted lamp as representing a completed vision of formerly incompletely recognized elements, such as time, family, or persons. But the lamp may also be understood as bringing to light the precariousness of relations beneath the surface of an ostensibly harmonious plantation life, an inner disharmony to which the Fairchilds are simply oblivious, as when Aunt Jim Allen recognizes the scene of the burning town on the lamp as actually a disaster and yet still views it as "pretty": "Only to light it, and you see the Great Fire of London, in the dark. Pretty—pretty—" (46). It seems more than an accidental coincidence that the town on the lamp has "trees, towers, people, windowed houses, and a bridge, . . . the clouds and stars and moon and sun" (46), while in the town of Fairchilds, where the Fairchild plantation is located, certainly all these things are present—a bridge, a towered plantation home, and another home where children play "Go in and out the *window*,"[3] the scorching sun over the cotton fields, and a starry sky over the family picnic. In the earlier story of Pinchy being driven away by Troy, a comparison of Pinchy to "a matchstick in the glare" (150) suggests that she could pose a kind of incendiary threat to the peace and security of the Fairchilds, just as a match ignites the fire in the town painted on the lamp.

The most apparent inner disharmony and potentially destructive force that Welty brings to light in *Delta Wedding* derive, as Gretlund has shown, from the relations between the races, and even his enumeration of examples does not begin to exhaust the instances of Welty's acute but camouflaged criticism of this racist society. To begin with a rather obvious example, the Fairchilds' Negro servants and field hands are called by such awkward and often humiliating names as "Man-Son," "Pinchy," "Aunt Studney," "Root M'Hook," or "Pleas." Welty pointed out in interviews that the African Americans frequently name their children with very pretty, meaningful words; names are often the only things they can give to their children (a custom also adopted by the poor white characters in *Losing Battles*). Welty was apparently alluding to given names in the contemporary South, not the antebellum South where, as Richard Godden indicates, "planters were entitled to declare their title or property within a slave by naming that slave as they wished, and in so doing they deadened the slave's right by birth to human connections" (69). Yet considering Welty's strong awareness of the importance of personal names, especially for the poor, Welty's choices of the African Americans' names in this novel—whether given names or family names or just sobriquets—convey her tacit censure of the practice: that the African Americans working on the postbellum, or even early-twentieth-century, plantation are often still not "free" even in one of the few domains where they might have freedom of choice.

One of the features of the racial relations at Shellmound that Welty emphasizes is the incredible smoothness with which the racial separation is sustained even among the children. The white children play "Go in and out the window" in the yard where little black boys cut the grass for the wedding, the lawn mowers sounding like "Please . . . please." The author, through Laura's consciousness, adds, as if she were reporting something pleasant and commendable, "The children [that is, the white children, of course] were keeping out of mischief so that people could get something done" (73). Later in the novel we learn that the servant Howard's little boy, Pleas, is seen working hard like an adult. By contrast, Ranny, the Fairchilds' four-year-old boy, hollers for the maid before six o'clock every morning as if he were one of the adults: "Roxie! I need my coffee!" (208). Though apparently he does this for fun, imitating the adults, nonetheless his prank obliges the maid to come up cheerfully to humor him every morning. Patricia Yaeger capitalizes on Ellen's carefree reaction to her little son's daily ritual: "Given this deliberate ignorance of the costs of servitude, Ellen's lack of anxiety about the system of labor driving her family's plantation system may be expected, but Welty's ironic frame defamiliarizes this thoughtlessness, making it visible, unfamiliar, remarkable" (184).

Gretlund correctly points out that the Negro servants and field hands are treated by the whites like children, but it is also true that it is often the whites who actually *behave* like children. For instance, Laura witnesses Uncle George pacing up and down the sleeping porch smoking his pipe, apparently thinking of his runaway wife, while the servants downstairs are working busily in preparation for the wedding (73); it is as if he is being kept "out of mischief so that people could get something done." Yet "mischief" he most certainly creates: supposedly the most sympathetic Fairchild, he later walks unconcernedly in his muddy fishing gear onto the floor that Roxie had polished on her knees all that morning, saying, "Give [the fish] to the Negroes" (103–7). As the huge wedding cake is being brought into the dining room, the Fairchild women make a hysterical fuss while not even touching the cake, leaving the Negro servants to carry it in with the most intense care: "You watch that cake, Howard! Do you know what'll happen to you if you drop that?" "Yes, ma'am. *Dis* cake not goin' drop—no'm." "That's what you say. You have to *carry* it straight up too" (201). Again, Howard is suddenly ordered on the bride's father's whim to lay out a dancing place in the yard, to which he responds cheerfully: "'Mr. Battle sure love doin' things at las' minute, don't he, Miss Ellen?' laughed Howard from the top of his ladder, making it sound attractive, even irresistible of Mr. Battle" (207). Even for the preparation of the newlyweds' residence, the Fairchilds do no actual work. On the morning after the wedding Battle gathers "a back yard full of Negroes[,] . . . all sleepy and holding their heads" (227), to clean up the young couple's prospective residence, Marmion—the biggest of the three plantation homes on the grounds, "the magnificent temple-like, castle-like house" with twenty-five rooms. This mansion has never been inhabited since it was built in 1890, but Battle orders them to restore it in three days for the newlyweds to live in comfortably: "Men clear off and clear out, women do sweeping—and so forth. Want you all to climb over the whole thing and see what has to be done—I imagine the roof's not worth a thing. Don't you go falling through, and skittering down the stairs, haven't got the time to fool with any broken necks, Miss Dabney wants Marmion *now*. Take your wagons, shovels, axes, everything—now shoo" (227).

Although these and many other exchanges between the whites and the African Americans are made cheerfully and smoothly, often with a sense of playfulness, within the speech conventions of the society at the time, the callousness of the conventions themselves is patently evident. Furthermore, even all the cleaning, decorating, and cooking for the wedding represents only a few of the instances demonstrating that the actual tasks are performed by the African American servants and field hands, while the Fairchild men and women simply make known what they want. It is a clear presentation of the simple fact of plantation economy that the division of labor and management is based on race. The system has resulted in the family's almost inbred deficiency in understanding the cost of labor, as seen, among other places, in the fact that the Fairchilds have constructed an extravagantly large and expensive house such as Marmion, left it unused for over thirty years, and then ordered the unquestioning employees to restore it in three days. Because the African Americans are there to obey the orders of the Fairchilds and the overseer Flavin, who knows "how to handle your Negroes" (95), those who wish to stay on the plantation payroll are constrained to do so cheerfully.

It is not only by means of the incidents directly related to the wedding but the whole life at Shellmound that Welty illuminates "the fantastic complexity of racial relations in the Deep South," as Price put it. The story of Ellen's lost garnet breastpin, for instance, illustrates a threatening mixture of trust and mistrust, of love and disdain between the blacks and the whites on the plantation, although the breastpin passes only through the hands of the three whites, Battle, Ellen, and Laura. A few days before the wedding, Ellen has a dream in which she finds her garnet brooch, a present from Battle in their courting days (and that actually "had been lying around the house for years and then disappeared") (65) under a giant cypress tree in the far corner on the plantation. Soon afterward, on her way to visit her old Negro nurse Partheny, Ellen passes by the cypress tree, where she encounters a beautiful white girl hiding behind it. Ellen calls to her that she is looking for her lost breastpin, to which the girl quickly responds: "'I haven't seen *no pin*.' . . . 'Nobody can say I stole *no* pin'" (70–71). The two then part, Ellen showing the girl the road to Memphis. On a later day, Ellen sends her daughters Shelley and India along with Laura to Partheny to invite her to the wedding, but she also has Shelley ask Partheny if she had happened to see the garnet brooch when she came to cook for Battle's birthday. Partheny, apparently jokingly, starts looking for it in her cabin, patting the bed quilt, tapping the fireplace, looking under the dishpan, ransacking even the chicken house. In Ellen's exchange with the runaway girl in the woods, the author has shown that being asked about the whereabouts of something precious is likely to cause pain in a person of a lower status due to the fear of suspicion of stealing.

In the surface story, as the mistress of the plantation, Ellen is the compassionate mother figure to her biological children as well as to her relatives and to all the African American servants and field hands on the plantation. But on the subtextual level, Ellen is revealed as a careless, complacent mistress. She does not consider the possibility that the manner of her inquiry could be interpreted as an expression of mistrust of Partheny; Partheny's search, which one expects would be prompted by her concern for Ellen's loss, becomes seemingly a farce, an act of exaggerated defense bordering on sarcasm and carried on out of fear, an act certainly directed at the expression of Ellen's mistrust implicit in her inquiry. Seeing the unnaturalness of Partheny's response, Shelley on returning home reports: "Partheny's got something of yours, Mama, but she wouldn't give it to me for fear she didn't know what a garnet was" (150).

The brooch is accidentally discovered by Laura and Roy in the grass in the yard at Marmion. Laura retrieves it, but on their way home in a rowboat Roy playfully tosses her into the river, where she loses the brooch

forever. Laura never tells Ellen what has happened to the brooch. Ellen
will inquire about it in the future, and Partheny will remain suspect to
Shelley; everyone of whom Ellen will inquire will experience the same
feeling as did the girl in the woods and Partheny. Conversely, there is
something of Partheny's, precious in its own way, that also gets lost forever through the carelessness and irresponsibility of the Fairchild children.
Partheny asks Shelley to take to George her special patticake, which she
claims has power to recover Robbie's heart if George eats it at midnight.
Shelley lets India carry it, but when they meet Troy on the way, India
casually gives him the cake, lying that it was baked by Dabney. Taking a
bite, Troy does not like the taste and later finds Robbie does not like it
either. Seeing no use in keeping the cake, Troy tells Pinchy when he drives
her away, "Here, Pinchy—here's a cake. . . . Eat it or give it to the other
Negroes. Now scat!" (150). We hear nothing about the patticake for the
remainder of the novel: the children do not tell George about the cake,
nor does Troy say anything about it to Dabney. Partheny's effort and expression of concern are forever lost. She is never informed of the whereabouts of the cake, nor does she try to find out, as Ellen had tried to find
out about her garnet pin.

Ellen's feelings of maternal concern and care extend to the greenery
on the plantation, but these qualities also undergo an ironical transfor-
mation. The morning after the wedding Ellen strolls around the yard
examining each plant with the sympathy and joy a mother would bestow
on her child. Yet for any physical gardening work she calls on Howard,
in the same way the actual tasks of preparing for the wedding are performed by the servants. Welty does not fail to give us a glimpse of both
sides' feelings:

> "Howard, look at my roses! Oh, what all you'll have to do to them."
> "I wish there wasn't no such thing as roses," said Howard. "If I had my
> way, wouldn't be a rose in de world. Catch your shirt and stick you and
> prick you and grab you. Got thorns."
> "Why, Howard. You hush!" Ellen looked back over her shoulder at him
> for a minute, indignant. "You don't want any roses in the world?"
> "Wish dey was out of de world, Miss Ellen," said Howard persistently.
> "Well, just hush, then."
> She cut the few flowers, Etoiles and Lady Hillingtons (to her astonish-
> ment she was trembling at Howard's absurd, meek statement, as at some
> *impudence*), and called the children to run take them in the house. (226,
> emphasis added)

Diana Trilling has pointed out Ellen's reaction as an instance of the source
of her distaste for *Delta Wedding* (103). Had she read a little more care-

fully, carefully enough to observe that the word "impudence" is effectively carried over to reflect back upon Ellen herself in the novel's next
paragraph, Trilling might have appreciated the presence of Welty's "moral
judgment." As she steps inside, Ellen's "maternal" concern returns from
plants to the human, and she thinks about the future for her niece Laura:
"(Should she keep Laura? Billie McRaven [Laura's father] was solid and
devoted, but he had *no imagination*—should she take Laura and keep her
at Shellmound?)" (226–27). For her to think that Laura may be happier
living with the Fairchilds at Shellmound than living with her own father
in Jackson reveals an "impudence" and a lack of *"imagination"* on Ellen's
part. Indeed Laura has been considered a virtual "orphan" by the
Fairchilds, since to their minds Laura is the child of the deceased Annie
Laurie Fairchild—her father's existence in Jackson being completely ignored. His letter to the Fairchilds that Laura brought has been lost while
being passed around among them before Ellen and Battle ever read it,
and nobody cares about it.

Only Laura knows the insularity of Shellmound, a knowledge derived
from her experience of living outside the plantation. Even at the beginning of the novel she suspects that the Fairchild men and women are no
"freer" than the tropical birds in the great bowerlike cage in the zoo her
father had shown her (15). From this viewpoint, the moving episode of
Laura and her eight-year-old cousin Roy's exploration of the uninhab-
ited Marmion makes for an ironical reverberation. Marmion, when the
two children visit, is presented through consistent archetypal allusions.
It stands facing the Yazoo River, the name of which means "river of death"
in the local Indian language. From a rowboat Laura and Roy see the
elderly Negro woman Aunt Studney—so called because she continually
says "Ain't studyin' you"—with her sack, which Roy thinks is "where
Mama gets all her babies" (173). Seeing her entering Marmion, the children get out of the boat and follow her. On the entrance step Laura and
Roy find a dead mockingbird, reminiscent of the earlier comparison of
the Fairchilds to caged birds. Inside, the children see Aunt Studney with
her sack on the floor; she does "not move at all except to turn herself in
place around and around, arms bent and hovering, like an old bird over
her one egg" (175). This strange, almost primordial, atmosphere makes
Laura cry, "Is it still the Delta in here?" Roy answers, "Sure it is!" (175).
After a while Laura notices numerous bees swirling around the room, apparently having escaped from Aunt Studney's sack. In the next moment
Roy, up in the lookout tower, cries out, "I see Troy! I see the Grove—I
see Aunt Primrose, back in her flowers! I see *Papa! I see the whole creation*" (176, emphasis added). Apparently, Marmion is where life and
death come together in a whirlwind; one sees the panorama of "the whole

creation." But this symbolic perception can be subverted by another perception, this one ironic, that actually Roy is *not* seeing "the whole creation" at all but merely the Fairchild plantation, that the Fairchilds cannot even bring their own offspring into the world without the help of the African American woman. Roy's perception can be taken as representing the insularity of the Fairchilds and the lack of freedom to move and see beyond the boundaries they have prescribed.

To Laura's eye, the Fairchilds' captive condition has rendered her beloved Uncle George, who is also loved by all the Fairchild men and women, a slave to their possessive love, and she fiercely wishes to rescue him: "She would have liked to clear them away, give him room, and then—what? She would let him be mean and horrible—horrible to the horrible world" (76). It is this lack of freedom of the inhabitants to admit the horror of their "horrible world" that runs through the subtexts of *Delta Wedding*, especially those concerning racial relations.

Welty's focusing on this aspect of Southern society in *Delta Wedding* may have been inspired by an essay in the 19 September 1942 issue of the *Saturday Review of Literature*, a special issue on "The Deep South," to which Welty herself contributed a book review. In the title essay, entitled "The Deep South," David L. Cohn, himself a native of the Mississippi Delta country, states:

> The life of every white man [and woman] in the area is profoundly affected by the presence of the Negro, just as the life of every Negro is profoundly affected by the presence of the white man. There has never been a free white man in the Deep South—as there is in Vermont—because his entire life and ways of living individually and institutionally are conditioned by the presence of multitudes of Negroes (in Issaqueena County, Mississippi, there are five thousand Negroes and five hundred whites), and consequently no one knows precisely what a Deep Southerner is since he functions in an environment of which he is a prisoner.
>
> This is no fault of the Negro. It is simply a fact. Consequently the Deep South writer—who is himself affected by the environment—is dealing with distorted whites suffering from more or less severe psychological aberrations. (3)

What I have been enumerating as instances of Welty's critical view of the racial relations at Shellmound may all come down to the matter of this lack of freedom. Dabney speculates on the enigma of George's personality: "Sweetness then could be the visible surface of profound depths—the surface of all the darkness that might frighten her" (37). *Delta Wedding* can be considered an attempt to expose that frightening darkness of lost freedom and the resulting psychological aberrations not only of the

African Americans but of the whites as well under the surface of the romantic pastoral scenes of the Southern plantation.

It is thanks not only to the labor and skill of the African American servants and field hands at Shellmound that Dabney's wedding can be put on successfully, but also directly or indirectly to the sacrifices of whites who are marginal to the Fairchilds or outsiders. As the uneasy racial relations illuminate the inner disharmony and threat of breakdown at Shellmound, so also do the relations between the central Fairchild family members and these marginal people. Maureen's renunciation of Marmion secures the newlyweds this castlelike house, twice as large as Shellmound, with "the lookout tower, and twenty-five rooms, and inside the wonderful free-standing stair—the chandelier, chaliced, golden in light, like the stamen in the lily down-hanging," and outside "the garden—the playhouse—the maze" (122). Yet the negotiation over this "alienation of property" between Dabney and Maureen, her nine-year-old retarded cousin, who has no idea of private property, had been accomplished with almost criminal informality and unfairness:

So Dabney had said to Maureen, "Look, honey—will you give your house to me?" They had been lying half-asleep together in the hammock after dinner. Maureen, hanging over her to look at her, her face close above hers, had chosen to smile radiantly. "Yes," she had said, "you can have my house-la, and a bite-la of my apple too." Oh, everything *could* be so easy! Virgie Lee, Maureen's mother, was not of sound mind and would have none of Marmion. (31)

Later the reader is introduced to a crude skeleton story of Maureen, the daughter of Virgie Lee and Denis Fairchild, who died in the war:

Maureen had been dropped on her head as an infant, that her mother, Virgie Lee Fairchild, who had dropped her, ran away into Fairchilds and lived by herself, never came out, and that she wore her black hair hanging and matted to the waist, had not combed it since the day she let the child fall. "*You*'ve seen her!" Their two lives had stopped on that day, and so Maureen had been brought up at Shellmound.
"Why, she's Denis's child!" they all said. (61)

This is the surface story, the Fairchilds' version. The reader cannot but discover in this story a subtext parallel to what is happening to Robbie Reid Fairchild and Laura McRaven, and remotely even to what happened to Ellen's mother when she eloped with a man, when Ellen was nine, and was gone for three years. From the way the Fairchild women treat Robbie, it is easy to imagine that they had never really approved of the marriage

of Denis, the Fairchilds' favorite son, to Virgie Lee either, and that especially after Denis went to war and was killed they valued the infant
Maureen far more than the mother. Virgie Lee, who must have been a
normal, attractive woman, could not endure, one surmises, the Fairchild
women's insolence, which deeply affected her mind: "A circle is ugly
without you" (73). Dropping her own baby on its head must have been
a perverse act of resistance and anger toward the Fairchilds. Moreover,
the Fairchilds had kept the child, "Denis's child," for themselves despite
Denis's death, believing the child would be happier with them than with
her non-Fairchild mother, just as Ellen thinks of Laura as an object of
pity because she is with her father. The guilt consciousness of the attempted murder, or accident, and the virtual loss of her child may have
very well left Virgie Lee "not of sound mind." The Fairchild girls giggle
about Virgie Lee's hair being eternally uncombed and tangled, and Battle
Fairchild, agreeing, gives "a hearty and rather prolonged laugh[,]
. . . groaning, as if it hurt his side" (62).

The history of the disposal of Marmion illustrates the arbitrariness of
the Fairchild women. Marmion had originally belonged to Annie Laurie
Fairchild, Laura's mother, and when Annie Laurie had married and left
the Delta, she had given it to Denis. On Denis's death, it should have
become his wife Virgie Lee's property, but Annie Laurie had felt "that
wild concern some ladies feel for little idiot children" (145) and had given
it to Maureen, "with her own child cheated" (145). Yet Annie Laurie,
having made a doll for Laura and named it Marmion, must have meant
the house eventually to belong to her daughter. But now Dabney has
taken it from Maureen to keep for herself.

Still, the most tragic blow the Fairchilds have dealt Virgie Lee
and Maureen is to their mother-daughter relationship. On a street in
Fairchilds, upon coming across Shelley, Laura, and Maureen in their car
on the Sunday morning after the wedding, Virgie Lee Fairchild says, "'Go
away! Go away! Don't tamper with me! Go home to your weddings and
palaver'" (235). Maureen, leaning out over the side of the car, laughs
aloud at her own mother, undoubtedly a response stemming from an
attitude instilled in her by the Fairchilds. Yet in her "wild way"—according to Shelley's characterization of her, "her cheeks painted red as if she
were going to meet somebody, and in the back, with her hair tied up in
a common rope" (235)—Virgie Lee *is* made up and dressed to go to her
church. In contrast, the girls are on their way to do grocery shopping
on the Sabbath, the day commercial activity is supposed to be suspended
in Mississippi.

Only Laura, with a sensibility free of the smug insularity of the
Fairchilds, is terrified by the scene of Maureen laughing at her own

mother: Laura "[throws] her arms around Maureen as if to pull her back from *fire*, and [holds] her, calling her as if she were deaf, 'Maureen, Maureen!'" (235, emphasis added). At home, talking about Laura's future repossession of Marmion, Ellen wonders, "Do you ever trust Virgie Lee not to *flare up?*" (237, emphasis added). Thus, like Pinchy, Virgie Lee is presented as a possible threat to the peace and security of the Fairchilds, just as the "fire" is to the town painted on the lamp. Virgie Lee's remonstrance to the children, "Go home to your weddings and palaver," arises as probably the sanest criticism of the Fairchilds when one recalls that etymologically "palaver" is a parley between persons of unequal social standings—specifically, between European colonizers and African natives. Finally, it is when she hears Battle's scornful remark and how he laughs about the whole matter concerning Virgie Lee that Laura feels that "in the end she [will] go—go from all this, go back to her father" (237). It can be said that Laura's decision-making process reflects part of Welty's implicit "moral judgment," if one, along with critics like Trilling and Pierpont, demands it from this novel.

The episode of the beautiful runaway girl whom Ellen meets in the bayou woods signals another moral threat to the Fairchilds. To Ellen's eye, the girl is pure and fresh, embodying nature's primordiality, like an ancient spirit of the woods, the entity to whom the word "beauty" may have been originally applied. Ellen's order to the girl to "stand still" is an expression of awe at this moment of the sublime, an echo of Faust's "Stand still, you are so beautiful!" But this sense of awe and humility engendered in nature's primordial vegetation is violently destroyed upon her return to Shellmound. When she mentions her encounter to George, he informs her that he had met the girl on his way to Shellmound and "took her over to the old Argyle gin and slept with her" (79). (Later incidents suggest that the gin is probably the one that went out of use because of a *fire*, a disaster Ellen suddenly recalls when she sees George is about to find out that Robbie has come back to him.) In her shock, Ellen tries to reason out the situation: "Sometimes he, the kindest of them all, would say a deliberate wounding thing—as if in assurance that nothing further might then hurt you. . . . Then impatiently, as if you were too close to a *fire*, he pulled you away from your pain" (79, emphasis added). Then George adds, as a consolation, "'She's older than you thought'" (79).

The girl is a complete stranger to the Fairchilds, but she becomes the "fire" in the lamp with the town scene, illuminating what will be seen as George's and Ellen's partiality toward themselves alone. Although it is unknown which of the two proposed the sexual act, it is clear that George stepped beyond what he could have prevented. Yet neither Ellen nor George is really concerned with the plight of the helpless outsider who was taken advantage of by a man of a higher social and economic status; both Ellen and George are only trying to plumb and protect each other's feelings. George's last remark reveals no sense of guilt or remorse toward the girl, while his revelation of male aggression leads Ellen to voice her concern, not for the girl but for her own daughter: "Oh, George! . . . Sometimes I'm so afraid when Dabney marries she won't be happy in her life" (80). If one accepts Gretlund's reading of the Pinchy-Troy story, Ellen's anxiety comes from her admission of what Robbie and Dabney in their married lives have to tolerate. It is one of the darknesses of a system in which women socially and institutionally weaker than Robbie or Dabney can be used to satisfy George's or Troy's random sexual desires—but a system in which, for that very reason, Robbie and Dabney both are helpless to prevent either their husbands' possible betrayals or other women's misery. It is a system that creates, as Cohn pointed out in 1942, an environment in which women in either position are prisoners. Yet it may be that men like George or Troy are just as much prisoners of this environment in which such dissipation is tacitly permitted; the more sincere and proud the men are at heart, the more severe will be the "psychological aberrations" (in Cohn's words) they suffer.

Within the Fairchild family, Robbie and Laura, because of their very marginality, are far more perceptive of the family's smug complacence. But living within the institution as they do, their behavior and thinking cannot in every instance remain free from the mores they despise. For instance, however strongly she may feel victimized by the Fairchilds, Robbie feels no guilt in ejecting Pinchy from the cotton shed into the glaring sun so that she herself can rest in its shade on her walk to Shellmound. Laura's actions, despite her childish thinking, certainly reveal evidence of the Fairchild women's selfish possessiveness toward their loved ones. She wishes Shellmound to burn down so that she would have an opportunity to rescue Uncle George from the *fire* and thus prove her love to him. Laura, hoping to present George, rather than Dabney, with the "wedding gift" he will love most, actually hides George's favorite pipe so that she can present it to him later when he really misses it. Finding out the whole scheme when he is given his own pipe by Laura, the irony in George's response reveals his sense of helplessness faced with the human relationships he has to deal with in this family: "'Thank you,' he said. 'You're growing up to be a real little Fairchild before you know it.' / [Laura] was filled with happiness" (209).

Besides the presence of the current fires illuminating the disharmony and moral threat that have surfaced on the occasion of Dabney's wedding, historically the Fairchilds had created their plantation atop the ashes and cinders of another fire, one that had been violently trampled out. As the name Shellmound suggests, their home is built on an Indian mound, a sacred place for the tribe who had once inhabited the area before they and their culture were wiped out. Although the existence in the distant past of Native Americans on the land the Fairchilds now occupy seems to play no role in the Fairchilds' self-recognition, their historical presence occasionally turns up in the Fairchilds' consciousness. Talking about the ghost haunting The Grove, one of the Fairchild plantation homes, Aunt Jim Allen reasons: "It's not an Indian maid, for what would she be doing, breaking our window to get out? The Indian maid would be crying nearer your place [Shellmound], where the mound is, if *she* cried" (45). Moreover, when Ellen passes through the bayou woods, where she will encounter the beautiful girl, she senses how ancient the woods are and is reminded of the memory of the people who once lived there: "There were trumpet vines and passion flowers. The cypress trunks four feet thick in the water's edge stood opened like doors of tents in Biblical engravings. How still the old woods were. Here the bayou banks were cinders; they said it was where the Indians burned their pottery, at the very last" (69).

The name of the tribe who had lived here—the Tunicas, the Yazoos, the Ofos, the Koroas, and the Tioux all had dwelled on the lower Yazoo River—is not specified, nor is how they met their "very last"; the "cinders" are all that is left from the smothered fires of an extinct civilization now symbolized by its pottery. Welty had expressed her sympathy for the extinct local Native Americans in *The Robber Bridegroom* (1942) and her essays of that period, and here again in *Delta Wedding* the ghosts of these long-gone peoples linger in their old places: when Ellen has a glimpse of the girl, she at first feels that it is "someone who [lives] in the woods, a dark creature not hiding, but waiting to be seen, careless on the pottery bank" (70). It is in these virgin forests untouched by cultivation that one comes close to the ancient life of the land.

On a more factual level, Welty makes sure that the reader knows that the Fairchild plantation, like all the plantations, was developed by literally *deadening* this original ground and forest cover. The vast cotton field where the old Fairchilds began cultivation a hundred years ago is still called the Fairchild Deadening, the place where they "deadened off the trees to take the land" (144). "The old Fairchilds" comprised only two or three people—Mary Shannon and her husband, and probably his brother. Dabney tries to image what her Great-Grandmother Mary Shannon's life was like: "What if you lived in a house all alone and away from everybody with no one but your husband?" (41). Yet certainly they were far from being alone; they had dozens of African American slaves on the plantation to "deaden" and cultivate the land. Although Welty's novel does not attempt a Faulknerian directness in depicting the "deadening" project of the Fairchild plantation, the process must not have been so different from that of Sutpen's Hundred (Faulkner's *Absalom, Absalom!* was published exactly a decade before *Delta Wedding*). Dabney, for all her sensitive and sympathetic picturing of Mary Shannon's situation, ignores the reality that her fabulous wedding, and ultimately the existence of the Fairchild plantation itself, rest upon the foundations built with the labor and sacrifices of not only her ancestors but also the innumerable Native Americans and Negro slaves of bygone days.

Kreyling, in his "Eudora Welty as Novelist: A Historical Approach," eloquently identifies a unique feature of the narrative style of *Delta Wedding,* as we noted at the beginning of this chapter. It is the *spatial* juxtaposition of the visions of the central characters, which, he contends, has enabled Welty to produce her first full-fledged modernist novel. I believe the social subtexts that I have identified show that Welty has achieved the substance proper to a novel by layering several subtexts under the surface story. Social meaning, the alleged lack of which many critics charge Welty with even today, emerges by reading *vertically,* so to speak, the multilayered effects of incidents and themes. The surface story may be about "a charmed life" (166), but *Delta Wedding* rests upon its underlying layers, and these constitute "the horrible world" (76).

By clashing idyll with exploitation, sensitivity with selfishness, generosity with impudence, love with possessiveness, wealth with poverty, Welty clearly reveals the pervasion of contradictions in the society she depicts. Applying Balibar and Macherey's thesis as noted earlier, one can say that on the subtexual level *Delta Wedding* was produced through the effect of "ideological contradictions precisely because these contradictions cannot be solved within the ideology"—namely, within the unique form of capitalism called the plantation economy. In these French Marxists' idea, literary texts can at best, due to the lack of a real solution, provide only an *imaginary solution,* or replace real contradictions with *soluble imaginary contradictions.* In *Delta Wedding,* although these are imaginary— that is, fictive—cases of contradictions, they are not "soluble imaginary contradictions": Welty makes clear that these cases of contradictions in *Delta Wedding* remain *insoluble.* The final scene, that of the evening picnic at Marmion, where all the major characters gather and behave as though the event were the happy denouement of a great family drama— "All secrets were being canceled out, sung out" (241)—is a mock denouement; it is Welty's purposeful "mise en scene," simply *a presentation of the contradictions as mock solution.* The real purpose of the scene is to confirm the insolubility of the contradictions. Robbie and George are reunited, but at the cost of sacrifices by two parties: the first, by Robbie, who, giving up the privacy of city life, succumbs to what she had considered moral degeneracy by becoming a full-fledged member of the Fairchilds (her and George's purchase of a Hudson Super-Six on Sunday is the beginning of her adoption of the Fairchild way of life); and the second, by George's two spinster sisters, who will probably lose their old home when he repossesses The Grove. This may be a sign that George will no longer sacrifice himself for the Fairchilds, but the fact remains that the acquisition, repossession, and alienation of property will be a continuous source of anxiety, and often injustice, among the family members. George and Troy may introduce fruits and vegetables, and horses and cattle in addition to the cultivation of cotton to the ongoing economic prosperity of the Fairchilds, but the cultivation and farming will still depend on the labor of the African American workers, overseen by the whites, who know "how to handle your Negroes." Even during this picnic, Howard and six or eight servants waft smoke from a distant fire to drive mosquitoes away from the Fairchilds in the picnic space—another idyllic plantation scene, from the traditional viewpoint. But to create this space, Battle has had the servants clear away the brambles, thorny plants that Howard hates to encounter. Maureen is "tame as a pigeon" (241) during the picnic, and Laura senses that it is "only now and then that she [shows] what she [can] do, *just like most people*" (241, emphasis added), a scary prospect. Finally, Laura decides not to tell Aunt Ellen what became of her garnet pin. Thus, from racial relations to a girl's hiding a truth, *Delta Wedding* ends with conflicts unresolved, deceits unaccused, and contradictions unsolved. *Delta Wedding* embodies a Machereyan realization of the novel in its barest form. It owes its status as a novel to those insolubles and unresolvables, so to speak, which the author layers as subtexts.

Yet Welty *is* one of those writers represented as "the Deep South writer—who is himself affected by the environment—" (3), as David L. Cohn said in 1942. Or, rather, as her fellow Mississippian William Faulkner said of his feelings toward his home state—"Loving all of it even while he had to hate some of it because he knows now that you don't love because: you love despite; not for the virtues, but *despite the faults*" (499, emphasis added)—Welty pays tribute to the memory of the beautiful moments she has presented in her surface story. Near the very end of the novel, under the "radiant night" of falling stars, Ellen calls again, as in the bayou woods, but this time to her own daughter, "Stand still, India" (247). India, whom Dabney calls "so tacky" (247), does not stand still like the beautiful girl in the woods but runs to the Yazoo River—the waters of death—and stands "as if she saw some certain thing, neither marvelous nor terrible, but simply certain, come by in the Yazoo River" (274). India will witness the cycle of death and birth, she will grow to be a beautiful woman like Dabney, and the plantation will change. But *Delta Wedding* appeals to this passing moment in Southern history, as to the falling stars Laura witnesses, saying, "Stand still, you are so beautiful!" *despite the faults* it has revealed.

PART II

The Power of Language:
Lies and Reality

CHAPTER 3

ꙮ

The Robber Bridegroom:
A Fiction of Lies

Welty's novella *The Robber Bridegroom* (1942) opens with this problematic statement: "It was the close of day when a boat touched Rodney's Landing on the Mississippi River and Clement Musgrove, an innocent planter, with a bag of gold and many presents, disembarked" (1). What does the narrator mean by "innocent"? Could a man have sold his crop of tobacco "for a fair price" (1) without being cheated in a rough, boisterous New Orleans under the Spanish crown, as the succeeding passage implies, so that he can return home with "a bag of gold and many presents," and be innocent? Could he be so alert and cautious as to be able to avoid staying at the establishments of innkeepers with criminal pasts, as another passage reveals, and be innocent? In the course of the novella, Clement Musgrove becomes a planter of great fortune with acres of land and numerous slaves, surviving his two wives and two children (though one—Rosamond—is found alive at the very end of the novella), who shared the hardships of frontier life with him but eventually fell victims to it before his eyes. Yet at the end of the novella, the narrator still describes Clement Musgrove with the same modifiers: "He was an innocent of the wilderness, and a planter of Rodney's Landing, and this was his good. / So, holding a bag of money in his hand, he went to the docks to depart" (182–83). Could a man remain innocent having lived this kind of life?

The question of Clement's innocence has attracted the attention of certain critics, who place this topic at the center of their arguments. Michael Kreyling's view in his 1980 book probably stands closer to the more sympathetic end of the spectrum of evaluation of Clement's words and deeds. He takes Clement's innocence at its face value: "He is an innocent, like Don Quixote. . . . He enters with the naïve innocence of Don Quixote or Candide; and he grows, through the development of his conscience, memory, and foresight, toward an encompassing vision. Like the Indians, he is pushed aside by time and change" (42). Kreyling interprets Clement's carrying a bag of gold and many presents "in plain sight" (43) as proof of innocent vulnerability, his selling of tobacco for a "fair price" as demonstrating his honesty, and his trusting the innkeeper, who displays no outward marks of a criminal past, and the fortune-hunting Jamie as indicators of his gullibility. Kreyling also considers it proof of Clement's innocence that his fortune was gained not through greed on his part but through that of his wife Salome and regards Clement as ultimately innocent at the close, "leaving action to the Salomes and Jamies, violent resistance to the Indians" (48). At the opposite pole one finds Deborah Wilson's more recent 1993 essay, which argues that Clement is *not innocent* but that his prosperity is "a result of patriarchal authority and imperialism" (64). She points out that Clement is guilty of assigning to his wife the blame of accumulating wealth when it is he who is actually engaged in it. Between these two extremes lie views that vary according to the definition and the degree of ironic implication each assigns to the word "innocent."

More than whether or not Clement really is innocent, I am intrigued by the fact that the author has adopted this fairy-tale convention in which, rather than providing the reader with evidence of his innocence or qualifying the definition of the word toward this end, the narrator plainly states that Clement is "an innocent planter." It is a fait accompli, and as such, the reader has no recourse but to accept it as a fact within this fiction. Although this "fact" is open to the challenge of the reader's interpretation and his or her likely suspicion of the fallacy on the part of the narrator, all such speculations would be based on the assumption that Clement's innocence is a narrative truth, solely because the narrator says so. One sees here an unrivaled power of authorship. The author, through the voice of the narrator, has *created* the character out of no reasonable material evidence but out of words. Rather than a "planter," Clement could be a "husband," "deuterogamist," "gentleman," "boat passenger," "traveler," "frontiersman," "tobacco grower," "pessimist," or "henpeck," or whatever; rather than "innocent," he could be "wealthy," "cautious," "honest," "middle-aged," or "middle-sized," or whatever. Instead, in the beginning, the author has simply *let there be* "Clement Musgrove, an innocent planter"; the character is nothing but a construct of the words that respectively name one of the many possible aspects the character could possess. This is an extreme example of what the author of a fiction does. What affords the author this power is words. As in "Powerhouse," Welty devises the opening sentence so as to imply an idea or scheme for the whole story and thus prepares the reader for what is to come. Throughout *The Robber Bridegroom* there extends a subtext on the unique nature of the power of words.

One of the most memorable statements by the narrator in this novella appears toward the end: "And as for [Jamie], the outward transfer from bandit to merchant had been almost too easy to count it a change at all, and he was enjoying all the same success he had ever had" (184–85). Decades later, Welty made a revealing remark in her essay "Fairy Tale of the Natchez Trace" (1975; originally a talk before the Mississippi Historical Society). She points out the theme of "doubleness in respect to identity that runs in a strong thread" (310) through *The Robber Bridegroom*: "Life was so full, so excessively charged with energy in those days . . . that leading one life hardly provided scope enough for it all" (310–11). Warren French, in his discussion on the historical shift of the New World from "the forest" into "the market-place," capitalizes on the above statement by the narrator about Jamie's transfer from bandit to merchant and observes that Welty "does not . . . equate change with progress," since she indicates that "the same talents are required for the two callings" (185). Some other critics regard the narrator's statement as Welty's more affirmative expression on the change. Thus Ellen L. Walker and Gerda Seaman argue that Welty considers Jamie's change "necessary" rather than "regrettable" in what she accepts as "the inevitable march of history" (58). In Barbara Carson's view, Welty presents a world where "life can only be lived fully with the acknowledgment of the harmony to be found in the co-existence of the contraries" (53) and that Jamie's becoming a wealthy merchant is a perfect way to embody that harmony. Yet on a different level, this statement by the novella's narrator as well as Welty's later remark on the necessity of using "doubleness in respect to identity" in the novella both testify to how words operate: words name-label the object with only *one* of its plural aspects.

J. Hillis Miller's analysis of *Oedipus the King* can be recalled as an analogy. Miller calls the tragedy "a story about generational confusion, in which a son is also a husband of his mother, a mother a wife to her son, Oedipus the brother of his own children, and so on." He continues, "Insofar as clear kinship names and identifications are necessary to a man's or a woman's sense of who he or she is and where he or she has come from, *Oedipus the King* presents a story in which the possibility of such clarity is questioned and suspended" (74). The same kind of cognitive confusion can occur, though with a much smaller traumatic impact or none at all, when one attempts to name-label a person with what, for instance, he or she does. In the narrator's view, the activities involved in commerce and robbery are fundamentally the same, the main difference depending upon whether or not society confers legality upon it. Just as the concept of incest comes from the distinctively human possession of language, which distinguishes among mother, wife, sister, and daughter rather than taking them all as possible sex objects, the words "merchant" and "bandit" name-label the person with the word that represents the lawful or unlawful aspect of one of the person's activities. Thus Jamie the bandit and Jamie the merchant are both verbal constructs; Jamie could be not only double but infinitely multiple, as long as he can be name-labeled with different words.

Another kind of double identity, one not so explicitly presented as Jamie's but one that is all the more noteworthy due to its apparent un-reality, is the one seen in the Amalie/Salome characterization. Echoing their homophonous names, their doubleness is indicated in passing by Clement as he expresses his feeling toward the double identity of Jamie: "All things are divided in half—night and day, the soul and body, and sorrow and joy and youth and age and sometimes I wonder if even my own wife has not been the one person all the time, and I loved her beauty so well at the beginning that it is only now that the ugliness has struck through to beset me like a madness" (126).

Although Clement outwardly appears to be a calm, stable person, he at times reveals an aspect of his psyche that is close to hallucinosis,[1] and this is one such occasion. His remark derives from his inward understand-ing that, to survive as a wife confronting the hardships of the frontier, any sweet, beautiful woman is doomed eventually to become an ugly, greedy woman. He knows to the marrow the kind of physical and psycho-logical stress that weighs heavy on the people of this era—"Life was so full"—so heavy as to change wholly the personalities of many of them. The thought of such people leads him to this maddening idea that the sweet Amalie and the ugly Salome are one and the same woman. In Clement's hallucinatory perception, Amalie name-labels his wife with the sweet, beautiful aspect of her personality and Salome the ugly, greedy aspect. It comes down to the same kind of usage of words as the narrator's calling Clement "an innocent planter."

The power of words is exhibited in *The Robber Bridegroom* not only in the name-labeling of the characters' personalities and callings but in their lies; it is not too much to say that this novella is basically made up of lies, setting aside the recognition that a fiction is itself a lie. Most im-portantly, the plot development in *The Robber Bridegroom* is energized by some sort of lie at each stage, because, though lies are nothing but pure verbal constructs, they affect reality to no less a degree than truths would when the lies are believed, and sometimes even when they are not believed. To take the concept Clement becomes obsessed with, lies are reality's *doubles:* just as Dr. Jekyll and Mr. Hyde live one life interchange-ably, reality and lies contribute to one plot line interchangeably in *The Robber Bridegroom.*

From the beginning, Jamie's outwitting Mike Fink and winning Clement's trust are based on his lies, and both Rosamond and Jamie lie to each other at their first meeting and those that follow; thus major human relations, which are real in this novella, start from lies. Aside from the various lies creating the events in the course of the novella, the sur-vival of the lovers to a happy dénouement is secured by lies. Rosamond would be raped and killed by the Little Harp if the robbers did not lie to him that the Indian girl is Jamie's woman. Goat would not rescue Rosamond from the Indians if she did not lie to him that she will marry him. Meanwhile, all the animals Goat pretends to be—a woodchuck, a squirrel, a boar, a snake, a fox, a bear, a wildcat, a lion—sound real to the Little Harp, because for Goat and the Harp, as their names suggest, sounds have meanings as words and thus can name-label. Goat's lie to the world that the Big Harp's head on the pole in Rodney square is that of Jamie Lockhart, whom he says he has killed, frees Jamie completely from his old identity of the bandit of the woods and qualifies him to become a gentleman merchant. Rosamond's false promise of marriage to Goat is scrapped by Goat himself because of Jamie's lie that Rosamond is a terrible housekeeper. The final reunion of Rosamond and Jamie is achieved because of both lovers' telling lies to Mike Fink. Thus the plot line of *The Robber Bridegroom* is a process of a lie producing a reality and the reality in its turn producing another lie.

Among the lies mentioned above, the lie about the Big Harp's head especially pinpoints the awful power of words. This lie, which exploits the name-labeling faculty of words, leads to the understanding that whatever quality and power seems to be inherent in the object can be nothing but the product of cognition and that cognition can be achieved or nullified by simple name-labeling. The lie ultimately lays bare the fact that our cognition of the world and the self, which is pure discourse, cannot help being accomplished through constructs of words and being subjected to name-labeling.

Under the surface plot line of lies and reality, which proceeds to the happy reunions of the lovers and of father and daughter, Welty constructs a subplot that also consists of an interlacing of lies and reality. In "Fairy Tale of the Natchez Trace" Welty claims that *The Robber Bridegroom* is "not a *historical* historical novel" (302, 311), a fact that she assumes should be obvious to the reader from her use of the word "innocent" in the opening sentence. Incorporating European fairy tales and local

Mississippi legends into history, the novella certainly contains numerous
explicitly fictitious details. But probably the factor most contrary to actual
history is "the Indians." Although the tribe is never specified in *The Robber
Bridegroom*, these Native Americans are apparently "modeled on the
Natchez Indians" (Kreyling 1980, 37). Yet as Welty herself notes about
this tribe in her essay "Some Notes on River Country" (1944), the
Natchez had been wiped out and driven from the area by the French army,
either massacred or sent into slavery in Santo Domingo, by 1773, some
two decades before the novella takes place, if one dates it from the given
circumstances. The use of this extinct people as a living presence in the
novella, however, is not the result of the authorial neglect of historical
rigor under the pretext of the work not being a "*historical* historical novel"
but, I believe, of an extremely purposeful decision. The Natchez have to
be unreal. The opening passage of that 1944 essay, truly a gem among
Welty's nonfictions, conveys the *atemporal* atmosphere of the locale,
where the past becomes the present, the unreal the real, the very atmosphere that Welty seems to wish to engender in *The Robber Bridegroom*:

> A place that ever was lived in is like a fire that never goes out. It flares up,
> it smolders for a time, it is fanned or smothered by circumstance, but its
> being is intact, forever fluttering within it, the result of some original igni-
> tion. Sometimes it gives out glory, sometimes its little light must be sought
> out to be seen, small and tender as a candle flame, but as certain.
>   I have never seen, in this small section of old Mississippi River country
> and its little chain of lost towns between Vicksburg and Natchez, *anything
> so mundane as ghosts*, but I have felt many times there a sense of place as
> powerful as if it were visible and walking and could touch me. (286, em-
> phasis added)

Throughout *The Robber Bridegroom*, from behind its romantic present
of love and adventure, beings who could not be in existence cast their
somber silhouettes from the past upon the action and at times show up
in the light of the present to claim their vested rights.

It is noteworthy that in *The Robber Bridegroom* the whites are always
caught by surprise by a sudden emergence of the Indians; although the
whites should know very well the constant danger posed by the Indians,
it is as though they had never expected *this* assault, as though once again
the Indians' existence had been buried beneath their consciousness for a
moment *this* time. To the whites, the Indians are embodiments of lies,
though their lies are not made of words but in the fact that they disguise
and camouflage themselves. They assail the travelers by surprise, waiting
on all fours under their bearskins; their faces lurk behind the walls of leaves

and the bush at one's side becomes alive; under a mask of spotty leopard hides an Indian's face. Their emergence is like that of ghosts—silent and unexpected, but when they really appear one realizes one had known their existence all along.

Although the Indians' disguises and camouflages, made from the animals and plants found on the land, are a form of lying, we know the notion that "the land is there for the taking" (99), as Salome says, was a misconception. There were native people living on the land along with bears and spotty leopards among the leaves and bushes, not in disguise or camouflage. Welty poignantly indicates in the 1944 essay that the French regarded the Natchez as "either '*savages*' or '*naturels, innocents*'" (294) and yet took special notice of their cultured manners in certain social situations—for instance, that they never spoke except one at a time and never interrupted a speaker. Still, in the course of their contacts, out of mistrust and greed, both the Natchez and the French massacred each other and in the end the Natchez nation was annihilated by the French army. Although they may have been erased from the land, nevertheless the complex, exuberant memories of this extinct people, Welty seems to say, endured upon the land as if a living presence, remaining in the subconscious of the whites as a sense of guilt and horror. Like ghosts from the past, the Indians emerge from the chasms of nature—from between the leaves, from under the bearskins, to take their revenge. When this takes place, the whites know them well, as if they had emerged from their own minds. One of the subtexts of *The Robber Bridegroom* is the story of the ghostly Indians; it exposes a great lie of American history, a lie that is made up of such verbal constructs as "the New World," "the Great West," "sublime nature," "the frontier," and "the pursuit of happiness."

This Indian story subtext can be seen as playing the role of a double to the surface story of the love and adventures of the white characters. In this connection, one should recall Welty's remark in "Fairy Tale of the Natchez Trace" on the theme of "doubleness" to express the fullness of times when "leading one life hardly provided scope enough for it all." To resolve his confusion caused by his discovery of the double identity of Jamie, Clement meditates in a stone circle. But his meditation soon extends beyond the identity of one individual and leads to the doubleness of the age's identity; it involves both nature and humans alike:

> Two long ripples are following down the Mississippi behind the approaching somnolent eyes of the alligator. And like the tenderest deer a band of copying Indians pose along the bluff to draw us near them. Men are following men down the Mississippi, hoarse and arrogant by day, wakeful and dreamless by night at the unknown landings. A trail leads like a tunnel under

the roof of this wilderness. Everywhere the traps are set. Why? And what kind of time is this, when all is first given, then stolen away? (142–43)

In the same way, the subtext of the story of the Indians in *The Robber Bridegroom* becomes the product of the age's fullness and complexity that the author wishes to re-create. With the story of the Indians serving as the double for the surface story of love and adventure, Welty has added to the scope and depth of this frontier story.

After all the lies that have constructed this novella, as the last stroke of the master liar, Welty has the narrator cast one last great lie to the reader. Here she does not allow herself to reveal the deception but leaves the careful reader to suspect the perpetration of it upon him or her. When, at the end of *The Robber Bridegroom*, Rosamond and Clement are reunited at the docks in the still-Spanish New Orleans, among the things the daughter describes to the father is her and Jamie's now-fabulous lifestyle, gorgeous in its wealth and beauty: "They lived in a beautiful house of marble and cypress wood on the shores of Lake Pontchartrain, with a hundred slaves, and often went boating with other merchants and their wives, the ladies reclining under a blue silk canopy; and they sailed sometimes out on the ocean to look at the pirates' galleons" (183–84).

Before pointing out the absurdity of this passage, we should recall a similar situation earlier in the novella, in which Salome describes her dream home to Clement: "[We] can live in a mansion at least five stories high, with an observatory of the river on top of that, with twenty-two Corinthian columns to hold up the roof." To this, Clement responds: "'My poor wife, you are ahead of yourself'" (100). In "Fairy Tale of the Natchez Trace," Welty reveals the jest in this exchange between the wife and husband, pointing out that the mansion Salome describes is the real "Windsor Castle, out from Port Gibson, which did not get built until 1861" (305). This is why Salome is "ahead" of herself, for this exchange takes place long before the Louisiana Purchase. Welty's photo "Ruins of Windsor," taken in 1942—the year *The Robber Bridegroom* was published—and included in *Eudora Welty Photographs* (1989), and her mention of the ruins in the 1944 essay suggest that this relic of a planter's glory held a special fascination for her. Although Welty admitted in an interview that she played with historical chronology, she remained circumspect with regard to another playful liberty taken with historical accuracy to create a lie, one that we can consider a cousin to this one. Just as Windsor Castle would come into existence long after Salome describes it, so also no mansion "on the shores of Lake Pontchartrain" would be built until long after Rosamond describes one located there.

The city of New Orleans, which was returned by the Spanish crown to the control of Napoleon's France in 1800—only three years before the

Louisiana Purchase—consisted of what is the present Vieux Carré. In the early nineteenth century the city limits were redrawn, but this was done mainly to include the Faubourg Ste. Marie across the "commons," the present Canal Street, on the opposite side from the Vieux Carré. At the time when Rosamond speaks about their house on Lake Pontchartrain, apparently prior to 1800, the shores of Lake Ponchartrain should have resembled more closely a wilderness than "the place to live" (184) for a rich merchant's family. Besides, a merchant's residence with slave quarters in the city of New Orleans, however rich he might have been, could never have housed a hundred slaves. In fact "a hundred slaves" reminds us of one of Rosamond's earlier lies, in which she tells Jamie that her father killed "a hundred Indians" (49). The use of large round numbers follows fairy-tale convention, but the difference between the ahistorical situations of fairy tales and the actualities of American history involving the "Indians" and "slaves" is so great that Rosamond's carefree use of such a quantity, spoken with no more feeling for humans than one would have for cattle, is shocking. Moreover, sailing out to sea to see pirates' galleons for recreation would have been unrealistic to say the least, unless those galleons are now merchant ships, as Jamie is now a merchant. Yet the narrator reports that "it was all true but the blue canopy" (184). This means that not only Rosamond but the narrator is apparently lying: this is a fiction made up of lies.

Once the narrator's infallibility is suspended, what seems to be the ultimate "moral" the narrator wishes the reader to garner from this "fairy tale" becomes suspect. Following the blue-canopy episode, the omniscient narrator reveals Jamie's belief that "he [is] a hero and [has] always been one, only with the power to look both ways and to see a thing from all sides" (185). One may approve of this attitude as an inevitable necessity for survival in the "civilized" society of a market economy or as simply necessary if one is to live fully, acknowledging the harmony of the contraries. Yet to dub a successful bandit-merchant a "hero" implies the same kind of naming confusion inherent in the use of words that Miller identifies in his analysis of *Oedipus the King*. Earlier in the novella Clement already recognizes this confusion and remarks, "The appearance of a hero is no longer a single and majestic event like that of a star in the heavens, but a wandering fire soon lost" (143). The construct of the "hero" held in the old order that Clement had known is one whose achievement surpasses earthly, human limitations—it is "a star in the heavens"—and does not apply to a person like Jamie, whose achievement is the accumulation of worldly wealth. Although Clement is resigned to admit to the anachronism of his concept of the hero, the reader may not necessarily be expected to accept the narrator's endorsement of Jamie, since the narrator's fallibility and nonaccountability have already been explicitly demonstrated.

If we assume, as I have argued, that *The Robber Bridegroom* is on one level a fiction about the power of words, we find in retrospect a genuine hero who has fought to surpass human limitations with the power of this distinctively human possession. Salome, the character originally constructed to incorporate every possible evil borrowed from the mother/wife in such fairy tales as "Snow White," "Hanzel and Gretel," and "The Fisherman and His Wife," and of course by association the woman who had John the Baptist put to death, acquires one more attribute that I believe makes her a "hero" in this novella. Salome is characterized as one who firmly believes in the power of words and acts accordingly even in the teeth of death. From the start, the narrator seems to present Salome unfairly, and the author, very interestingly, somehow makes sure that the reader recognizes the unfairness. For instance, although the narrator emphasizes Salome's envy of the fancy dress, petticoat, and hairpins Clement has bought for Rosamond in New Orleans, in actuality Salome's response is more than understandable, since what he has bought Salome are articles that will tie her to household work; Salome also fears that such fancy possessions will cause Rosamond to become so vain as to run away from home: "You mark my *words*" (36, emphasis added), she says, a prediction that turns out true. Moreover, although Clement thinks of sending Rosamond to the Female Academy or getting her a tutor to cure her of lying in an effort to make her a lady, he never thinks of the hardships Salome underwent as a young woman, when such a luxury as going to finishing school was the remotest dream. Again, although Clement's complaint about Salome's greed for more land to cultivate is often noted in the narration, the narrator never expresses appreciation of the value of Salome's enterprising foresight, a foresight that has enabled the family to survive and prosper in the wilderness. In the presentation of Salome the narrator simply echoes the traditional pattern assigned to the wicked stepmother and the greedy wife. Finally, Salome's death is narrated as the natural outcome of this traditional pattern, namely, that the wicked mother/wife reaps the just harvest of her own evil sowing. It follows that the greater the pain and agony Salome endures, the more the reader should rejoice. Yet the overall effect of Salome's death is not this. Rather, it elicits a curious admiration for her in the reader.[2]

A self-chosen sacrifice to satisfy her vanity, or her self-esteem, perhaps, to be name-labeled the most beautiful, Salome defies the Indians with words. Welty makes comic use of the Natchez custom of speaking only one at a time:

> But before [the Indians] could say anything at all to her, Salome opened her mouth and gave them a terrible, long harangue that made them put their fingers in their ears. She told them all she knew.

"It is the command of our Chief," they told her, "that you be still."
"I won't be still!" said she, and told them everything over. (160)

Salome's words are so powerful that the Indians are afraid to touch her. She declares: "No one is to have power over me! . . . No man, and none of the elements! I am by myself in the world" (160–61), and she even commands the sun to stand still. This is an expression of the pride and arrogance of the enlightened, autonomous existentialist, who is certainly "ahead" of herself. Before her, the intimidated Indians from the past—those "*naturels, innocents*"—are pitiful like "feverish children" (161). Told to dance on till the sun obeys her words, Salome dances shouting to the sun to stand still. The narrator describes her as throwing off all her clothing during the dance so that she is "as naked as a plucked goose" ("geese" was, Welty tells us in her 1944 essay, the Natchez Indians' metaphoric description of the Europeans, whom they observed speaking together all at once so clamorously that they called to mind a flock of the squawking birds) till she stands "blue as a thistle" and falls over "stone dead" (163). Salome's attempt to fulfill her *words* at the risk of her life is a clear contrast to Rosamond's choosing the shame of walking home naked for the sake of saving her life, though this shows the stepdaughter to be no powerless *heroine* either. Moreover, the crude humor in the description of the dancing Salome presents a contrast to the complacent composure of the self-styled hero Jamie. Salome has aspired to surpass the human and control the universe with the distinctively human possession of words and has failed; Jamie has aspired to make himself wealthy among his fellow human beings, again with the distinctively human use of lies, and has succeeded. Which should be called more of a hero?

On the ahistorical fairy-tale level, deceits are openly justified and often commended for making possible the survival of the protagonist so that he or she may enjoy victory in the end; lying is an act of cleverness, the sole means by which the weak and good may defeat the strong and evil. In the novella's surface story, the otherwise innocent Jamie and Rosamond are justifiably, respectively, a hero and a heroine. But in the light of the novella's subplot of American frontier history, just as the hundred Indians and slaves become measures by which one can question the narrator's moral stance, Salome conversely becomes morally admirable. Is not the "hero" the greedy wife and wicked stepmother's double?

So far, I have been employing the word "double" rather loosely, as indeed Welty and her critics have done. Yet historically, when the word "double" has been applied to an individual, it has signified at least two differing concepts. Ralph Tymms in his *Doubles in Literary Psychology* (1949) distinguished between the type of doubles created by division and the type created by multiplication; in a similar framework Robert A.

Rogers in his *A Psychoanalytic Study of the Double in Literature* (1970) makes a distinction between the subjective double, that is, the divided self and the objective double, that is, two persons. In other words, one person could possess a different him/herself as a double, while two different persons could be the same person, being each other's double. Thus, the concept of the double derives from the discovery of instability in the cognition of sameness and difference, for, as Carl F. Keppler in his *The Literature of the Second Self* (1972) points out, the double is at once identical to and different from—often opposite to—the original. In *The Robber Bridegroom*, most of the doubles I have identified so far fall into the first, subjective, type, in which one person is two, one reality consisting of itself plus unreality. Yet the novella is inhabited by the second, the objective, type of the double as well—included, without doubt, consciously and purposely. The concluding section of this chapter attempts to clarify Welty's concept of certain aspects of fiction that I believe is represented in her use of these two types of the double in *The Robber Bridegroom*.

First, let us look at the subjective double, the various examples of which I have already indicated. If *The Robber Bridegroom* can be interpreted as a fiction about the power of words, which accounts for the novella's full use of that power's by-product—lies—how does this interpretation relate to the understanding, which we set aside earlier, that a fiction is *itself* a lie? Although Clement, Jamie, and Salome are all annoyed by Rosamond's habit of lying, the author seems to value her lies highly. The narrator tells us that Rosamond's lies simply cascade out of her mouth "like diamonds and pearls" when she opens it to speak (39). The allusion to Perrault's "The Fairies"—in which the beautiful heroine Rose on orders of her wicked mother goes into the forest singing to herself, helps a fairy disguised as an old woman, is rewarded with the gift of having jewels and flowers fall out of her mouth whenever she speaks, and in the end marries the prince who sees her passing through the forest—is not meant to be ironical, for Rosamond's lie about the kind mother panther does no harm to anyone and on the contrary amuses even the reader. The lie brightens up the weary hours of work that have been her real lot and transforms them into an exciting time that she would choose to dwell in. Besides, as we have seen, the happy ending to the lovers' romance is the result of the lies that Rosamond and Jamie had continued to tell at their times of hardship. Welty has spoken of her theme of doubleness as an expression of the fullness of the age when an enormous socioeconomic transition was taking place and people in effect lived more than one life. To defy the physicality of the one life allotted to each individual, the gift of imagination and the ability to create fiction with nonphysical words is as precious as the gift of pearls and diamonds. Is there a time in history that is not full enough to enjoy this gift? It is not only the days of the

Rosamonds and the Jamies but any time one wishes to taste the exuberance the world, which is ever in transition, offers.

Although the presence of the objective double is not as obvious in *The Robber Bridegroom* as that of the subjective double, the novella presents several instances in which the objective double appears, revealing a quite different aspect of fiction, namely, fiction as a form of repetition. I have already pointed out Clement's hallucinatory perception of his two wives, Amalie and Salome, as being one woman. Yet the narrator at certain points presents Rosamond as identical with Salome, despite the fact that Salome's main action in the novella is supposedly the mistreatment of her stepdaughter. Rosamond is kidnapped by Jamie at the same place on the bank of the Mississippi where Clement and Salome were married by an unholy priest. Once Rosamond begins living a wifely life with Jamie, she acts as the treasurer of her husband's earnings, sorting and labeling and storing the spoils, and certainly cherishes all the material wealth. If the tastier heron meat is not enough to feed the band, she chooses to share the preferred meat with Jamie alone, leaving the rest of the robbers to eat buffalo meat in silence. In the end, it befalls Rosamond to live in a gorgeous mansion with a hundred slaves, although we know this must be a lie, and yet this is the kind of life that was Salome's own dream. Thus the sweet and good Rosamond's and the lifestyle she is granted are no different from the wicked and greedy Salome's wishes. When it comes to deceiving her husband out of curiosity, Rosamond listens to Salome's proposal for a cunning strategy "like a blood mother and daughter" (122); finally the two women appear as "one shadow" (123). It is as if one life is cyclically repeated in the lives of the three women related to Clement—Amalie, Salome, and Rosamond—with yet another life suggested in the person of Clementine, Rosamond's daughter. What does this line of doubles mean?

Before attempting an answer to this question, one should note that the presence of the objective type of the double is suggested in other characters and concepts in the novella, though in subtler ways. The one being the husband of Amalie and Salome and the other the husband of Rosamond, respectively, Clement and Jamie, playing the same role as the other toward their wives, become at times doubles to each other; the Big Harp, his head falsely identified as Jamie's, can be considered Jamie's double in his bandit aspect. Besides, Clement's concept of the history of the New World, in which "the planter will go after the hunter, and the merchant after the planter, all having their day" (161), suggests in effect that humans in any historic phase are all doubles to those in the other phases. Yet probably more significant examples of doubles of the objective type are seen in the novella's appropriations of past literary works and archetypes. As the present discussion, as well as other criticisms and

Welty's own essay, show, *The Robber Bridegroom* replicates such character types and situations as those seen in the fairy tales transcribed by the
Brothers Grimm and Charles Perrault, in the biblical Salome and Joshua,
who had the sun stand still, or in the ballad "Young Andrew" (Pollack,
16–18). Although Welty certainly remakes the effects of the stories for
her own purposes, the sources are often clearly recognizable. Thus those
source stories and *The Robber Bridegroom* can be considered to constitute literary doubles of the objective type.

Getting back to the earlier question of the significance of the objective type of the double, one can say that it functions as the opposite to
the subjective type of the double. If the subjective type responds to our
desire for exuberance, the objective type answers our need for limita-
tion. The world is exuberant, and history complex, often too much so.
Placing an imaginary framework of what is known—a known story, a
known historical outcome, or whatever—upon the chaos of reality is an
easy and gratifying way to achieve a sense of control over one's life in
such a world and in the face of such a history. Even between the evil in
a wicked mother and the goodness in a sweet maiden, or between the
life of the planter and that of the Indian, if one can discern similarities
or even *create* an imaginary pattern with which an understandable order of things may be constructed, one is greatly freed from the fear of
chaos and assured that this and that have already occurred in human
experience so that reality is within one's grasp. To encounter the objective type of the double is to limit the expansion of the exuberance
and the deepening of complexity of the reality one faces. One should
be reminded that this impulse for order is so strong in us that even historians, scholars supposedly adhering to scientific discipline, find ways
to gratify its demands. For, as Hayden White points out, historians have
tended to "narrativize," rather than "narrate," events in the historical
record; "this value attached to narrativity in the representation of real
events rises out of a desire to have real events display the coherence,
integrity, fullness, and closure of an image of life that is and can only
be *imaginary*" (24, emphasis added). The objective doubles we see in
The Robber Bridegroom, then, can be considered one of the layman's
ways of narrativizing reality by utilizing preexisting narratives, which
include characters and concepts, exploiting the power of imagination.
The bridge between the reality and the preexisting narratives is fiction.

The Robber Bridegroom is a fiction about the power of words, this nonphysical human possession, with which one can create fictions to defy the
physicality of one's existence and create the sense of order in the fathom-
less chaos of time and space into which each of us is tossed.

CHAPTER 4

In Defense of Lies: "The Wide Net"

The title story of Welty's second collection of short stories, *The Wide Net and Other Stories* (1943), contains a passage that, at the time of publication, apparently amounted to nothing more than an offhand remark by one of the characters but was to fulfill a curious destiny in later years. Near the beginning of "The Wide Net," Virgil, the sidekick of the story's protagonist, William Wallace Jamieson, compares William Wallace's wife, Hazel, with her cousins:

> "She's a lot smarter than her cousins in Beulah," said Virgil. "And especially Edna Earle, that never did get to be what you'd call a heavy thinker. Edna Earle could sit and ponder all day on how the little tail of the 'C' got through the 'L' in a Coca-Cola sign." (171)

Who would have thought the author a decade later would develop this obscure passage into a fiction much greater in length than the story in which it originated? Welty's novella *The Ponder Heart* was published in 1954 (originally having appeared in the *New Yorker* in December 1953). In it the female protagonist, Edna Earle Ponder, runs the Beulah Hotel, considers herself the smart one of the family, and actually is quite a heavy thinker. The fact that Welty created a whole novella out of this short passage fortuitously throws light on the argument that I wish to make in the following discussion of "The Wide Net."

The story of "The Wide Net" is based on Hazel's short letter to her husband, William Wallace, a letter that, at the end of the story, is revealed to have remained unfinished because her husband came back unexpectedly. The letter was apparently written out of indignation at his staying out all night with his friends and leaving her, pregnant and alone, at home. In it she declares that she is going to the river to drown herself. This suicide note is fairly suspect, as people, including William Wallace himself, do not seem to take it very seriously. Thus, although William Wallace insists on dragging the river to recover Hazel's body with "the wide net" (170), which he will borrow from Old Doc, he walks leisurely with his friend Virgil to Old Doc's place, kicking at roadside flowers, catching a rabbit, reminiscing about his courting Hazel a year earlier. Yet like Virgil's precipitous remark about Edna Earle, a whole series of events is *made* to develop out of Hazel's suicide note by the very people who, apparently fairly convinced it is bogus, pretend to take measures to deal with the alleged tragedy.

The process of a lie producing a reality and the reality in its turn producing another lie is, as I have interpreted it, the pattern seen in the plot line of *The Robber Bridegroom*. In "The Wide Net" Hazel's *one* lie, a fiction, becomes a communal excuse to produce a reality beyond the daily life of the community in Dover, and this process constitutes a subtext concerning one role of fiction in relation to one's recognition of reality.

Having gathered enough men to join hands in the dragging—the Malones and the Doyles with their dogs—and followed by two white boys, Grady and Brucie, and two black ones, Sam and Robbie Bell, William Wallace and Virgil call on Old Doc, the community's guru figure and the owner of the wide net. Doc joins them with his net, and they all start down the Old Natchez Trace for a point on the Pearl River, from which they will drag upstream to a spot near Dover, where Hazel is considered to have jumped. The mythical-archetypal aspects of this river-dragging have long been pointed out by the critics. Ruth M. Vande Kieft sees in it an evocation of "the Dionysiac feasts, the fertility rites of primitive cultures, the folk ceremonies that marked the changes in season or the celebration of birth and marriage" (1962, 65). She continues: "The clan's ritual of dragging the river takes place at the turn of a season, shortly before a birth, at a time of change in the life of the young hero who is about to become a father" (65), while the "trials" of the hero are executed during and after the dragging (66). Zelma Turner Howard calls William Wallace "an unwitting humorous Dionysus followed by his tribe of 'satyrs,' . . . undergoing all the ordeals of the archetypal initiation" (37) to find his lost wife, in the mock-serious local situation. Howard also notes the author's appropriate use of the farming calendar in the Natchez Trace area; the dragging is to take place when the farmers have nothing to do till spring (39). Michael Kreyling, in his earliest book, *Eudora Welty's Achievement of Order* (1980), and his recent *Understanding Eudora Welty* (1999), sees reflected in the story's structure that of *The Divine Comedy:*

the locations of the river, the town of Dover, and William Wallace and Hazel's cabin, along which the protagonist follows the process of his initiation, are identified respectively as "the terrible" (corresponding to *Inferno*), "the prosaic" (*Purgatorio*), and "the sublime" (*Paradiso*), and the characters Virgil and Hazel as Dante's companion and Beatrice (Kreyling 1980, 19–21).

These mythical-archetypal approaches are based on the story's external form and internal structure, in which the process of the protagonist's change is traced in accordance with the change in season. The "change" in season and in the protagonist's life, however, can be interpreted more specifically as the *cyclic* change in them, when one considers the content of Hazel's suicide note, from which this dragging ritual originates. Hazel's suicide note is the outcome of her extremely serious, almost comical, consideration of the coming of a new life into their family and of her indignation at her husband's not appreciating its importance fully enough. To call attention to the gravity of the coming of the new life, Hazel has to renounce her own life, or at least to feign to do so. This life/death dualism of her situation cannot be resolved through the private domesticity of a young couple, for one must resort to a more universal application. During the course of the communal dragging, the life/death opposition is resolved through various manifestations of the cyclicity of life and death.

The prevailing tone is set by Old Doc, orating on the present change of seasons "from hot to cold" (176). He points out the ripeness of the farm animals, the fowl, and the fruits and nuts, and the autumn colors in the woods and yet already foresees the coming of winter. Seasonal change is the most obvious cyclic change one can observe in daily life. The equating of life and death with cyclic seasonal change must have been, also, one of the most common ways down through the ages that humans acquired a sense of immortality: the sense that the death of a life is necessitated by the birth of a new life and that, in fact, life, though in successively new incarnations, continues on through deaths, in a cyclic progression.

Old Doc's oration reminds the river-dragging party of this seemingly trite but nevertheless irrefutable folk belief. Earlier, Virgil had expressed men's common complaint that "it's a pity for [pretty girls like Hazel] to grow old, and get like their mothers" (171). In the light of Doc's oration, even this observation should be reconsidered; aging and becoming a mother should not be "a pity" but a welcome step for following generations of pretty girls. The cyclic viewpoint subverts what one had taken as reality and reconstructs a new reality. To William Wallace, now completely attuned to looking for the new reality, the river before him is no longer the familiar Pearl River but some alien stream: "What is the name of this river?" (176), he has to ask. Despite the people's reassuring responses, William Wallace expects the river to be "still a mystery" (177), a mystery he will challenge.

The succeeding passages of the story include instances of the cyclicity of life and death revealed by the river. The draggers see three generations of alligators—big ones, middle-sized ones, and a little baby one, which Old Doc warns will become just as big. Grady and Brucie, the white boys who have been allowed to join the adults' dragging because their father had been drowned in the Pearl, see their reflections in the surface of the river. In the reflecting water Grady feels he is seeing the image of his own drowned father, "with arms open, eyes open, mouth open" (180). The image impresses the reader with its expression of urgency compounded with earnest effort to try to communicate beyond the boundary of mortality. Grady, unlike the younger Brucie, sees unrequited desire in the open eyes and hears a voiceless cry from the open mouth.[1] He perceives the repetition of life passing from his deceased father to himself, his own living image and the image of his father's dead body overlapped.

The most dramatic discovery is made by William Wallace. Retaining, as Kreyling suggests, the Dantean allusion to Virgil, who is "to keep [him] on the track" (172) to recover "the prettiest girl in Mississippi" (175), William Wallace first has to descend into his inferno all alone: he dives for the bottom of the deepest spot of the river. His long submersion is described as a virtual death, during which time he comes close to becoming one with the mind of Hazel, who has died her own virtual death, and when he finally ascends to the surface, it is at the spot where Grady sees the image of his own dead father. The nature of William Wallace's discovery under water, "about which [Hazel's] words in a letter could not speak" (180), is implied by the narrator:

> How (who knew?) she had been filled to the brim with that elation that they all remembered, like their own secret, the elation that comes of great hopes and changes, sometimes simply of the harvest time, that comes with a little course of its own like a tune to run in the head, and there was nothing she could do about it—they knew—so it had turned into this? It could be nothing but the old trouble that William Wallace was finding out, reaching and turning in the gloom of such depths. (180)

The content of his discovery is not expressed in words, just as Hazel's true feeling could not be. Nor does Grady give expression to what he has seen. The secret the river reveals is something beyond the conventional mode of verbal representation, in which change and continuity, life and death, husband and wife, father and son are all separate entities. The river reveals a different kind of reality, in which these oppositions are grasped as one, as in Hazel's case, in which a profound change—her pregnancy—ensures the same sort of richer continuity as nature embodies at harvest time. To direct attention to this "contradictory" mode of conception by means of words, however insufficient, a letter based on a lie is appropriate. Once William Wallace learns, in the depths of the river, how to share the secret of this new reality with his wife, he eats and sleeps his fill on the bank.

The episode of "The King of the Snakes" (182) has been considered by most critics as an archetypal form of a "test" performed on William Wallace before he can become a hero, or a full-fledged husband and father. He, who now knows the secret the river revealed to him, passes the test by staring down the King of the Snakes.

The thunder and lightning that ensue confirm the change of seasons. The occasion also presents another manifestation of cyclicity, this time in the two black boys, Sam and Robbie Bell. The boys believe that being struck by lightning runs in the family: a "pitchfork" mark had been etched on their grandfather's cheek, and their father had lain "dead" for three days, both struck by lightning. Sam and Robbie Bell express fear that this may now be their turn (183). Yet instead of being struck by lightning and left with a physical mark, the boys, together with the others, find themselves covered all over with torn leaves blown by the gusts. About this an unwittingly insightful remark is made: "'Now us got scales,' wailed Sam. 'Us is the fishes'" (183). At the same time that they are aware of being in the family cycle of death, they see that they and the fish in the river belong to the same great family, being all part of ever-changing nature. Doc and Virgil scold the boys for talking too much, but again Sam makes a cogent observation: "We always talk this much . . . but now everybody so quiet, they hears us" (183). These black boys are able to put into words the kind of ultra-real awareness that William Wallace and Grady could not. Marginalized in social status because of age and race, Sam and Robbie Bell display a sensitivity and speech that are not confined within the conventions of the society. Their speech crosses the border between the mundane reality and another, (ultra) reality, so to speak, with natural ease, and expresses what they intuitively sense.

The last section of "The Wide Net" is set once again in Dover, to which the river-dragging party returns. The refreshed atmosphere of the town, where the thunder storm has washed everything clean, reflects the party's perception of the new reality to which it was exposed during the dragging. In the festal mirth among the dragging party and the townspeople over the big catch, only William Wallace is still discontented; he yells, "I don't want no more of 'em [the fish]. I want my wife!" (185). It is now all out in the open that even Old Doc had "nary once" (186) believed that Hazel was drowned in the river and that the dragging had been intended to catch fish. William Wallace has to claim that the river-dragging was originally to catch his wife, not the fish, and that the wide net was *his* net. Although William Wallace makes Virgil say this through physical coercion, it is also clear that in the world of the new reality that the river has revealed, to catch the fish and to catch Hazel are intrinsically identical actions, since humans and fish are taken as belonging to the same great family, and since William Wallace was the one who brought about the use of the wide net for this purpose.

The little lunar rainbow he sees over the roof upon arriving home is comparable to the rainbow after Noah's Flood, "the token of the covenant" of trust between God and humankind, which is to be succeeded to by the cycles of "perpetual generations." Ostensibly, the rainbow is the token of the covenant of trust between Hazel the celestial and William Wallace the terrestrial, but ultimately it is between his family—William Wallace, Hazel, and their future posterity—and nature with its ever-repeating cycles. Inside the house, Hazel welcomes her husband back, but smiling in the crook of his arm, she says, "I will do it again if I get ready. . . . Next time will be different, too" (188). There will be crises like the one just resolved in their married life in the years to come, but since William Wallace is "trying to look where she [looks]" (188), each crisis will be overcome so that their married life may continue, through ever-changing stages.

The role of Hazel's suicide note is to open up a passageway to a reality that the mundane domesticity of a young married couple has not known. The fact that in content the note is a lie suggests that the note prescribes a mode of perception of the world different from the ordinary modes. Hazel's lie forces William Wallace to see that the oppositions in the ordinary world—life and death, change and continuity, humans and fish, summer and winter—are actually different phases of the same cycles, and they correspond to the greater, universal cycles of nature. It enables him to see why Hazel would kill herself for the sake of a new life. Thus, taken positively, lies, or fictions, liberate us from the materiality of our existence in which the one set pattern of the passage of time, aging, and ultimately death is firmly established: lies afford us other ways of seeing our existence, other realities in which to place ourselves. This subtext of "The Wide Net" is Welty's testimony to the power of fiction, showing that this nonmaterial, purely verbal construct can *produce* a new reality by influencing our recognition of the world around us. It testifies to the situation that fiction preexists reality. The casual remark about Edna Earle's limited mental abilities that Welty the author inserted in "The Wide Net" influenced Welty herself in the same way and produced a new reality brought to fruition in her novella *The Ponder Heart*.

CHAPTER 5

A Hilarious Destruction:
The Glory of *The Ponder Heart*

When Terry Eagleton said, "'Our' Homer is not identical with the Homer of the Middle Ages, nor 'our' Shakespeare with that of his contemporaries. . . . All literary works, in other words, are 're-written,' if only unconsciously, by the societies which read them" (12), he may not quite have had in mind the kind of situation *The Ponder Heart* has fallen into. Eudora Welty's novella has been "rewritten" by members of her own society with exceptional frequency for the past half-century since its publication in 1953 and particularly frequently within the last fifteen years.

The Ponder Heart was literally "rewritten" in 1956 into a Broadway play, naturally erasing all the effects of the original first-person narration; the play entirely re-created the extraordinary half-witted hero into a rather rational repentant. The original author, who had upheld the reader's complete freedom of interpretation, be it regarding the question of Phoenix Jackson's grandson's death or anything else, expressed her uneasiness over this "rewriting" in a letter to the playwrights.[1] The succeeding years witnessed more moderate interpretations by critics. The swirl of comedy and terror in the work was noted by critics early on; Michael Kreyling adds to this a new focus on the narrator's foreboding of her family's extinction with the passage of time. Jennifer Lynn Randisi and Carol Manning, among others, discuss the novella's narrative technique, the former relating it to the Southern romance, the latter noting the aspects of the southern tall-tale tradition in it. The past decade, however, has seen a rush of criticisms on *The Ponder Heart,* each of which takes quite a strong stand within a unique view; the situation gives an impression that the novella has been going through a series of radical "rewritings."

Probably none of the earlier critics, including Rachel V. Weiner in "Eudora Welty's *The Ponder Heart*: The Judgment of Art," and John L. Idol, Jr., in "Edna Earle Ponder's Good Country People"—sympathetic defenders of Edna Earle—has evaluated the narrator's character as highly as does Barbara Harrell Carson, who "rewrites" *The Ponder Heart* into a testimony of Edna Earle's moral integrity, selfless courage, and above all, intelligence and creativity backed by an understanding of human nature: "The thinking and feeling one, she is the real possessor of the pondering and the ponderous heart of the title" (621). Lynn Snyder in her "Rhetoric in *The Ponder Heart*" calls the novella "a short saga of family declining" (18) in which the narrator, using her finest rhetoric, tries to present a family that possesses "affection, tenderness, pride, and love" (25). From an entirely different perspective, Gerda Seaman and Ellen L. Walker have identified a sensational Freudian story that sees Edna Earle as, in effect, glossing over two, not one, deaths, if not murders, caused, if not committed, by a retarded pervert: "The reader must admit a sense of the perverse in our dim-witted hero's sexuality" (72). Marilyn Arnold's "rewriting" is even more radical: Edna Earle's narration is a "strategy" to trap the narratee as "Daniel's next bride" (70).

What gives rise to this incessant "rewriting"? None of Welty's other works has engendered such a succession of complete metamorphoses. I attribute the cause to what I see as a subtext inherent in the whole scheme of the work, a strategic subtext designed to exploit to the limit the possibilities of a peculiar narrative device—the dramatic monologue, in which every "fact," every choice of material, every motive for action, is based on the narrator's subjectivity. It is a subjectivity, however, left entirely to each reader's subjective scrutiny and assessment. For *The Ponder Heart* Welty has chosen to explore how far indeterminacy, rather than any determinate message, can reach. In the twenty-first century this experimental attitude does not strike us as especially unfamiliar. Although at the creation of *The Ponder Heart* such words as "deconstruction" or "deconstructionist criticism" did not exist in the American academic vocabulary, what Welty did in this novella is curiously oriented toward this now esteemed (or notorious) critical practice.

The charge of murder against Daniel Ponder is based on his own verbal message to his wife, who had kicked him out from home almost a year earlier. The words, entrusted to Big John, his old employee, are, "I'm going to kill you dead, Miss Bonnie Dee, if y'don't take m' back" (91). The public prosecutor, Dorris R. Gladney, capitalizes on the fact that Bonnie Dee was found dead two days after the message was sent and, moreover, at a time when Daniel and her niece Edna Earle Ponder were visiting her. Edna Earle, called to the witness stand, testifies that as a "perfectly normal household," threats like this flew all the time in the Ponder household; its members meant no real threats at all. She cheerfully illustrates her argument: "[Grandma] said 'I'm going to kill you' every other breath to him—she raised him. Gentlest woman on the face of the earth. 'I'll break your neck,' 'I'll skin you alive,' 'I'll beat your brains out'—Mercy! How that does bring Grandma back. Uncle Daniel was brought up like anybody else" (111).

Jennifer Lynn Randisi, in her *A Tissue of Lies: Eudora Welty and the Southern Romance*, identifies "the distance between what Edna Earle says and what the reader hears" (57) as one of the main effects of the work. To take it a step farther, Edna Earle's refutation of the seriousness of Daniel's words suggests that she herself is attesting to the distance between utterance and understanding, or, to borrow Saussurean terms, attesting that the same signifier carries with it two different kinds of signifieds between the Ponders and Gladney: what is to the one a request embellished with the highest degree of endearment is to the other a blunt death threat. Actually, Edna Earle's perception of this discrepancy is so radical as to be called "poststructural." Agreeing with Barbara Harrell Carson, who takes Edna Earle's mature, compassionate, courageous character as that of a truly enlightened being, I wish to argue that Edna Earle clearly sees, through her understanding of human nature, that the meaning of language depends on the context in which it is used and on the users or communities of users. Thus Edna Earle says of Uncle Daniel's message, "With some people, it's little threats. With others, it's liable to be poems" (117).

Throughout Edna Earle's narrative, there exists a solid subtext that Welty constructs with numerous instances in which language's supposed one-to-one correspondence between the signifier and the signified is utterly destroyed. Probably one of the crudest discrepancies occurs in the use of personal names. For everyone in and around the town of Clay, "Mr. Ponder" means Mr. Sam Ponder, Daniel's father and Edna Earle's grandfather, and not Daniel Ponder, who is referred to as "Mr. Daniel," "Uncle Daniel," or "Daniel." But outside this community, at the Jackson asylum, when Daniel Ponder, back from an overnight stay at home, quite guilelessly refers to his father accompanying him as "Mr. Ponder," Sam Ponder is mistaken by the asylum staff for Daniel Ponder and is forcibly put in confinement, while the real patient is left free to go home— an incident causing a hilarious "conniption fit" (19) throughout Clay. Later in court, when Prosecutor Gladney, an outsider to Clay, calls Daniel "Mr. Ponder," Uncle Daniel looks "over his shoulder for Grandpa. Nobody had ever called him Mr. Ponder in his life" (132). Another ridiculous failure of language in personal identity occurs when DeYancy calls Johnnie

Ree Peacock as a defense witness. Intending to implicate Bonnie Dee's behavior while she was still alive, DeYancey asks Johnnie Ree to tell the court about a trip to Memphis she had enjoyed "with [her] sister" (122). Apparently not understanding the real purpose of the interrogation, Johnnie Ree spends hours going into details of their conduct in Memphis; only at the end of her testimony does the court find out that Johnnie Ree had taken that trip not with Bonnie Dee but another of her many sisters, Treva, while Bonnie Dee had stayed at home, as a good "married lady" should (126). To Johnnie Ree, DeYancey's "your sister" does not necessarily mean the person obvious to him and everyone else.

The destruction of the correspondence between a personal name and a person occurs even beyond the human boundary. In the lobby of Edna Earle's Beulah Hotel, there is a mysterious plant that Edna Earle regularly enters in the contest at the Fair under the category "Best Other than Named." Around the Beulah Hotel the plant has been called "Miss Ouida Sampson," after the lady who gave it to her grandmother. Thus when Uncle Daniel carries "Miss Ouida Sampson" to the fair for Edna Earle, he takes a plant (21). Only toward the end of the novel does the listener/reader suddenly hear about the human "Miss Ouida Sampson," who is so old that she "wanted to be *carried*" (145, emphasis added) to the courtroom, giving rise to an exorbitant fancy that the old lady has been named after the plant. In this novella not only personal names but simply names of things, or signifiers, can become completely arbitrary, depending upon how the speaker looks at the signifieds. Thus, talking about Bonnie Dee's numerous gorgeous dresses, as reported by Edna Earle, her proud maid, Narciss, says, "[There are] evening dresses and street dresses and hostess dresses and brunch dresses—dresses in boxes and hanging. Think of something to wear. Bonnie Dee [has] it" (67). Although one daily uses these words for distinguishing types of dresses, we are led to acknowledge that these categorizations for differentiating kinds of dresses are no less arbitrary than the way a donor names a plant.

Even professional titles cease functioning as such. The late "Professor Magee" of Clay, as Edna Earle tells us, "wasn't professor of anything, just real smart. . . . He'd never worked either" (21); and Judge Tip Clanahan "is not really a judge. What he is is a splendid lawyer and our best friend" (83). Yet the most incredible discrepancy between a professional title and its bearer's qualifications is the blind coroner of Clay. A sightless coroner is in itself a total betrayal of whatever meaning or reference the word denotes as a vehicle of expression, or, in Derridean terms, a betrayal of the "presence" presupposed behind the word "coroner." Besides, Coroner Truex Bodkin's professional testimony on the cause of Bonnie Dee's death is just as agnostic and indeterminate as his first name ("True X"): "'Heart failure,' he said. 'Natural causes—I mean other than natural cause, could be. That's what I meant—could've been other than natural causes'" (89).

Beyond names and titles, Welty's use of troping figures in *The Ponder Heart*, often very trite clichés, constantly destroys their presupposed trite meanings. Her technique is to expose the textuality of those expressions that can be compared to what Roland Barthes calls the "stereographic plurality of the weave of signifiers" (159). For instance, early in the novel Edna Earle, describing Uncle Daniel's appearance, says, "He dresses fit to kill, you know, in a snow-white suit" (11). Uncle Daniel dresses impeccably as a socially established gentleman, in the innocent color of pure snow, in the torrid Mississippi summer, so appropriate to commit murder: all these contradictory, ominous connotations cancel out in each other their respective presupposed meanings and create a new multiple, yet irreducible, plurality of meaning. Of course, the gluttonous Daniel could "eat [Bonnie Dee] up" (34, 57). While "Narciss all at once dies laughing" (100) in court, poor Bonnie Dee literally "died laughing" (141); she was *tickled to death*. At the Peacock woman's death, the doctor exclaims, "'You don't mean she's flew the coop?'" (143).

Some passages not even meant to be tropes by the narrator exhibit such reverberations for the reader due to their textuality. For instance, when DeYancey is taking his leave of the Ponder household after seeing Bonnie Dee quite at home there as Daniel's new wife, Welty drops in a seemingly trifling scene involving Narciss: "Narciss had the fattest chicken of all down on the block, and hollered at him, 'We's going to keep her [Bonnie Dee]!' and brought her ax down whack" (40). At this point, Narciss's words are an expression of joy mixed with a possible hint of defiance toward whatever objections this marriage might face in the family; the maid demonstrates her approval of the marriage by cooking the fattest chicken. As the story unfolds, however, the Ponders and their well-wishers (Narciss, Tip Clanahan, Dr. Eubanks, and others) certainly resort to various means, from playing jacks with her to paying her allowance, to keep Bonnie Dee Peacock in the Ponder House; in the end, when all else fails, she is finished off just as a fowl is killed, with a "whack." The scene creates such multiple layers of contradictory images as celebration, defiance, love, marriage, confinement, wife/fowl, and murder.

Although the author and the reader thoroughly enjoy savoring the plurality of meaning in *The Ponder Heart*, the narrator, however "enlightened," sometimes grows weary of it. At such times, Edna Earle opts for the least possible plurality of meaning:

I was up there in my room, reading some directions. That's something I find I like to do when I have a few minutes to myself—I don't know about you. How to put on furniture polish, transfer patterns with a hot iron, take

off corns, I don't care what it is. I don't have to do it. Sometimes I'd rather
sit still a minute and read a good quiet set of directions through than any
story you'd try to wish off on me. (73)

Edna Earle, this person who calls herself "a great reader that never has
time to read" (55), who brags that she can read in the dark (55) and
who versifies a classified ad—all nothing but betrayals of the "presupposed presences"—is the sort of person who knows and feels the burden of the kind of language she has to face in daily life. Her own
narration can never spare a moment of serenity, like "a good quiet set
of directions," but rather is permeated with the instability of meaning.

While *The Ponder Heart* celebrates the destruction of the so-called
presupposed presence behind language, by so doing it also destroys its
characters. What the main characters undergo is hardly a "growth" or even
a "change," such as often takes place in the traditional novel, but a
destruction of being. Early in the novella, the hero of Edna Earle's narrative is presented as an extremely generous, loving, kind-hearted, nice-
looking, well-dressed, good-mannered gentleman of great material
fortune. But under Edna Earle's lavish panegyrics, the reader also sees a
different portrait of Uncle Daniel. Putting aside the fact that Edna Earle
"was liable to have passed anybody" (10), she "did pass him in the seventh
grade" (9), and we do not know how far Daniel progressed beyond that.
When all was said and done, he had been committed to the asylum, although later discharged, again due not to any merit of his own. He has
indeed been generous, but from what the reader gathers from Edna
Earle's narrative, Uncle Daniel had been so rich that his generosity really had not affected his lifestyle, except when he has given away all of
his bank savings toward the end of his trial. Indeed, for a person who
does not possess great mental resources, showing his goodwill by gift
giving could be the easiest way to earn the respect and love of the
community.

He is hardly a well-mannered gentleman if he says in public to a
strange woman less than half his age, "I've got a great big house standing empty, and my father's Studebaker. Come on—marry me" (30), or
if he pulls the corner of the dress of his late wife's sister from under the
stile and asks for a date only a few weeks after his wife's death. Actually
at the very beginning, Edna Earle says of Uncle Daniel, "When he sees
you sitting in the lobby of the Beulah, he'll take the other end of the sofa
and then move closer up to see what you've got to say for yourself; and
then he's liable to give you a little hug and start trying to give you something. Don't do you any good to be bashful. He won't let you refuse"
(7). She creates an impression that the point is his friendliness and generosity. But as the story develops and especially after the incident at the

stile, the reader may regard such behavior as uninhibited sexual aggressiveness in return for a material reward. Again, Daniel's manner at the Beulah Hotel dining table is far from being "good as gold"; also, to leave his wife alone at home in the country every night while he comes in to town and to give his wife no money to spend are not acts of kindness, to say the least.

The shining portrait of Uncle Daniel created by Edna Earle at the beginning is thus gradually dismantled and finally destroyed by her own narration. When almost all the money, which has supported whatever commendable qualities Daniel Ponder has displayed so far, is lost, the exemplary character Edna Earle first creates in her narrative literally melts away: rejected by Johnnie Ree as a dirty penniless old man, "for a minute [Daniel] just stood still in the bright sun, like the cake of ice that was melting there that day" (152). Uncle Daniel's final remark in the novella shows that he is no longer that optimistic, innocent, impervious person but a sober, experienced, pitifully hurt person, one whose story now could never come close to being as hilarious as *The Ponder Heart*: "You fooled me up yonder at Court this afternoon, Edna Earle, I declare you did. But never mind—I'm staying just the same. You didn't fool me as bad as Bonnie Dee did" (154).

In a reverse manner, Bonnie Dee comes to gain the reader's understanding and sympathy as the narrative proceeds, despite the narrator Edna Earle's presumably adverse opinion of her. What is interesting is that Edna Earle is essentially so fair-minded that she cannot help noticing the unfair lot that has befallen Bonnie Dee by her having married Uncle Daniel, although Edna Earle has appointed herself to be on Uncle Daniel's side. Reporting Bonnie Dee's having run away from home after her "marriage trial" of five and a half years, for instance, Edna Earle makes a comment that cancels out whatever criticism she has leveled at Bonnie Dee's behavior:

> The way I look back at Bonnie Dee, her story was this. She'd come up from the country—and before she knew it, she was right back in the country. Married or not. She was away out yonder on Ponder Hill and nothing to do and nothing to play with in sight but the Negroes' dogs and the Peppers' cats and one little frizzly hen. From the kind of long pink finger-nails she kept in the ten cent store, that hadn't been her idea at all. Not her dream. (48–49)

Edna Earle also reveals, as something quite funny, that Uncle Daniel didn't give Bonnie Dee any money, that she herself would pass Bonnie Dee some every now and then or would buy her "something ladylike to put on her back" (49). Edna Earle is certainly kind in her generosity, but her acts also confirm to the reader an underlying bias against Bonnie Dee, since it is within Edna Earle's power to halt Daniel's inconsiderate treatment of his wife. Thus Edna Earle's narrative, in effect, refutes itself and suggests that Bonnie Dee's subsequent behavior might be understandable. Moreover, it might occur to one that later, when Bonnie Dee is living separately from her husband, a sudden cutoff of her weekly allowance represents a serious breach of trust between husband and wife, a betrayal that Edna Earle has initiated—or at least the way the business is narrated invites the reader to consider such a notion. As the last stroke, at the end of her narration, Edna Earle unwittingly reveals her true feeling about Bonnie Dee: "Ordinary as she was and trial as she was to put up with— she's the kind of person you do miss. I don't know why—deliver me from giving you the *reason*. You could look and find her like anywhere" (156). Edna Earle may not know the reason for liking Bonnie Dee herself, but behind her words the reader has been gathering clues all along.

As for her own self, Edna Earle paints a quite favorable image. Apparently she is "the smart one of the family" (9): she fixed up the run-down Beulah Hotel when it was given to her and ran a good business; she is resourceful, with good ideas on how to secure the welfare of Uncle Daniel and others around her, and possesses the vitality to pursue and bring to fruition those ideas. Moreover, she is proud of her conviction and courage, as she says of her acts in court: "I never lied in my life before, that I know of, by either saying or holding back, but I flatter myself that when the time came I was equal to either one" (143). Going on, she describes herself as a fully eligible woman, with a boyfriend who regularly stays at her hotel and takes her out. But throughout her narration incidents are mentioned that bring into question the reliability of her self-portrait. Although the reader will have no doubts about the integrity of her efforts to protect Daniel, she is blind, or chooses to be blind, to certain aspects of the whole affair concerning Uncle Daniel's marriages and trial, leading the reader to perceive the gradual destruction of the original images of Daniel Ponder and Bonnie Dee, as we have noted above.

Toward the end of the novella, Welty includes an episode that effectively and aptly destroys the self-image of Edna Earle as she has created it. It occurs as Edna Earle runs to fetch ammonia, possibly to revive Bonnie Dee: "In the bathroom I glanced in the mirror, to see how I was taking it, and got the fright of my life. Edna Earle, I said, you look old as the hills! It was a different mirror, was the secret—it magnified my face by a thousand times—something Bonnie Dee had sent off for and it had come. I ran back, but the laugh didn't go away—" (142).

Up to this point Edna Earle does not seem to have had any doubts about her self-appointed role as guardian of Uncle Daniel from whomever or whatever would do him harm. But Bonnie Dee's death, apparently, is something utterly unexpected. It had never occurred to her that her "good as gold" Uncle Daniel could do harm to the one whom she has all along believed to be doing harm to him. Edna Earle's whole raison d'être in life is shaken, and she has a glimpse of what might be the true image of herself, of which she has rejected acknowledgment so far. The mirror has simply magnified what she is.

Destroying language and character, Welty also rips asunder the central event of the novel—the murder. Although Edna Earle's first mention of Bonnie Dee's death is a bolt out of the blue, it is unusually terse: "Well, to make a long story short, Bonnie Dee sent him word Monday after dinner and was dead as a doornail Monday before supper. Tuesday she was in her grave. Nobody more surprised than the Ponders" (75). She cleverly skips over the cause of Bonnie Dee's death and draws the listener's/reader's attention ahead to the details of the funeral that follow. But Gladney indicts Daniel Ponder for suffocating Bonnie Dee to death, "out of a fit of pure-D jealousy from the well-springs of his aging heart" (98). To this DeYancy Clanahan, the Perry Mason of Clay, brings forward a counterargument that Bonnie Dee died of heart failure at the shock of a bolt of lightening, entering as evidence the top part of a lightening-struck fig tree from the Ponder garden. Defense witnesses, including Edna Earle, back DeYancy's argument, although as defense attorney he certainly blunders in leading off with his witness Johnnie Ree. Then, all of a sudden, Daniel Ponder volunteers to tell his story, and Edna Earle shouts out: "'Never mind, Uncle Daniel! Listen to Edna Earle,' I says. 'If you tell that, nobody'll ever be able to believe you again—not another word you say. You hear me?'" (139). Now, to her present guest, Edna Earle tells the "truth," which she had prevented Uncle Daniel from telling in court—that Bonnie Dee died of the combined stress of the terror of the storm and of Uncle Daniel's tickling her. Thus, Gladney's indictment, DeYancy's clever defense, and the reversal now reveal that Daniel Ponder, after all, killed his wife—all of which have made up for a good light mystery story so far. But in Welty's conception this novella far exceeds the depth of a Perry Mason mystery, of course. The "truth" about the lightening, which DeYancy has proved; the "truth" about Bonnie Dee's laughing to death, which Edna Earle has confided; and all the other minor "truths" that have constituted a "true" story about Bonnie Dee's death crumble in the face of Daniel Ponder's next act.

His giving away almost all his money to those in the courtroom and outside it (the dogs) nullifies all the efforts to conduct a proper trial (and Edna Earle's confidential revelation later in the Beulah lobby). Everyone in the courtroom—the Peacocks, the friends of the Ponders, the jury, and "everybody and his brother . . . and then people not knowing the Ponders but knowing *of* them" (86)—uniformly rejects, in effect, the court process by accepting the money. Friend and enemy, truth and falsehood, guilt and innocence no longer stand in opposition. Uncle Daniel, presumably the most guileless character of *The Ponder Heart*, using what one would consider the most shameless and unethical path, succeeds in destroying such binary oppositions and hence the validity of his murder charge.

In the end, the topics of Edna Earle's narrative come to naught: Daniel Ponder is acquitted of the murder but is wifeless as before, while Edna Earle still keeps the hotel and is not to be married to her boyfriend, Mr. Springer. Not only the townspeople but even Uncle Daniel has deserted the Beulah lobby. Although Edna Earle calls to Narciss and Daniel, their response is not heard, at least not yet: "Narciss don't cook good any more" (155), and Daniel "comes down a little later every night" (155). The novella ends with only the narrator's voice echoing in the empty room. What will follow her calls? Will they revive the former hilarity of the Beulah, will the guest stay, or will the lobby remain empty and silent "like the grave" (10)? The ending of *The Ponder Heart* is as indeterminate as the blind coroner's testimony.

What, after all, does Welty do in *The Ponder Heart*? The "smart" Edna Earle is left not in the past but ahead of her time in asserting that words change meaning according to the speaker and the listener. Welty shows that if language is to function, signification is not a phenomenon of one-to-one correspondence perceived jointly by speaker and listener but of a plurality of meaning produced independently, in varying degrees, by the speaker/writer, the listener/reader, and the context. Due to the essential indeterminacy that exists between the narrator and the listener/reader of the dramatic monologue, Edna Earle's narration, if one may borrow Derridean flamboyance to describe it, "multiplies words, precipitates them one against the other, engulfs them too, in an endless and baseless substitution whose only rule is the sovereign affirmation of the play outside meaning[,] . . . a kind of potlatch of signs that burns, consumes, and wastes words in the gay affirmation of death: a sacrifice and a challenge" (274). As Derrida implies, destruction comes along with this exuberant plurality: to admit plurality means to destroy the possibility of any single "presence." To use language is to create a meaning and, by so doing, to nullify the rest of the possible meanings (if we are to know what the rest encompasses). But this newly created meaning is destined to be destroyed, or "sacrificed and challenged" by another meaning, and yet another, and another.

Welty amplifies this concept beyond words and expressions to extend it to the characters and events and ultimately the work itself. *The Ponder Heart* can be read as a heart-warming story of family love, a saga of a declining family and a declining tradition, a psycho-criminological analysis of niece and uncle, a matchmaker's sales talk, and who knows what else as well. Welty thrusts before us the uncertainty of language and text and at the same time the vitality of the uncertainty that endlessly rejuvenates them through destruction. *The Ponder Heart* is a self-reflexive meta-narrative that embodies that strange glory of literary art that destroys as well as creates.

PART III

Transforming the Genre:
The Reader

CHAPTER 6

The Mystery of the Narratee
in "Old Mr. Marblehall"

Noel Polk calls "Old Mr. Marblehall" "as much a tour de force as William Faulkner's 'Carcassonne'" (261). Indeed, the richness of this brief story of a little over six pages has, in its turn, inspired some genuine *critical* tours de force, each of which sheds new light on Welty's narrative devices and the thinking underlying them. Although Welty clearly said in an interview in 1978 that Mr. Marblehall's double life is not meant to be a fantasy life but "*is* an actual story" (Prenshaw 1996, 26), critical speculations on this question never seem to cease. Whether Mr. Marblehall's double life is regarded as real or as a fantasy of the narrator (including the possibility of Mr. Marblehall himself being the narrator), the discussions in some way or other assume that duality of the human psyche that psychoanalysts claimed to have discovered in the early decades of the twentieth century. They contend that not only the character and the narrator but also the city of Natchez, Mississippi, where the story is set,[1] can be seen as the reflections of a pair of conflicting or compensatory desires, desires that could be reworded more specifically by such pairings as the conscious and the unconscious, the id and the ego, the shadow and the persona, etc. In the course of their discussion, many of the critics focus on the mysteries of the identity of the narrator and of the relationship between the character—Mr. Marblehall, or Mrs. Marblehall—and the narrator.[2]

Widespread interest in these mysteries is natural, since seeking to understand the purpose and meaning of the unnamed narrator's narrative act seems to touch to the core of the authorial intention. I believe, however, that the author is challenging the reader with yet another mystery layered as a subtext under the surface story of "Old Mr. Marblehall." It is the mystery of the identity of the narratee, and solving this mystery will deepen an appreciation of the richness of this multilayered story and demonstrate Welty's concept, at least in this story, of the status and role of fiction in general.

The identity of the narratee in "Old Mr. Marblehall" depends largely on what the reader conceives the overall scheme of the story to be. In my view, "Old Mr. Marblehall" resembles "Powerhouse" (1941) in many ways. Considering the fair amount of revision from the original version, "Old Mr. Grenada" (published in *Southern Review*, spring 1938), to the 1941 definitive redaction of "Old Mr. Marblehall" included in *A Curtain of Green and Other Stories,* as indicated by McDonald (1987), one can safely say that the periods in which Welty conceived "Old Mr. Marblehall" and "Powerhouse" in their final forms were not far apart and that her interest in "playing" on the scheme of things observed in "Powerhouse" seems to have been operating just as strongly in "Old Mr. Marblehall." As with "Powerhouse," in which the author employs "another language" (132) and camouflages serious anti-racist messages, "Old Mr. Marblehall" conceals the importance of the narratee under the conventions of the psychological suspense mystery, whereby the identity of the protagonist and/or narrator is revealed only at the end.

Accepting the validity of projecting onto this narrative such psycho-analytical dualisms as those mentioned above, with the understanding that the psychological factor is an important issue in it, one might take into consideration another Freudian-Jungian assumption in interpreting the plot. This is the assumption that the human psyche in the present is soaked in the residues of the past and often bears never-disappearing scars from the past. If the dualisms reveal the state of the psyche, this assumption deals with the process. The psychoanalyst attempts to uncover the analysand's past in search of the cause why his or her present state is as it is, analyzing the significance of signs presumably originating in the past. Thus psychoanalytical practice is an effort to reconstruct logically the analysand's life story. From the literary viewpoint, as Peter Brooks points out in his *Reading for the Plot,* this practice resembles the act of reading a detective story. The reader of a detective story, through the perceptivity and doggedness of the detective, makes out how the present mysterious circumstances have come about (which usually involves commission of a crime), by reconstructing the past out of the various more or less ambiguous signs, which acquire meaning as a pattern of causality is determined by the reader-detective (269–70). What occurs in both psychoanalysis and the reading of a detective story is *retroaction,* action that proceeds in the reverse direction, conferring upon each retro-sequential event a meaning that did not exist earlier, in hopes of solving the mystery existing in the present.

With mystery and a crime apparently present in the story, one must ask whether "Old Mr. Marblehall" works in this way—that is, as a traditional detective story. Hardly, from the conventional viewpoint. For Mr. Marblehall "never did anything" (91) until he got married, at sixty, when his act of bigamy—the crime—also commenced. The reader is offered no past event with which to retroact in order to find the cause of the bigamy. Only the fact that he did nothing seems to be attributable to his bigamy, or so says the narrator: "Before [he was sixty], he'd never done anything. He didn't know what to do. Everything was for all the world like his first party. He stood about, and looked in his father's books, and long ago he went to France, but he didn't like it" (94). For our lack of knowledge of Mr. Marblehall's past, save for this one statement volunteered by the narrator, the narrator is, of course, made to be solely responsible. According to the narrator's logic, it was Mr. Marblehall's realization that he had never done anything in his life that propelled him to marry two women at the same time at the age of sixty and sire a son in each marriage, also at the same time, the two conceptions apparently occurring immediately after the marriages. The ridiculousness of the reporting of even these facts testifies to the narrator's lack of credibility and of a sense of reality.

Polk indicates that due to these and numerous other ridiculous instances that do not make sense "Old Mr. Marblehall" is "a story that seems *not to permit itself to be read,* both literally and metaphorically" (267); rather, he maintains, the story should be understood as a "brilliant rendering . . . of nightmare's dreamwork" (268). Polk's argument eloquently explains these apparently illogical occurrences and incredible coincidences in the story, and I believe his interpretation also explains the presence of strong sexual connotations underlying these incidents. Just as dreams can be interpreted as suppressed sexual desires in Freudian and Jungian psychoanalytical theories, the narrator's reporting reveals his or her own concern for sexuality in every aspect of life. For instance, in the narrator's view, whether Mr. Marblehall *did* or did *not* do anything before the age of sixty amounts to whether he married and propagated his seed or not. On this suppressed psychosexual level, the allusion to "his first party" suggests an inability on the part of Mr. Marblehall to make social or sexual approaches to women; the narrator also seems to imply that Mr. Marblehall had not liked France because he had not succeeded in having gratifying encounters with women there. The passage also indicates that Mr. Marblehall could find no answers to "what to do" in his father's books but that he found an answer somewhere at the age of sixty. Later the reader realizes that he has found what he needed in such pulp magazines as *Terror Tales* and *Astonishing Stories.* The fact that

Mr. Marblehall derives an intense pleasure from reading these magazines suggests an imagination chronically obsessed with the kind of violent psychosexual desires such fiction deals in. From this viewpoint, the strange descriptions of his two marriages can be interpreted as telling signs of the outcome of his discovery of "what to do."

If one takes the story as narrated in the language of the nightmare by a person with suppressed sexual desires, the descriptions of Mr. and Mrs. Marblehall's married life are marked by signs of psychosexual disorders such as sadism and masochism. Apparently, Mrs. Marblehall, like a sniffing retriever, had discovered her husband's shocking sexual perversion and even learned to participate in his private pleasure. As if "cruelly trained" (91), she never discloses their private act; all the same, when she thinks about what he does during the night, she often loses her sense of reality, looking "remote and nebulous, out of fringe of habitation" (91). Though in public life she engages in club activities as a respectable Southern lady, her singing voice somehow transmits the reverberations from the libidinal reservoir inside her, which tickles the senses of ladies and men alike who hear it. Mr. Marblehall continually learns about various new forms of sensual pleasure from his pulp fiction, and Mrs. Marblehall learns them from him in turn; they are the source of "her perpetual amazement" (92), although the sense of shame and fear of discovery torment her "back in safety . . . in the domestic dark" (92). The wife trapped in her husband's nightly act of sadistic/masochistic sensuality is the "servile, undelighted, sleepy, expensive, tortured Mrs. Marblehall, pinning her mind with a pin to her husband's diet. She wants to *tempt* him, she tells him. What would he like best, that he can have?" (92, emphasis added). Her concern over her husband's "diet" is thus her desire to satisfy his *sexual* appetite.

Just as Mrs. Marblehall's singing voice tickles the hearer's libidinal senses, the sight of the Marblehall home is curiously tempting: "You always look toward it, the way you always glance into tunnels and see nothing" (92). With the precarious circumstance of its location with regard to the peculiar double-tiered topography of the city of Natchez, the house emits a treacherous attraction of decay: the rear garden has crumbled away into the river, and yet the box maze is there "like a trap, to confound the Mississippi River," and the front door has "a knocker shaped like a gasping fish" (92).

When the narrator mentions the Marblehall son, the sexual connotation of "do nothing" is confirmed: "Natchez people do nothing themselves, and really, most of them have done or could do the same thing. This son is six years old now" (92). The Marblehall son certainly exhibits some measure of his parents' psychosexual propensity as he flattens a little green worm under his boot on his way to the Catholic school, an incident that ludicrously fits the logic of the nightmare when one later realizes his father is to become a *butterfly*. Is this the son's act of "vindictiveness" (93)?

As the narrative proceeds to the story of the Birds, the nightmarish mixture of fear and ludicrousness infiltrates the narrative ever more clearly. In the narrator's analysis, Mr. Marblehall wishes to show he has done something extraordinary so that people will take note of him, but what the narrator tells about the Birds is a strange mixture of the horrible and the comic, things too frightening and grotesque to be real. Along with the incoherent, tantalizingly evasive expressions, the section on the Birds exhibits almost childishly crude, ludicrous coherences, which only the logic of the nightmare could tolerate. For instance, in one of Mr. Marblehall's (or Mr. Bird's) pulp magazines, Mrs. Bird reads that "when the characters open bureau drawers, they find a woman's leg with a stocking and garter on" (95), scaring her to death; coincidingly, after talking to the neighbors, she "rolls back into the house as if she had been on a little wheel," and her son supposes that "his mother was totally solid, down to her thick separated ankles" (95). Corresponding to the fact that Mrs. Marblehall writes and sings "O Trees in the Evening" (91), the Bird boy climbs a tree in the Marblehall garden in the evening to peek through the window (96), an action she might happen to notice. The "enslaving blaze" (95) of which the spectacle of the screaming Mrs. Bird reminds her son entraps Mr. Marblehall, making him "a great blazing butterfly" (97). In contrast to Mrs. Marblehall, who tries to hide Mr. Marblehall's perversion, Mrs. Bird "does tell the truth" (95). In the same way, the Marblehall son quietly mashes his father—the little green worm—to death, while the Bird son will ruin his father openly by writing on the fence about the old man's double life. In addition, the "stone figure of the pigtailed courtier mounted on the goat" (96) in the Marblehall garden can be considered an image of bestiality, another example of the "what to do" Mr. Marblehall has discovered. The grotesquery created by these crude instances of coherence can be characterized as "richness without taste, like some holiday food" (93), as in the comparison the narrator uses to characterize the stories in Mr. Marblehall's pulp magazines.

If to show off what extraordinary things he has done is one of Mr. Marblehall's strong compulsions, another compulsion, one just as strong, is to postpone the disclosure as far into the future as possible. His greatest pleasure, and the narrator's greatest source of excitement, seems to be to dream about some spectacular moment of great revelation (97) that is yet to come. Until then, Mr. Marblehall would rather scorch himself in the "enslaving blaze" (95) of the self-made inferno of the constant fear of disclosure: "[H]e is a great blazing butterfly stitching up a net; which does not make sense" (97), the narrator reminds us. Yet it does make sense; a remark by Freud in *Beyond the Pleasure Principle* (1920) provides an insight into this contradictory behavior:

> We have found that one of the earliest and most important functions of the mental apparatus is to bind the instinctual impulses which impinge on it, to replace the primary process prevailing in them by the secondary process and convert their freely mobile cathectic energy into a mainly quiescent (tonic) cathexis. While this transformation is taking place no attention can be paid to the development of unpleasure; but this does not imply the suspension of the pleasure principle. On the contrary, the transformation occurs on *behalf* of the pleasure principle; the binding is a preparatory act which introduces and assures the dominance of the pleasure principle.
>
> . . . We have all experienced how the greatest pleasure attainable by us, that of sexual act, is associated with a momentary extinction of a highly intensified excitation. The binding of an instinctual impulse would be a preliminary function designed to prepare the excitation for its final elimination in the pleasure of discharge. (62)

I do not wish to apply Freudian theory indiscriminately here, but as I have indicated, Mr. Marblehall's double life is, in the narrator's view, all a matter of his sexuality, and the narrator's vision of Mr. Marblehall in the following passage curiously corresponds to the sexual act Freud describes above: "[D]eeper and deeper he speculates upon some glorious finish, a great explosion of revelations . . . the future. / But he still has to kill time, and get through the clocking nights" (97). Freud's well-known association of sexual "consummation" with dying and his idea of "détour" as a form of resistance to dying also figure here. Mr. Marblehall's "détour" is to kill time by reading *Terror Tales* and *Astonishing Stories*, fancying the shock and the horror people would feel were they to discover that his life is like those stories. Whether the narrator is someone other than Mr. Marblehall, as suggested by Howard and by Schmidt, or the narrator and Mr. Marblehall are one and the same person, as speculated by Pitavy-Souques and by Polk, at least the story about the Birds should be considered the narrator's fantasy. Mr. and Mrs. Marblehall may or may not be infatuated with sadistic/masochistic pleasure, but this would simply be their private matter. The disclosure of Mr. Marblehall's life, then, would mean the revelation of the truth that Mr. Marblehall is *not* leading a double life, the truth that would end the narrator's fantasy. The narrator is a Shahrazad, promising to the Sultan, the narratee, an exciting ending but unable to allow that ending to come, for, as soon as the ending does come—and when what has purported to be the story is revealed to have amounted to naught—the narrator's raison d'être will cease to be, just as Shahrazad's will end, upon which the Sultan will have her killed. What is most pressing for the narrator all the while has been to retain the narratee's interest.

Has the narrator been successful in this? To provide the answer, Welty plays on the reader a hilarious trick. Toward the end of the story, the narrator supposes the most spectacular situation, namely that Mr. Marblehall himself will confess his double life, whereupon the narrator exclaims, "What an *astonishing,* unbelievable, electrifying confession that would be, and how his two wives would topple over, how his sons would cringe! To say nothing of most men aged sixty-six. So thinks self-consoling Mr. Marblehall" (96, emphasis added). The narratee has certainly been listening to what would become Mr. Marblehall's confession, this *"astonishing"* story, and the narratee is none but "you" the reader, the author would say. It is not only Mr. Marblehall and/or the narrator who enjoys the kind of fiction one finds in *Terror Tales* and *Astonishing Stories* but you yourself, who must have been looking down smugly upon them, the author chuckles at you in your dismay. It is not only Mr. Marblehall but you who have realized that people, including yourself, "endure something inwardly—for a time secretly; they establish a past, a memory; thus they store up life" (97). "Old Mr. Marblehall" ends with this suggestive sentence: "If people knew about his double life, they'd *die*" (97, emphasis added). "Die" reminds one of the Freudian "consummation" behind its colloquial meaning of extreme surprise: as Mr. Marblehall has chosen the "détour," rather than "consummation," and continues to lead an astonishing life in his fantasy, so will you the reader. Actually, the kind of "détour" of fantasy incited by the act of reading stories has been considered a universal attribute of fiction in general, not limited to pulp fiction, of course, as confirmed by Mikhail Bakhtin in his description of the effect of the novel upon the reader: "In place of our tedious lives we are offered a surrogate, true, but it is the surrogate of a fascinating and brilliant life. We can experience these adventures, identify with these heroes; such novels almost become a substitute for our own lives. . . . It follows that we might substitute for our own life an obsessive reading of novels, or dreams based on novelistic models" ("Epic and Novel," 32). Only, Welty's story reminds the reader that the model the reader simulates is not always a brilliant, fashionable, socially admired hero or heroine but one who can be a base, egoistic, sexual pervert whom he or she would never choose to be in real life.

In the end, the story comes round to its beginning: "Old Mr. Marblehall never did anything." He may have married at sixty, but that is all. Whether or not Mr. Marblehall is leading a double life, all the horrible things related to the narratee will never be known to the people of

Natchez, at least as long as the "great explosion of revelations" does not occur, which it is most likely never to do. Thus one might as well say those things never happened. Mr. Marblehall *never did anything and never will* until he dies. His life is not an astonishing story but a humdrum one. It is his fantasy that makes his life, only for him, unique and worth living. By means of fantasy Mr. Marblehall/the narrator doubles living and delays dying. What he learned at sixty may be called the joy of sexual perversion; yet it is a form of the most basic *thing to do* in life—namely, to resist dying.

Just as a starkly bare bulb glares over the pages of *Terror Tales* and *Astonishing Stories* in the Marblehall mansion high on the bluff as well as in the Bird house in Natchez-under-the-Hill, the Sultan—the reader—has unwittingly been drawn into a "low-class" horror story and spent a blazing night of psychosexual desire that the waking daylight would put to shame. The "enslaving flare" of the story has not been weakened by time, as attested by the fact that the story was reprinted along with other "regular" horror mysteries in *Ellery Queen's Mystery Magazine* in the eighties. "Old Mr. Marblehall" shows, in an extreme situation, the role and status of fiction, which multiplies the reader's life and offers a "détour" from life's real course toward death.

Ultimately, "Old Mr. Marblehall," using itself to blur the borderline between sophisticated high-modernist fiction and crude pulp fiction, challenges the traditional concept of literature with its generally accepted distinction of highbrow and lowbrow. In this sense, this brief story truly embodies what Jacques Derrida identifies as the role and status of literature, in his explication of Kafka's parable "Before the Law" (used as an epigraph for the present book). "Old Mr. Marblehall" "does not *belong* to the field [of literature], it is the *transformer* of the field" (215, emphasis added). "Old Mr. Marblehall" entices the reader through the forbidden gate of the Law into the vacant space beyond, which the author has left as an "ellipsis" and which the reader might "transform" into his or her own dazzling garden.

CHAPTER 7

"Everybody to Their Own Visioning": Connection through Dispersion in *The Golden Apples*

Harold Bloom's *The Western Canon* (1994) names four books by Welty: *Collected Stories, Delta Wedding, The Robber Bridegroom,* and *The Ponder Heart*. If Welty had not insisted that *The Golden Apples* (1949) is not a novel but "inter-related" *stories* (Kreyling 1991, 136), Bloom surely would have singled it out rather than regarding it as a part of the *Collected Stories*. This may suggest how short stories are considered somewhat less note-worthy than novels in our culture. Nevertheless, Welty chose to avoid that "first tier" for this work. Her almost obdurate stance regarding the genre, or nongenre, of *The Golden Apples* for over half a century leads one to recognize the strength of her confidence in the viability of her new creation as well as to appreciate her resistance to the conventional hierarchy of genres, an authorial claim that most critics over the years have respected.[1]

Whether they are seen as a novel or not, one cannot but detect a certain unity or perceive links among the stories beyond simply place and character. The author herself publicly indicated the existence of "something additional coming from [the seven stories] as a group with a meaning of its own" (Prenshaw 1984, 43) and privately wrote to her literary agent expressing her "hope that some over-all thing would emerge from the group that might have a significance greater than that of the stories taken one by one—by virtue of accumulation and familiarity and so on" (Kreyling 1991, 137). Thus, since Thomas L. McHaney capitalized on Welty's own use of the word "cycle" and applied the word to the relationship of the stories in his "Eudora Welty and Multitudinous Golden Apples" (1973), "cycle" seems to have been accepted as a happy coinage: Ruth M. Vande Kieft, among others, refers to the work as "the short story cycle" (87) in her revised *Eudora Welty* (1985). Apart from its structural unity as a "cycle," the topics of the discussions on the thematic unity of the work range from the role of the artist to more recent ones of feminist concern.[2] McHaney grapples squarely with this question in his "Falling into Cycles: *The Golden Apples*" (1989). Dismissing the challenges of Bakhtin's writings on the novel as inapplicable to *The Golden Apples,* he speculates on the meaning of Welty's nongenre claim, asking "Could it be, then, that *The Golden Apples* is that post-modern event, a text? Could it be that Welty herself is not just a reluctant deep-South object to which the smart signifying of post-modern criticism may be applied, but a post-modern consciousness herself?" (175). So saying, McHaney examines the nature of this "tradition of her own" (175) from the perspective of the author's cyclic consciousness of life and art.

Fiction that consists of several, or numerous, stories that are "interrelated" in one way or another is not so rare in modern literary tradition. When she was writing what was to become *The Golden Apples,* Welty surely must have been familiar with such works as Ivan Sergeevich Turgenev's *A Sportsman's Sketches* (1852), Sherwood Anderson's *Winesburg, Ohio* (1919), and William Faulkner's *Go Down Moses* (1942), to name only a few. To assess whether Welty really discovered the "tradition of her own," I believe it necessary to know exactly how Welty conceived and distinguished between the traditional genres of novel and short story. The following two remarks by Welty, the gist of which she repeatedly expressed on different occasions, seem to shed light on this matter:

> A short story is more [than a novel] a single thing, more one sustained effort, which has a beginning, a rise, and a fall. Of course, a novel has so much wider scope, greater looseness of texture, and so much more room to expand. Many rises and falls are possible, and even necessary. . . . In the case of the short story, you can't ever let the tautness of line relax. It has to be all strung very tight upon its single thread usually, and everything is subordinated to the theme of the story: characters and mood and place and time; and none of those things are as important as the development itself. Whereas in a novel you have time to shade a character, allow him his growth, in a short story a character hardly changes from beginning to end. (Prenshaw 1984, 45)

And:

> I'm quite certain that by nature I'm a short-story writer rather than a novelist. I think in terms of *a single impulse*, and I think of a short story as being

a lyric impulse, something that begins and carries through and ends all in the same curve. (Prenshaw 1984, 308–9, emphasis added)

Considering intellectual movements at the time of her early literary career and the people she associated with then, especially her mentors at the *Southern Review*, it is understandable that Welty's idea of literature echoes the mood of the New Criticism. Her conception of "impulse" in the passage above reminds one of I.A. Richards's concept of "impulse" articulated in his *Principles of Literary Criticism* (1924). This book and his *Practical Criticism* (1929) became one of the major sources of the theoretical and pedagogical developments of the New Criticism in the United States in later years. Moreover, what Welty regards as the most important quality of the short story, as expressed in both passages above, is comparable to the idea of "organic unity" embraced by the New Critics.[3] As the New Critics were concerned mainly with poetry, which for them was more or less synonymous with literature, Welty characterizes here, as elsewhere,[4] the process of creating a short story as lyric and its achieved effect as similar to that of a lyric poem. In Welty's view, the short story, rather than the novel, was the prose fictional genre in which she could achieve the kind of effect she had learned to value. Nonetheless, she was well aware of the difficulty of developing character in a short story, as she reiterates more specifically in a 1955 essay: "Characters in a short story have not the size and importance and capacity for development they have in a novel, but are subservient altogether to the story as a whole" (*Eye*, 112).

In the eighties, Welty threw light on the origin and nature of the links among the stories in *The Golden Apples* in interviews and in the autobiography *One Writer's Beginnings*. Michael Kreyling's *Author and Agent: Eudora Welty and Diarmuid Russell* (1991), a narrative documentary on Welty's growth as a fiction writer, largely based on her letters to her literary agent Diarmuid Russell, further clarified the situation. Her letters written around the time she was working on those stories reveal that she had been under pressure from publishers to write a novel rather than stories and that she had been unable to fulfill their expectation. Her creative inclination toward a single lyric impulse shunned what she believed to be "the burden of the novel, with all that tying up of threads and preparing for this, that and the other" (quoted in Kreyling 1991, 137). Kreyling indicates, based on her letters, that Welty was a great admirer of E.M. Forster and that a talk she addressed in 1947 to the Northwest Pacific Writers' Conference owed much to Forster's *Aspects of the Novel* (Kreyling 1991, 129). Her essay based on that talk, "Looking at Short Stories" (1949), attests to the accuracy of Kreyling's observation. Indeed, her

discussion of plot in this essay is based on Forster's well-known definition of the plot in a novel as "a narrative of events, the emphasis falling
on causality" (86). It is noteworthy that at the time Welty was preparing
the talk she was also working on the stories that were to become parts of
The Golden Apples. Rather than worry about devising causality and closure in a work of a much bigger scale—a novel—Welty would write short
stories "just as they actually [were] in [her] head" (136).

In an interview in 1981 Welty quite candidly expressed her surprise
when she saw these stories that had been written in this manner were
"inter-related, but not inter-dependent" (136):

> I did not realize until I'd written half of these stories that all these people
> really did live in Morgana. So I was just showing different phases of it, dif-
> ferent aspects. They were all under the same compulsion. I realized that the
> stories were connected. It was a marvelous moment with me when I real-
> ized that a story I'd written really was about a character from an earlier story.
> My subconscious mind, I guess, had been working on the same lines all the
> time. Everything slid into place like a jigsaw puzzle. It all worked out. I
> loved it because I felt that I could get deeper into all the people through
> using a number of stories and different times in their lives than I could hope
> to do using one story. (Prenshaw 1984, 332)

The excitement Welty recalls here and that is expressed more vividly in
her letters (Kreyling 1991, 135–46) is well justified, since she believed
that she was creating a work combining the tightly strung unity of the
short story and the scale of character development that she had believed
possible only in a novel. *The Golden Apples* allowed Welty to go beyond
the genre boundary to harvest the fruit of the novel, while reaping that
of the short story, and this new double yield formed the "tradition of her
own." In effect, the work turned out to have accomplished even more
than that; its unified imaging of theme, which exemplifies the New Critic's
contention of the inseparability of form and content, and the inevitable,
rather than incompatible, coexistence of intensely individual feelings and
cosmic impersonality are two other qualities that have made *The Golden
Apples* by all accounts Welty's masterpiece.

One might, thus, consider that Welty's objection to calling *The Golden
Apples* a novel derives from her rather rigid conception of genres, a conception fostered under the influences of the New Critics and writers like
E.M. Forster, and that she saw the possibility of surpassing such genre
divisions by connecting the stories in such a way as to create a new
"whole" beyond the "whole" of each story taken individually. As a finished work, *The Golden Apples* creates in the reader a compound impression of dispersedness as well as connectedness. Each story certainly exhibits

the New Critical sense of centripetal force directed onto a single plot line, the quality Welty seemed to value most in the short story, but some elements in the plot leap beyond one story's borderline, often across two or three borderlines, and contribute to another story's plot in a situation completely removed from the one in their original story. It is this kind of dispersedness that plays a significant role in engendering the connectedness of the stories of *The Golden Apples*.

This compound impression of dispersedness and connectedness reminds one of a technique Forster, again in *Aspects of the Novel*, coins "rhythm." Taking as an example the "little phrase" in the music of Vinteuil used in Proust's *A la recherche du temps perdu*, Forster analyzes its effect:

> It is almost an actor, but not quite, and that "not quite" means that its power has gone towards stitching Proust's book together from the inside, and towards the establishment of beauty and the ravishing of the reader's memory. There are times when the little phrase—from its gloomy inception, through the sonata into the sextet—means everything to the reader. There are times when it means nothing and is forgotten, and this seems to me the function of rhythm in fiction; not to be there all the time like a pattern, but by its lovely waxing and waning to fill us with surprise and freshness and hope. (167)

Forster, then, defines "rhythm" as "repetition plus *variation*" (168, emphasis added). When the complete manuscript of what was to become *The Golden Apples* was sent to the publisher, Welty still did not want to call it a novel but suggested calling it "something like '*Variations* on a Portfolio' or something from the other arts where such groupings are more common" (Kreyling 1991, 146, emphasis added). It is not simply the coincidence in wording Forster and Welty chose but the similarity in actual usage and effect between Forster's "rhythm" and Welty's dispersed elements that make me suspect that Welty had recognized the possibility of creating a new genre of her own by advancing what Forster indicated to be a more or less traditional technique of the novel.

At the conclusion of the essay "Looking at Short Stories," Welty seems to reveal what her sentiment was toward the "inter-related" stories she was then working on: "I think it ought to be said that a fiction writer can try anything. He has tried a great deal, but presumably not everything. The possibilities are endless because the stirring of the imagination never rests, and because we can never stop trying to make feeling felt" (105). The tone and the gist of this statement is a clear echo of the conclusive chapter of *Aspects of the Novel*, the only difference being that while Forster is speaking from an observer's viewpoint, Welty speaks from a creator's, and this seems to me to confirm my suspicion that Welty had recognized the possibility of creating a new genre. The following section will show how Welty attempts to achieve connectedness through dispersedness and how this device metafictionally reflects her conception of literature.

The first story, "Shower of Gold," which actually was written after Welty had begun to see the connectedness of the four stories written earlier—"Whole World Knows," "Golden Apples" ["June Recital"], "Music from Spain," and "Moon Lake" (Kreyling 1991, 136)—sets out this seemingly contradictory scheme of connection through dispersion. Relating Snowdie MacLain's apparently undisturbed attitude toward her husband's having absconded, the narrator, Katie Rainey, contrasts herself with Snowdie: "But it didn't seem to me, running in and out the way I was, that Snowdie had ever got a real good look at life, maybe. Maybe from the beginning. Maybe she just doesn't know the *extent*. Not the kind of look I got, and away back when I was twelve years old or so. Like something was put to my eye" (8).

Whether Katie experienced a sexual awakening or was raped (the latter case I believe unlikely from her casual tone, "twelve years old *or so*") and learned "the extent to which men abuse women" (Mark 40), what she acquired then has grown into a more universal insight. Literally, what is most likely to be "put to one's eye" is a telescope. In *One Writer's Beginnings* Welty now recalls her father's telescope brought to her eye a new, closer vision of the moon (10). The "telescope" as if put to Katie's eye has enabled her to see the far-reaching meanings and consequences of mundane events in life beyond their surface appearances. Katie's "extent" covers not only the very near past and future—including King's possible "copy-cats" who would desert their wives, his offspring past and future in the county orphanage, and King and Snowdie's married life to come— but also mythological times, indeed time immemorial. Although Katie's background provides no resources for making any sophisticated references, her words function often like those of a medium who sees through the temporal and spatial bounds of human cognizance and narrates her *fata morgana* over the sea of the Mississippi fields. Thus the albino Snowdie's conception and King's abscondence are described employing explicit mythological allusions. Katie's "telescope" even surmounts spatial limits: "I believe he's been to California. . . . I *see* King in the West, out where it's gold and all that" (11, emphasis added), and she adds, "Everybody to their own visioning."

In fact, King's return is witnessed by neither Kaitie nor Snowdie: Katie admits that her seeing King in the West is only her personal visioning, while Snowdie, who had put "her eyes straight out[,] . . . making curtains for every room" (6) and whose albinotic eyes have to be protected from the strong western sun with the western window curtained, would never *see* King in the West. Indeed, in addition to the often-noted allusion to Morgan le Fay found in the characterization of Katie, the atmosphere of personal visioning or *fata morgana* is felt throughout "Shower of Gold." The central event in Katie's narrative is, as she confesses clearly, "only a kind of *near* thing" (11). The narrator Katie has not actually seen King's coming to and looking into the house or his being scared away by the boys. The event could be a made-up ghost story, fit for Halloween. Katie's vivid narrative of the incident is based on the reports of Old Plez and the little MacLain children, all of whom are marginal members of Morgana society, whose credibilities need to be substantiated by such persons as Lizzie Stark and Katie herself. Neither has Katie really seen the night meeting of King and Snowdie in the woods; she has merely heard about it from Snowdie. Katie has never spotted King in the various places where the Morgana men say they have. Above all, Katie is the only person, as one will see reading through *The Golden Apples*, who mentions the possibility of "children of his growing up in the County Orphan's" (4), the only ground for her contention being that "so say several" (4). Accordingly, King MacLain with his flamboyant, playboyish lifestyle and all the other people and incidents Katie describes and narrates in "Shower of Gold" are simply her re-presentation of reality constructed with the materials she has acquired, *evaluated*, *selected*, and even *tainted* with her imagination. "Shower of Gold" is a vision gained through Katie's personal "telescope."

Right after she finished "Shower of Gold," Welty wrote to Russell about her idea of interrelated stories saying: "I believe if I went ahead with this in mind, then the trouble I've had trying to get too much into a single story would lay off me, for I'd know I'd have another story and another chance to get it into [those characters'] lives if I needed to" (Kreyling 1991, 137). "Shower of Gold" self-reflexively announces the device for this authorial scheme: each story of *The Golden Apples* will be limited to a re-presentation of reality constructed by a particular visioning of it by a person or persons. "Everybody to their own visioning" suggests that each element in reality is seen and evaluated differently by each person, that *reality is pregnant with numerous possibilities of itself. The Golden Apples* amplifies Katie's remark and embodies the idea that an element that remains insignificant and has but a dispersing effect in one person's vision/story may become central to or play a different role in another's and that human relations criss-cross the field of those elements.

Many studies have directed attention to motifs from Greek, Roman, Celtic, or Teutonic myths, or Yeats's poems, seeing how the myths and poems connect the stories of *The Golden Apples*. Besides these major motifs from more or less authentic sources, the stories are scattered with various minor motifs, which are made up of the kind of elements I have indicated. Using the terminology we have adopted for this book, these motifs—minor as well as major ones—constitute numerous subtexts, which run through the stories of *The Golden Apples*. I believe Welty was well aware of a possible weakness in that a sense of a "whole" might fail to emerge due to the fact that the stories could be read as independent works. She worked these minor motifs into the stories to create such subtexts so that they might function to ensure the "inter-relatedness" of the stories.

A real telescope appears from the outset in "June Recital," the second story. Loch has been allowed to use his father's telescope while he must stay in bed with malarial fever. Since the telescope had been brought out, as Loch remembers, for the eclipses of the *moon* and when an "airplane *flew over with a lady* in it" (23, emphasis added) and because for the latter occasion his father had gripped it "like a *big stick,* some kind of protective weapon for what was to come" (23, emphasis added), one cannot help sensing the suggestion of a hostile phallic reaction toward the female beyond the reach of the male. Although Loch's innocence does not engender such sexual antagonism, not only is he compared with Argus with the thousand eyes but in effect he uses his position with the telescope like a panopticon, with which he surveys the acts of two women, Virgie Rainey and Miss Eckhart. Yet Loch neither possesses the controlling power of the Foucauldean panopticon over the two women nor understands the *extent* of their acts, largely because he has not lived long enough in Morgana. When Loch recognizes Virgie, the reader recalls the baby Virgie's swallowing a button, an insignificant incident in "Shower of Gold," and realizes that fifteen years or so have passed; Loch, however, does not know about the incident. Nor does he understand the meaning of Virgie and the sailor's position "like a big grasshopper lighting" (30) on the bed that he sees through the telescope. Although he unconsciously feels the old melody of "Für Elise" and the paper decorations the old lady is making as things he had heard and seen a long time ago, he cannot really tell what they mean. The power of the "poor old telescope" (30) is limited simply to bringing close what is physically there then. This does not mean Loch lacks the innate ability to grasp the *extent*: he can imagine various outrageous childish pictures and sounds within the confine of his bedroom. He needs to "just bide [his] time" (77), as his mother once remarked.

In contrast, his sister Cassie is fully able to see the *extent*. Without a telescope, she recognizes, upon hearing the opening melody of "Für Elise," its far-reaching meaning in the lives of Miss Eckhart and Virgie, and later even in those of certain people, known and unknown, whom she regards as Miss Eckhart's and Virgie's spiritual kin: "And there were others of them—human beings, roaming, like lost beasts" (96). She has the kind of observant and sympathetic eye that enables her to gain insights into human nature, the kind most other Morgana characters do not seem to have. In this sense, Cassie does *not* submit herself, contrary to Donaldson's contention, to "the re-reading and the re-listening of Morgana stories about Miss Eckhart and Virgie" (499). Her awareness of possessing these insights deprives her of any sense of belonging; she stands "homeless-looking" (37), overwhelmed by the enormity of the Cassandrian solitary knowledge.

Cassie certainly knows "Morgana stories" about Miss Eckhart and Virgie, but she has also seen various other things that "Morgana" overlooked or missed the chance to see, or even expunged. When on a speaking night Miss Eckhart was listening to Mr. Sissum's cello and letting Virgie tug a loop of clover chain over herself, Cassie could feel Miss Eckhart's hidden terror and pain, with the two people she must have truly loved simultaneously in view. Yet Cassie's recollection of the scene reveals the even deeper significance that she was at the same time gazing at herself and discovering that she, biologically and emotionally a separate existence, could feel the pain of another so vividly, probably because of that very separateness. On another occasion Cassie also had had a glimpse of Miss Eckhart's hidden passion when the teacher had played the piano before Cassie, Virgie, and Jinny Love on a stormy morning. Cassie had witnessed the impersonality of a dedicated artist in Miss Eckhart's face: "the face a mountain could have, or what might be seen behind the veil of a waterfall[,] . . . a sightless face, one for music only" (56). Cassie, not Virgie as Miss Eckhart's musical protégée, could even visualize how such a quality had revealed itself: "[Miss Eckhart] had been pricked and the music came like the red blood under the scab of a forgotten fall" (57); she had understood the kind of emotion in the teacher that "was more than the ear could bear to hear or the eye to see" (57).

Separateness is an important theme in *The Golden Apples*, not only in the relation between Miss Eckhart and Virgie but also in the author's representation of the artist in general, as shown in Danièle Pitavy-Souques's classic essay on this theme, "Technique as Myth: The Structure of *The Golden Apples*." The *extent* to which Cassie's eye reaches is of a kind different from Katie's. Cassie's eye recognizes her separateness from every other individual, and this solitary knowledge enables her to see the others objectively in their subjective as well as social existence, placing them in relation to each other in a broader perspective: "[A]ll seemed to Cassie to be by their own nature rising—and so alike—and crossing the sky and setting, the way the planets did. Or they were more like whole constellations, turning at their very centers maybe[,] . . . maybe often upside down, but terribly recognizable" (58). Cassie needs no telescope or panopticon to survey those constellations. She knows her naked eye becomes a receptacle for them if she is observant: "All kinds of things would rise and set in your own life, you could begin now to watch for them, roll back your head and feel their rays come down and reach your open eyes" (58). Cassie will recognize them night after night, year after year as she will the hummingbird whom she will let come back each year for a hundred years (67). Cassie's "vision" is of familiarity and cyclicity in the separate human beings with their glory and torment. Her "vision" extends, though in her dream, beyond the particularity of Miss Eckhart and Virgie to "the grave, unappeased, and radiant face" (97) of an unknown, yet familiar, person, who lives through time in the poem.

Loch comes into possession of Miss Eckhart's metronome when it is thrown out of her window in the confusion following the fire; he takes the ticking instrument for a time bomb, which may be interpreted to mean that her passion is to be succeeded by Loch. The cloud he sees in the early evening sky, which he feels is like "a golden and aimless bird" (95), foreshadows his future. He feels in his dream his own frown, his own growl and gnashing of teeth, not the face of the stranger in the poem, in "a color and a fury" that exceed those of even the radiant Morgana summer. This is the essential difference between Loch and Cassie. Cassie sees the meaning of others' acts with the objectivity of a separate existence; Loch in his dream sees his own act in the tumult of his passion.

The juxtaposition of the two third-person points of view, or discourses, of Loch and Cassie is not only an appropriate representation of the author's avowed structural device—"everybody to their own visioning"—but also a demonstration of the expected effect of the device. I believe this effect can be understood well by drawing on the Bakhtinian dialogism. Bakhtin defines the novel, which we should take as the quality of "novelness" observed in prose fiction in general,[5] as "a diversity of social types (sometimes even diversity of languages) and a diversity of individual voices, artistically organized" ("Discourse," 262). The innate and fundamental quality of the novel, according to Bakhtin, is that these diverse languages/voices acknowledge and respond to each other: "[T]his movement of the theme through different languages and speech types, its dispersion into the rivulets and droplets of social heteroglossia, its dialogization—this is the basic distinguishing feature of the stylistics of the novel" ("Discourse," 263). Although Bakhtin's concern extends to a global scale taking into account the diversity of national languages, dialects, or the languages of social classes, the same mechanism can be applied to "authorial speech, the speeches of narrators, inserted genres, the speech of characters" ("Discourse," 263). In "June Recital" this kind of dialogism occurs within Loch's and Cassie's respective discourses, but between their juxtaposed discourses a different level of dialogization is induced, the kind of dialogization that is achieved by the reader's apperceptive ability. It is as if the reader were surveying the psychological prison cells of Loch and Cassie, with an even broader view of the whole social prison called "Morgana past, present, and future" as well. The reader is expected to experience the two discourses interacting and to relativize them in a way Loch and Cassie as characters could not do. The opening melody of "Für Elise," for instance, causes Loch to shed copious tears, the reason for which he cannot tell, and to recall the old days when he and Cassie lived in the same childhood world. The same melody causes Cassie to say aloud unwittingly, "Virgie Rainey, *danke shoen*" (34), and to recall the tragic relationship between Miss Eckhart and Virgie. So also magnolia blossoms, for another instance, play a completely different but commonly significant role in Loch's and Cassie's consciousness. By dialogizing the two reactions toward the melody or the magnolia blossoms or various other objects and incidents, the reader learns about such diverse things as sister-brother relationships, Cassie's gaze at and understanding of the Miss Eckhart–Virgie relationship, Loch's innocence and curiosity, Cassie's reflective and contemplative inclination, how it is to be a boy or a girl, a mother or an artist in Morgana, and the like.

Thus the effect of juxtaposing the two discourses is to induce in the reader a dialogic perception of the discourses and to deepen and broaden the extent of each discourse in a way that each discourse could never achieve independently. In this dialogizing process, what are to become minor motifs—a melody, blossoms, and whatnot—play no "minor" roles. If "Shower of Gold" sets out the structural scheme of *The Golden Apples*, "June Recital" demonstrates its expected effect throughout the stories.

"Sir Rabbit," the third story, was written in a single night in February 1948 (Kreyling 1991, 141) after Welty had already confirmed with herself and Russell her plans for a book of "inter-related" stories. Probably for this reason "Sir Rabbit" contains numerous elements that are to appear over and again throughout *The Golden Apples*.

The most important motif in "Sir Rabbit" is that of rape or fornication initiated by the woman. It is only in this story that Katie Rainey's claim of King's promiscuity is substantiated, although that part of her claim regarding his children growing up in the county orphanage is never proven in any of the stories. The story also demonstrates how King's amorous, carefree lifestyle, of which we learn from Katie in "Shower of Gold," is widely known and acquiesced in by the people of Morgana. In

all the seven stories of *The Golden Apples*, some kind of rape or fornication takes place, under diverse circumstances and in diverse forms. Yet if
one follows this motif, a powerful feminist subtext emerges from this
collection: none of the raped women or female fornicators suffers as a
victim or feels remorse; rather, all of them defeat the violence and control to which one normally expects this kind of sexual act to subject the
woman, and in most cases they savor its affirmative aspect of fertility and
procreation. Mark's *The Dragon's Blood: Feminist Intertextuality in
Eudora Welty's "The Golden Apples,"* among others, offers detailed discussions and speculations on this unexpected turn of fortunes.

Although when "Sir Rabbit" was written it was still half a decade before Hugh Hefner would institutionalize the traditional image of the pro-
miscuous rabbit as a cultural icon, another central motif that hops about
the pages of *The Golden Apples* is this jaunty animal in relation to the re-
puted playboy of Morgana, King. King is first introduced to the reader
in Katie's dramatic monologue, "Shower of Gold." Although no rabbit
appears in this first story, Katie's self-introduction "My name is Mrs.
Rainey" (3) may remind the reader of Gertrude "Ma" Rainey, who was
also known as Madame Rainey, the creator of the classic blues style. For
years in the early decades of the twentieth century Madame Rainey toured
the South with a company called the Rabbit Foot Minstrels, and they
became widely known throughout the region. In fact, this minstrel
company's name is mentioned by a character in Welty's *Delta Wedding*
(9). King's frequent long business trips throughout the South reported
by "Mrs. Rainey" and his marrying a woman "with pink eyes" (4) will
be appropriately recalled when King is compared to Sir Rabbit in this third
story. Yet already in "June Recital" a connection is established between
King and the rabbit, when Loch confuses King for Mr. Voight, who had
promised him a bird that can say "Rabbits!" Finally, in "The Wanderers"
King is seen wearing the "stiffest-starched white suit[,] . . . the lapels alert
as ears" (253).

In King's connection to the rabbit, there is a curious passage in "Sir
Rabbit" that relates how a white letter falls out of King's coat pocket
before Matie Will's eyes. Mark offers an extensive discussion on this
"letter . . . whiter than white" as a "tabula rasa" (108). Whether one accepts this interpretation or not, as far as the story line goes, when one
recalls King's custom of "sending word" to his wife before he returns from
a long trip (4, 6), as mentioned in "Shower of Gold," one finds this very
likely one of his letters to be sent to his wife. Mattie Will also knows that
King's custom is to "appear at any time and then, over night, disappear"
(104), as was the situation in which a letter was sent in "Shower of Gold."
It *is* a "letter," not a blank sheet, in a white envelope, and its physical

whiteness emphasized against the background is associated by Mattie Will with Sir Rabbit. For a deeper effect, this incident of the letter confirms King's carefree attitude toward sex and fidelity, which even the existence of his own love letter to his wife in his pocket and his plans to bring home some fowl as a surprise gift from the trip do not alter. In the same way, Mattie Will's strange vision of "a little boat . . . going out on a lake, never to come back" (99), can also be taken as the connecting image to Cassie's vision of a boat on Moon Lake in the preceding story, "June Recital," and with the actual boats on Moon Lake in the following story, "Moon Lake," all having connotations of sexual initiation.

The lighted cloud Loch sees in the early evening sky toward the end of "June Recital" reappears in two later stories, and in this "Sir Rabbit," the middle story among the three, it is given solid materiality. On the cloud Loch imagines "a golden and aimless bird" flying over, his vision overlapping with his boyish aspiration for some unknown adventure and achievement. The same bird flies over Mattie Will and King as the couple finish making love and lets drop a feather as if to commemorate the occasion: "A dove feather came turning down through the light that was like golden smoke. She caught it with a dart of the hand, and brushed her chin; she was never displeased to catch anything" (108–9). In the last story "The Wanderers," the bird and cloud motif appears again before Virgie's eyes as she floats in the river with a sense of total liberation: "She hung suspended in felicity. Far to the West, a cloud running fingerlike over the sun made her splash the water" (249). Furthermore, Virgie's posture in the water is also connected with that of the hummingbird Cassie saw and thought to let come back for a hundred years (67) some thirty years earlier, on the same day Loch saw the cloud.

"Sir Rabbit" also contains cosmic sound as a motif that appears repeatedly in later stories. Mattie Will listens to "the world go round" (110), as she watches King snoring peacefully after their lovemaking. This euphoric sound changes in "The Whole World Knows" to an abominable sound of the world's garbage splashing in the Mississippi, which Ran, descending in his car down the Dantean circles of the riverbank, hears "on the floor of the world" (177). In "The Wanderers," the children at the vigil listen to the locusts, which sound "like the sound of the world going around them as they suddenly beat their cupped hands over their ears" (244); at the end Virgie and the old beggar woman listen to the cosmic symphony of the constellations (277). In the cases of Mattie Will, Ran, and Virgie, they also experience an epiphanic vision, the scale and nature of which reflect each character's situation. At the end of "Sir Rabbit," Mattie Will looks from the hilltop into "the big West" and over the stretch of the fields and the river, and at "Morgana all in rays, like a

giant sunflower in the dust of Saturday" (111)—a realistic as well as euphoric vision that leads me strongly to believe that the author intends
Mattie Will's sexual encounter with King as real and gratifying, and not,
as some critics contend, as a fantasy caused by infatuation. In contrast,
Ran's vision of East and West being in his eyes (175) at sunset by the
canal in Vicksburg is a presage of the infernal scenes to follow. Virgie's
perception of the enormity of the falling rain and of King's "hideous and
delectable face" (277) cast on the screen of the falling rain reflect her
recognition of the cyclicity of life and death and attune her ear to the
cosmic symphony. Especially in the presence of such motifs as these and
the golden bird/cloud, though presented as "everybody to their own
visioning," one cannot but feel a powerful sense of oneness running
through the whole of *The Golden Apples*, a oneness enclosing the inhabitants of Morgana beyond time and space.

As seen so far, "Sir Rabbit," despite its brevity, incorporates some effective "connectives" that function to relate the stories of *The Golden
Apples* to each other. Also, I hasten to add, we have not even begun to
exhaust the possible list of motifs originating in "Sir Rabbit." When she
hit upon the idea of "inter-related stories," Welty completely changed the
identity of the protagonist in "Music from Spain," originally a person
unidentified with Battle Hill (the name Welty had originally used for what
was to become Morgana), to Eugene MacLain in order to include the
story in the prospective book (Kreyling 1991, 141). If she went that far
to arrive at a connectedness among the stories, it is almost certain from
our observation that one of the important roles the author has cast for
"Sir Rabbit" is as a reservoir of "connectives."

One more example from "Sir Rabbit," namely Welty's use of personal
names, can show how widely the variety of these "connectives" ranges.
"Old Man Flewellyn," who is mentioned only once in "Sir Rabbit"—but
this once is enough to be remembered—is a *dirty old man* who had ap-
proached the fifteen-year-old Mattie Will in the dewberry patch with a
smiling face, only to be kicked out by her (100). Yet the name Flewellyn
has been casually mentioned once in "June Recital" also; the Flewellyns
are the people out in the country whom Kewpie Moffit, Virgie's lover, is
assumed to be visiting (90). The name Flewellyn plays only the most
minor of roles in either story, but, appearing twice as it does in the different contexts, "by virtue of accumulation and familiarity" as the author
said, the image of "out in the country" becomes heavily colored with
libidinal desires.

Another name that originates in "Sir Rabbit" and passes through
strange vicissitudes of fortune is "Sojourner." In "Sir Rabbit" Sojourner
is known to be the maiden name of Mattie Will or Mrs. Junior Holifield.

In "The Whole World Knows," supposedly set some twenty years later, Maideen, the girl Ran MacLain eventually sleeps with, informs him that her mother's maiden name was Sojourner. The mother seems to be very worried about her daughter being out with Ran as he monologizes, "[Maideen] slept sitting up in the car going home, where her mama, now large-eyed, maiden name Sojourner, sat up listening" (174). In "The Wanderers" the reader learns that when Maideen committed suicide after having a sexual encounter with Ran, she was buried with the Sojourners (262). It is a possibility that the author is hinting that the story of "Sir Rabbit" is not finished at all but lives on in a continued subtext running beneath the legitimate, titled stories. This surreptitious other story may go as follows: "Maideen was the child King impregnated Mattie Will with. That was why Maideen's unnamed mother—Mattie Will—was so disturbed about her daughter's relation with Ran. When Maideen learned about this secret after her physical union with Ran, she committed suicide. She was buried with the Sojourners because Mattie Will had been divorced from Junior Holifield probably due to her encounter with King, and, further, with King's child had remarried a Sumrall." (Or, for a gloomier version, Junior had never come to after striking his head on the fallen tree and the ground and died of a brain contusion!) Is Mr. Holifield in "The Wanderers" (presumably Junior, if we can suppose that he did not die) mowing the grass at the Sojourner grave out of lingering feeling of love for his deceased ex-wife and her child (a melodrama indeed), or does he just happen to be the cemetery caretaker making his rounds (a comical irony)? In any case, dispersing the name Sojourner in the three stories, the author stirs in the reader's imagination an exorbitant Faulknerian story of incest running under the surface stories of *The Golden Apples*.

It is not the purpose of this chapter to attempt an exhaustive listing of "connectives" in *The Golden Apples*, but special attention in this regard should be paid to "The Wanderers," which was written, along with "Shower of Gold" and "Sir Rabbit," after Welty's decision in favor of a collection of "inter-related" stories and with the clear intention of placing it as the last story.

In "The Wanderers," the funeral of Katie Rainey, who professed the authorial scheme of "everybody to their own visioning," occasions the conditions for the revelation of the major characters' life stories. Prenshaw suggests that the skit "Bye-Bye Brevoort," upon which Welty was working in tandem as she was conceptualizing the organization of *The Golden Apples*, influenced the thematic pattern of this last chapter's "elegiac account of a passing Morgana life" (115)—that the theme of the skit is, despite its farcical surface, "the mutability of human life, the inevitable,

unavoidable passage of time and its consequence for human beings"
(110). Along with the outcomes of the major characters' lives, "The
Wanderers" presents some minor incidents that correspond with the incidents in "Shower of Gold," effecting a sense of continuity in their respective ways. For instance, the prime event in "Shower of Gold," the
return and departure of King MacLain, occurs while Katie and Snowdie
are cutting fabric for the babies' clothes, whereas Katie's death occurs
while Virgie is cutting out her own dress. Again, in the confusion after
the funeral, Virgie sees her and her brother's baby clothes, which Katie
had kept for all those years, being stolen by a woman who had come to
help. In "Shower of Gold" Virgie, as a baby, is introduced to the reader
through the accident of her swallowing a button and having her bottom
pounded to cause her to spit it up; this episode is subtly brought to a
resolution at the moment of her mother's death. For, when she sees her
mother has died, Virgie holds "her head, her mouth [opens], and one
by one the [fabric marking] pins [fall] out on the floor" (236). It is as if
the alien object she had ingested as a baby had after all remained within
her being and had developed some harmful and yet feminine growth, like
the tusks of the Medusa, to be liberated only when she is finally released
from her mother by the latter's death.

The motif of the radiant face is given the final stroke in "The Wanderers." The "night-blooming cereus" (267) an old lady offers Virgie is
apparently a Dutchman's pipe cactus (*Epiphyllum oxpetalum*), whose fra-
grant great flower starts opening after sunset and already starts wilting
past midnight. The flower's unusual shape and pale color with its trac-
ings like human blood vessels create an effective comparison to a human
face: "Virgie looked at the naked, luminous, complicated flower, large and
pale as a face on the dark porch" (267). This striking image reminds the
reader of "the grave, unappeased, and radiant face" (97) of Yeats's poem
that had appeared to Cassie always only in her dream. It was the face of
those who wander on the earth on unsolaced quests, the face of all those
who were like Miss Eckhart and Virgie.

Now, decades later, the face appears to Virgie herself, in the middle of
the night, as if in a dream; it has taken this long for this wanderer to see
the face that is her own, but she sees it not in a dream as Cassie did but
in real life. The evanescence of the flower pointed out by the old woman
is a warning: "After Miss Eckhart, after Katie, you are next, don't forget, see the beauty of life while it is living." The vision is so real and poignant that it frightens Virgie into throwing the flower away in the weeds.
But although she has thrown the flower away, the vision of it and the
warning will stay with her. The days when the ignorant Virgie impressed
the people of Morgana with the beauty of her piano performances are

long and forever gone; now what can Virgie do, confronted with the knowledge of her own face, of its evanescence? The inevitability of this question deriving from the motif of the radiant face, among other motifs, shows that through accumulation the short stories have brought about character development in the protagonist, the capacity Welty had originally believed only the novel possessed.

Welty's device of numerous minor motifs connecting and relativizing the discourses in the seven stories of *The Golden Apples* is backed by the thought that reality depends upon perception—or, in Katie's words, "Everybody to their own visioning." As I suggested earlier, this conception of the relation among reality, perception, representation (writing), and ultimately, comprehension (reading) is expressed well in Bakhtin's concise statement: "Reality as we have it in the novel is only one of many possible realities; it is not inevitable, not arbitrary, it bears within itself other possibilities" ("Epic," 37). The effect of this device upon the reader is that the reader gains a significant meaning, probably deeper than each separate story would offer, by dialogizing the accumulated given discourses. Yet the act of dialogizing itself confirms that the gained meaning is still only one of many possible realities, that a closure can never be hoped for.

The final scenes of *The Golden Apples* can be interpreted as a self-reflexive representation of this effect of dialogization. Firstly, Cassie's vision of the constellations in "June Recital" and Virgie's auditory image of the constellations at the end of "The Wanderers" clearly evidence the difference between the natures of the two women's perceptions. Cassie's perception is the observer's, and it is based on recognition of the self and the other. Cassie is able to recognize the separateness of the self from others and of others from each other. By dialogizing the lives of those separate beings, including herself, she is able to place them objectively in time as well as space. Thus in this final section, she retains a clear idea of herself and others: "'You'll go away like Loch,' Cassie called [to Virgie, who was leaving town,] from the steps. 'A life of your own, away— I'm so glad for people like you and Loch, I am really'" (272). Virgie, on the other hand, grasps the self and the other not as Cassie does but in three modes of existence, namely, the self, the other, and the self-other composite. Perseus slays the Medusa with the aid of the mirror shield that reflects the horror of the Medusa, and he acquires her lethal power by holding in his hand her horrible head, the sight of which is still able to petrify, in his hand; thus Perseus the hero simultaneously becomes the sight of horror. By the heroic act of killing the Medusa, Perseus holding the head becomes the monster, just as Siegfried simultaneously becomes the Dragon by gaining its strength when he bathes in the blood of the

Dragon he has slain. Virgie understands, at this point toward the end of "The Wanderers," why Miss Eckhart had hung the picture of Perseus holding the Medusa's head on her studio wall and said, "The same thing as Siegfried and the Dragon" (275). Virgie identifies this horrible relation between the hero and the victim with the relation between Beethoven and Miss Eckhart and that between Miss Eckhart and Virgie herself.

Virgie, as a young girl, had not understood the nature of the blood poured over her again and again as she taught Virgie her Beethoven. Yet Virgie's genius, which shone in her as Miss Eckhart's young protegée, "had accepted *the* Beethoven, as with the dragon's blood" (276): she had absorbed the hero and the victim from her teacher. Now in her mid-forties, relieved of the familial bonds and standing alone, Virgie understands that in the heroic act the self and the other become one composite being of the two, that the true meaning of heroism is to absorb the other within the self. Virgie has learned, as Miss Eckhart did, to dialogize the self and the other to bring about the self-other composite, namely, to see the other—Miss Eckhart covered with the Dragon's blood—within herself. Virgie is not an observer like Cassie; she is an actor, because she has absorbed the other. In this sense, the rhythms of the constellation Virgie hears at the end of *The Golden Apples* is not simply a vision like Cassie's, something merely witnessed, but a sensuous involvement.

Now recognizing within her own self Miss Eckhart's gift given with the Dragon's blood—the plunder of heroism—Virgie sees far back into time immemorial, envisioning the succession of heroic acts of conquering the separateness of the self and the other, Beethoven being only one of those heroes and Miss Eckhart also one, in however small a way. She sees how the heroes stood bathed in the blood of the victims and how each composite being of the hero and the victim, of the self and the other, created each civilization, each piece of art, each melody: "Every time Perseus struck off the Medusa's head, there was the beat of time, and the melody. Endless the Medusa, and Perseus endless" (276). Virgie sees the magnitude of the October rain falling "maybe on the whole South, for all she knew on the everywhere" (276), the everywhere in a temporal as well as a spatial sense. The "extent" to which Virgie's visioning reaches is human history itself.

Yet the author's visioning never deserts the local and historical specificity of Morgana, Mississippi, in the 1940s, and here again a dispersed motif plays its role. Earlier in "The Wanderers" Virgie protests to Juba, an African American maid sent by Mrs. Stark to help Virgie move out of town, that she saw Minerva, another African American maid, steal her mother's "hair switch" (270) along with her and her brother's baby clothes. Loch's stealing of Miss Eckhart's metronome in the confusion following the fire in "June Recital" suggests, as we noted earlier, that Miss Eckhart's passion is to be succeeded to by Loch, who performs a heroic act in "Moon Lake" and eventually goes to New York. Minerva's theft of Katie's wig seems to suggest that Katie's head—her heroic passion—is to be succeeded to by this poor African American woman, whose story would be added, we assume, to the chronicle of Morgana. Another African American woman who listens to the cosmic music of the falling rain with Virgie under "the big public tree" (277) is to be a main character in another would-be story; since she is granted the privilege of listening to the music, her being old, a beggar, and above all, a thief like Loch and Minerva and Prometheus the fire stealer, must qualify her to succeed to someone's passion. "The stroke of leopard" (277) in the cosmic music can be the sound of the sacred beast in her ancestral land of Africa not only that in the New World. The last scene of *The Golden Apples* is not a closure; it is an ending left open to many possibilities. Even Virgie's story is not finished; she is only now departing. Nor is the story of Loch in the Big Apple, nor the story of Easter. What has happened to Mrs. Morrison, whose ghost has no head, like the beheaded Medusa, or to Mr. Morrison, who now surveys the street with that "poor old telescope" from the confinement of his upstairs corner room? What about the people who lived before Katie's generation—people like King MacLain's grandfather? Virgie speculates, "Didn't he kill a man, or have to, and what would be the long story behind it, the vaunting and the wandering from it?" (274). All these past and future stories are left to be told someday. Yet one cannot but feel the author's special sentiment for including specifically these African American women of low social standing as the protagonists of future stories of Morgana, Mississippi.

I hope I have shown that these dispersed minor motifs play a crucial role of holding together the stories of *The Golden Apples* structurally and thematically and of bringing about subtexts pregnant with meanings that the respective stories could not have done when read independently. I should repeat that the role those minor motifs play is no "minor" one compared to that of the "major" motifs from myths or famous poems. Only, here the author counts greatly on the reader's apperceptive comprehension, for the dialogization of the separate discourses induced by those motifs takes place within the reader: representation functions through comprehension. Pitavey-Souques in her "Technique as Myth" sees the image of the artist in the image of Perseus with the mirror shield and with the Medusa's head in a convincing argument. In the course of my argument, Perseus with the Medusa's head is the image of the reader, the space where originally separate meanings on the pages interact dialogically to become composite meanings. When the reader is cast into this role, the fiction writer renounces a closure, because the reader is also Virgie, who stands before numerous possibilities, as Bakhtin's earlier quotation may be recalled to show: "Reality as we have it in the novel . . . bears within itself other possibilities." A "tradition of her own" realized in *The Golden Apples*, with which Welty attempted to surpass the existing genre boundaries, is self-reflexively embodied in Virgie the character and ultimately in the reader's act of comprehending this text. In this sense, *The Golden Apples* transforms the tradition of fiction through the agent of the reader. Yet it is doubly a great irony that, to create a "tradition of her own," one other than the novel, Welty seems to have made use of what Forster indicates to be one of the traditionally novelistic techniques— "rhythm"—and the effect she has achieved is what Bakhtin designates as the fundamental quality of the novel, or its "novelness."

PART IV

"Everything and Nothing":
The Author

CHAPTER 8

Sideshadows of Life:
The Bride of the Innisfallen and Other Stories and "Other" Stories

In his *Narrative and Freedom: The Shadows of Time*, Gary Saul Morson, inspired largely by the ideas of Mikhail Bakhtin and Isaiah Berlin, presents an intriguing statement on our conception of reality:

> Whereas foreshadowing works by revealing apparent alternatives to be mere illusion, sideshadowing conveys the sense that actual events might just as well not have happened. . . . Sideshadowing relies on a concept of time as a field of possibilities. Each moment has a set of possible events (though by no means every conceivable event) that could take place in it. From this field a single event emerges—perhaps by chance, perhaps by choice, perhaps by some combination of both with the inertia of the past, and in any case contingently. (117–18)

Welty's "Circe" (1949)[1] in *The Bride of the Innisfallen and Other Stories* (1955) can be considered a typical example of what Morson calls a "sideshadow" of a myth. To use an established literary term, it is a kind of parody—a "beside song"—of the well-known Odyssean legend involving the enchantress Circe, who transforms mortal drifters to her island into beasts with her magic broth and wand. Welty's story is narrated not from the hero's perspective (as by Homer) nor his companion's (as by Ovid) but from the enchantress's. The sideshadowing effect is most apparent in Welty's subversion of the traditional moral/power system attributed to the relation between Odysseus and Circe, a subversion that results in the exchange of the roles of victim and victimizer.

In the traditional framework Odysseus is first the victim; then, due to his valorous intention, worthy of divine assistance, and to his handsome appearance, he defeats the victimizer, and thus Circe's devoted service becomes Odysseus's lawful booty. What Welty does in "Circe" is to place her characters, as it were, in Morson's "field of possibilities" and light them from the side so that they cast sideshadows, rather than foreshadows or backshadows along a monologic "authorized" temporal line. Welty's Circe is a refreshingly spunky female immortal who cannot help laughing at the stupidity of mortals' valor and virtue, their total inability to achieve spatial and temporal transcendence: mortals don't see where their vision doesn't reach, nor do they know what will happen a moment hence. Yet vulnerable as all lovers are, Circe endures Odysseus's nightly boast of his own insightless (in her view) "heroic" acts, continues to provide for the crew's swine-like appetite, and after a year finds herself abandoned, suffering from the morning sickness of carrying Odysseus's child. Circe is the victim, Odysseus the victimizer. Welty has told an "other" story about Circe.

Welty's story of the Greek Madame Butterfly has inevitably invited strong feminist critiques.[2] But this feminist emphasis has, in my view, often obscured another serious theme of the story: that of the relationship between humans and literature. The critics who deploy feministic arguments on the theme of literary production in "Circe" stress the story's concern with the difference of woman's narrative from man's; typical examples are Ann Romines's "How Not to Tell a Story: Eudora Welty's First-Person Tales" (100–102) and Peter Schmidt's *The Heart of the Story: Eudora Welty's Short Fiction*, in which the latter holds that Circe is an extreme, in fact inhuman, example of "the freedom from the inherited bonds of male-centered narrative" (191). Yet Welty's concern in this story, I believe, is first the relation between the plight of humans and literary production; gender is not the question here, as revealed in the fact that the male sun god is categorized together with the female Circe due to his immortality (105). To ignore this out of overzealous feminist emphasis would dismiss a crucial point of the story.

Welty's Circe laughs at the mortals' lack of omniscience; for Circe, as with all immortals, there are no surprises, no moving events, since everything is foreknown—or "foreshadowed," to use Morson's word. Yet despite all her scorn for mortals, Welty's enchantress admits to recognition of "a mortal mystery" (105) that immortals cannot experience, for which actually she is burning with envy of mortals. The secret comes from mortals' life of contingency; immortals, omniscient, knowing only necessity, cannot experience contingency. What does contingency bring to the mortal? Stories, countless stories.

Thus Odysseus proudly tells Circe his story of poking out the eye of a one-eyed monster, but Circe knows "the monster is growing another

[eye], and a new man will sail along to blind it again" (105). Odysseus's men are also full of stories as to their beastly experience and their amorous spree after regaining human form, all of which are old stories to Circe. Circe's foreknowledge even extends to how Odysseus's death will be brought about by the child she is presently carrying: "We were a rim of fire, a ring on the sea. [Odysseus's] ship was a moment's gleam on a wave. The little son, I know, was to follow—follow and slay him. That was the story. For whom is a story enough? For the wanderers who will tell it—it's where they must find their strange felicity" (111).

The "felicity" of telling a story—literary production—is "strange" to immortals, since they experience no surprise or wonder. Mortals are all "wanderers," "seafarers," and "star-gazers," since they have no sure knowledge of their destination, nor their route, nor their fate of a moment later. If we reword this situation following Morson, mortals live only in the present, casting sideshadows on the "field of possibilities," where a single event emerges for each person contingently. Surprise and wonder being the natural outcome of contingency, how could the event not be worthy of a story? From this viewpoint, Welty's "Circe" is not only a sideshadow of a myth but also a metafiction, a story about the essence of "story" as sideshadowing.

The most common general comment on *The Bride of the Innisfallen and Other Stories* seems to have concerned each story's increased complexity in meaning and obscurity of focus relative to earlier of Welty's works.[3] One early reviewer candidly characterized the authorial intention as "undecipherable" (Peden 18), and even in the late eighties Harriet Pollack called the book "obscure, elitist" (75). This might be one of the reasons why the book had not attracted as much critical attention as Welty's other works until the past decade, when the feminists as well as others revived new interest in the stories.[4] In this chapter, however, I hope to call non-gender-oriented critical attention to how Welty's idea of metafiction concurs with this elusiveness of authorial center in these stories.

Reading them in the light of what "Circe" suggests to be the essence of story, one notices in the stories collected in *The Bride of the Innisfallen and Other Stories* a striking clarity of common understanding that a multitude of possibilities underlie life and that the actual events occur contingently. Often in these stories the enumeration of details and incidents seems to obscure the weight of what ought to be pertinent to the theme event; actually, however, we discern in the narrative Welty's subtext that life, or the present moment, unfolds and reveals a number of possibilities of which "mortals" are unable to distinguish, or foreknow, which will be pertinent.

Welty's protagonists in these stories usually continue to be exposed to such pertinent or impertinent details of the moment. These irrelevant details at best suggest numerous open-ended events, but possibilities of meaningful stories are there; only, the protagonist might not know this fact, from his or her "mortal" non-vantage point. Yet in the process of absorbing the mass of such details indiscriminately the protagonist acquires a certain knowledge that is pertinent to the protagonist's future. Thus, the unnamed woman and man in "No Place for You, My Love" (1952) during their drive through southern Louisiana see numerous people and objects, with whom or which they never really become personally involved, but the hallucinatory visions and horror that the woman and man face, though separately, during the night ride and on returning to the hotel are apparently the results of what they have seen during the day.

Again, Dewey Coker in "Ladies in Spring" (1954) sees during and after the fishing outing various people, such as the town's postmistress and rainmaker Hattie Purcell, a lone strange lady, Miss Hattie's niece Opal, and his own father and mother, along with the various bright-colored objects and animals the rain reveals, none of whom or which directly affects Dewey's present situation. But one sentence, which leaps across time to fifteen years into the future, thrown in toward the end of the story, confirms the mysterious density of each moment the boy (and the reader) suspects: "Fifteen years later it occurred to him it had very likely been Opal in the woods" (99). The reader sees that Dewey himself has reached the stage in his life at which he is able to understand the desire, anxiety, and sorrow those people must have felt, probably because he himself is experiencing similar feelings now.

In "Going to Naples" (1954), although the story follows the protagonist Gabriella Serto's growth from a naïve, playful girl to a somewhat pensive young woman during her voyage from New York to Naples, the author never goes into Gabriella's psychology itself but confines herself to describing the people, including Gabriella, and the incidents that come before her eyes, even during her brief intimacy with a young man on board ship. But in this story also, as in "Ladies in Spring," the narration makes an *unusual leap*, not this time into the future but into the emotions of the unspecified people present at that moment. The following passage, one of the most exquisite in the story, crystallizes the meaning of the numerous things Gabriela sees on board:

> And it lifted the soul—for a thing like crossing the ocean could depress it—to sit in the sun and contemplate among companions the weakness and the mystery of the flesh. Looking, dreaming, down at Gabriella, they felt something of an old, pure loneliness come back to them—like a bird sent out over the waters long ago, when they were young, perhaps from their same

company. Only the long of memory, the brave and experienced of heart, could bear such a stirring, and awakening—first to have listened to that screaming, and in a flash to remember what it was. (166)

Just as the various unspecified passengers' memories of their younger days are called back by Gabriella's screaming, so do the possibilities of Gabriella's own days to come vary. Yet as the only sure thing held in common among these passengers is aging—"the weakness and the mystery of the flesh"—so will the copassenger Gabriella's life voyage be a process of aging, a progress toward death. Her voyage to Naples, echoing the old saying "See Naples and die," becomes a metaphor of her life, in which she enjoys its beauty and eventually dies. Thus in all these stories, the specific effect of the respective encounters upon the protagonist's psychology and his or her life is never explained by the author, but the density of each moment in respect to "possibilities" and the mystery of contingency are strongly felt by the reader.

In the book's title story, "The Bride of the Innisfallen" (1951), the subtext on this density of "possibilities" in each moment functions as the very power source of plot development. Except for the last three pages of the forty-page story, the unnamed young American wife traveling from London to Cork, Ireland, does not seem to contribute to the plot development, as if she were not the main protagonist. Rather, the details about people and things, presented presumably through the American wife's perspective, are what propels the story ahead. Welty dwells on the wife's eight copassengers in the compartment of the train from Paddington to Fishguard but pays extremely little attention to the American wife herself; the only thing the reader learns about her early on is that she has left London without her husband's knowledge. Actually, this is the clue to the assumption that she is the main protagonist, since this is the only inner revelation that could not have been ascertained from her outward appearance.

Her copassengers exhibit each their distinct characters through their appearance and remarks: a middle-aged, talkative woman in a bright-colored raincoat with a huge appetite; a passionate-looking, exclamatory man from Connemara; a young boy with a harmonica and a young pregnant woman related to him, who have been to a wedding in London; and a pair of lovers who dwell mostly in their own quiet world; a Welsh schoolgirl who only reads a book and eats a banana during her short ride; an inquisitive Welsh gentleman who volunteers nothing about himself. While the lively exchanges occasion glimpses into the passengers' personalities and lives, the corridor beside the compartment becomes the scene of unexpected incidents: two greyhounds in plaid blankets rushing silently as if not to be noticed, an English nurse holding a beautiful Irish baby whom these passengers worry she is kidnapping: "Railway trains are great systems for goings on of all kinds. You'll never take me by surprise" (54), says the lady in the raincoat. But to the reader, and undoubtedly to the American wife, the things going on and being talked about even within this compartment certainly offer surprises and possibilities. For example, the man from Connemara talks about his clever parrot, which learned to talk very well but died suddenly because of its peculiar feeding habit:

> "There've been times when I've dreamed a certain *person* may have had more to do with it!" the man from Connemara cried in crescendo. "That I've never mentioned till now. But women are jealous and uncertain creatures, I've been thinking as we came this long way along tonight." (75)

Could he be implying that his wife killed the bird, or some other woman whose jealousy the parrot's talking had evoked? Had the bird been poisoned with its peculiar food? What will this man do now that he has confirmed this suspicion? Nothing is answered within this story, but all the things are left as possibilities for "other" stories.

The man also talks about the ghosts who appear regularly on a castle wall in Connemara (63), and another passenger occasions a hearty laugh when she tells about a man who insists that while he was eating in the diner the carriages were shifted and his carriage has disappeared; for all she knows, he is still wandering through the train (69). Due to the way Welty presents them, even things unsaid seem to present themselves as curious materials for possible stories: "They never let [the Welsh gentleman] tell what he was doing with himself in either end of Wales, or why he had to come on this very night, or even what in the world he was carrying in that heavy case" (76). Welty's method of depicting these passengers reminds us of what Mikhail Bakhtin calls "polyphony" in his *Problems of Dostoevsky's Poetics* (1929):[5] "Not a multitude of characters and fates in a single objective world, illuminated by a single authorial consciousness; rather *a plurality of consciousnesses, with equal rights and each with its own world*, combine but are not merged in the unity of the event" (6). Toward the end of the train ride, the reader is told about a slight change in the American wife, who has been sitting silently but apparently absorbing all the exchanges in the compartment: "As they talked, the American girl laid her head back, a faint smile on her face" (76). The reader sees, along with the American wife, that the people in the compartment are, in Bakhtin's words, "*free* people, capable of standing *alongside* their creator" (6).

At Fishguard, the passengers transfer onto a ferry, the *Innisfallen,* for Cork. Having crossed the channel during the night, the passengers wake up to find themselves in the bright morning sunlight sailing inland on the River Lee. The enumeration of dazzling scenes on the banks—color-ful houses, trees, birds, people waving—seen from the decks continues, this time with the American wife's earlier copassengers dispersed among others. At this point, this story's seminal "event" takes place—an event that, however, is actually too brief and trifling in itself to amount to a full-fledged event. Someone exclaims, "'There's a bride on board! . . . Look at her, look!'" (79). Although the narrator offers "Sure enough, a girl who had not yet showed herself in public now appeared by the rail in a white spring hat and, over her hands, a little old-fashioned white bunny muff" (79), it is not at all "sure" that the girl is a bride. It is sim-ply because of the dazzling whiteness of her outfit and her shy but ex-pectant posture that everybody who has heard the exclamation seems to believe it. The possibility of her being a bride emerges out of various other possibilities to become almost a sure fact, although nobody on board will know of her actual whereabouts after landing.

The reason one assumes an extra significance in this seemingly insig-nificant moment is that of all others, the author has made this the title event. The "bride" obviously reflects the American wife's state of mind, for the author indicates later that walking around Cork all day by herself the American wife "had felt no lonelier than that little bride herself, who had come off the boat. Yes, somewhere in the crowd at the dock there must have been a young man holding flowers: he had been taken for granted" (81). The journey from Paddington to Fishguard and on to Cork has changed her from a frustrated, "nearly destroyed" (81) wife who had to desert her husband to a hopeful "bride" who is entering a new life.

The only factual detail given, later in the story, regarding this woman's married life in London is that she and her photographer husband had "made a little dark room in [their] flat" (75). The reader notices a clear contrast between what the couple's own dark room implies and what the wife has seen during her journey in the lighted train compartment filled with people, and on board the *Innisfallen* in bright daylight, and in the town of Cork. The American wife recalls that her husband said, "You hope for too much" (82)—that had been, in his view, her trouble. Now she knows that he was wrong, that the world is filled with possibilities and that she may hope for countless encounters. She thinks of sending her husband a telegram with only the words "Don't expect me back yet" (82). Yet "The Bride of the Innisfallen" ends with her throwing even this mes-sage into a stream and walking into a pub, "into the lovely room full of strangers" (83). At this final moment of the story, the American wife is a "free" character, just like her fellow passengers, casting sideshadows onto a field of possibilities where new stories are to originate. "The Bride of

the Innisfallen" is a paean to the richness of *mortals'* lives and their freedom to savor it to the full.

In contrast to "The Bride of the Innisfallen," in which the protagonist projects her desire onto the unknown future, "Kin" (1952), another
story in the collection, is concerned with the protagonist's glance projected back onto the past. Yet here again the past is presented not as a
monologic, linear time but rather as a multilogic density made up of layers
of possibilities.

In this story, the characters are "kin," certainly by blood or marriage,
yet even more so by the depth of emotion they attach to their home in
rural Mississippi, the fictional Mingo on the River Hushomingo. Only two
of the kin now live there: Uncle Felix, actually the great-uncle of the
narrator, Dicey Hastings, and Sister Anne, his remote kinswoman, who
is taking care of him. But the way Dicey's Aunt Ethel pronounces the
word "Mingo" when she receives a letter from there tells of the richness
of memory and sentiment she still holds about this old home place: "The
name [Mingo] sounded in my ears like something instead of somewhere"
(112). Reading that old Uncle Felix's health is declining fast, Aunt Ethel,
who, also ill in bed, will probably never see Mingo again, asks her daughter
Kate and Dicey to visit Uncle Felix on her behalf. Dicey, recently engaged
to be married in the North, to which she and her family had moved long
ago, has been back for a short visit with her aunt and cousin. Dicey and
Kate gladly depart for Mingo. Dicey herself has her own cherished memories of Mingo, where their many kinfolk used to gather, all dressed up
and lively, at Uncle Felix and Aunt Beck's home for Sunday dinners. But
this visit is to reveal to Dicey possibilities of Mingo's past quite different
from what she had known.

Upon their arrival, Dicey and Kate are dismayed to learn that Sister
Anne has given an itinerant photographer permission to use Uncle Felix's
parlor to make portraits of the people in the community; in exchange,
Sister Anne will have her picture taken free of charge. Just about the whole
countryside has turned out for this rare opportunity, filling the house,
while, to the two girls' indignation, the invalid Uncle Felix has been
moved to a shabby storeroom in the back. There they find Uncle Felix,
who in Dicey's childhood memory had been a dandy, an active man; now
he is lying all disoriented due both to old age and sudden dislocation from
his bedroom. When he sees the girls, he only keeps on saying, "Hide"
(138). He seems to be living at some moment in the past when he had
to protect his women from the enemy. The reader can speculate, from
what Dicey observes in the storeroom, that the disturbance of the many
people crowding the house, the constant photo flashes, the gunpowder-
like smell traveling from the parlor, and very likely the Civil War musket

standing in the corner of the room have created in Uncle Felix the illusion of combat. It is part of Uncle Felix's past Dicey had known nothing about.

In this unfamiliar room, a curious thing happens, one that is to give Dicey rare insight into the human mind. By a gesture Uncle Felix asks Dicey to pick up a pencil from the floor, and with it he painstakingly writes a note, which he forces into her hand. Later, coming out of the storeroom, Dicey shows Kate the note, which says "River—Daisy—Midnight—Please" (148). Dicey interprets it as a note requesting a tryst with a certain Daisy by the river at midnight, while Kate flatly rejects such a possibility, pointing out that his wife's name was Beck, that people all went to bed at dark in the country. Yet Dicey insists on "her story."

A clue to the reason for Dicey's conviction seems to have been provided a few pages earlier, in a passage describing the parlor being used for the photography. The photographer's backdrop is hanging there so that the background for each portrait will be "a scene that never was, a black and white and gray blur" (146). Dicey realizes the backdrop is now covering the portrait of her Great-Grandmother Evelina on the wall, and she recalls this painting was made by an itinerant painter in the same way:

> [Evelina's head] had been fitted to the ready-made portrait by the painter who had called at the door. . . . The yellow skirt spread fanlike, straw hat held ribbon-in-hand, orange beads big as peach pits (to conceal the joining at the neck)—none of that, any more than the forest scene so unlike the Mississippi wilderness (that enormity she had been carried to as a bride, when the logs of this house were cut, her bounded world by drop by drop of sweat exposed, where she'd died in the end of yellow fever) or the melancholy clouds obscuring the sky behind the passive figure with the small, crossed feet—none of it, world or body, was really hers. She had eaten bear meat, seen Indians, she had married into the wilderness at Mingo, to what unknown feeling. (147–48)

Dicey sympathizes with the Evelina in the portrait, since she also is going to enter into married life, "to what unknown feeling." Although Dicey's married life will be nothing like Evelina's in the genuine wilderness of Mingo in the long past, Dicey can feel the grotesque gulf between the carefree romantic figure of the painting and Evelina's actual married life.

To Dicey, who understands the existence of possible multilayers of a person's life and feeling, the idea of Uncle Felix's tryst is not unnatural: he might have loved a woman other than Beck, one to whom he had had to send a pleading note secretly. He might have married Daisy, not Beck, if the situation had allowed, or perhaps Daisy was a married woman he loved in vain—the reader speculates that Dicey thinks of such "other stories," because she is sensitive enough to feel Uncle Felix's pain: "It was the 'please' that had hurt me" (152). The special compassion between the two has already been symbolized in the scene when Dicey picks up the pencil for him: "My Great-Uncle Felix, without his right hand ever letting me go, received the pencil in his left. For a moment our arms crossed, but it was not awkward or strange, more as though we two were going to skate off, or dance off, out of here" (140).

Yet there is perhaps one "other story" of which Dicey is unaware, and to which even the author does not allude but rather leaves to the careful reader's imagination: Dicey's own name, pronounced with a Southern accent, could have sounded to Uncle Felix like "Daisy," and her youth and beauty, together with the name, could have reawakened Uncle Felix's memory of a long-lost past. It is now the reader's turn to confirm the richness of possibilities of the lives in Mingo, including Dicey's. Compassion may upset the monologic, linear time, and Uncle Felix and Dicey, three generations apart, can very well be soul mates who depart from the confines of age and space to an open world, their arms intercrossed to support each other.

In this respect, the story suggests that the other characters also have their "other stories." Their unrevealed stores of the past are implied in situations and incidents that the author no doubt purposefully leaves not fully elucidated in the text, such as Aunt Ethel's affection for Uncle Felix since childhood, the maid Rachel's complex homesickness, or Sister Anne's falling in the well and coming out on someone else's wedding day. Thus the ultimate impression the reader gains from "Kin" is the uncertainty of the "past," the possibilities of sideshadows of the past: that *the past is never finalized.*

The prominent common characteristics of the stories in *The Bride of the Innisfallen and Other Stories*, compared with Welty's earlier works, are their complexity of meaning and obscurity of focus. In the present chapter, I have attributed these features to the author's deliberate blurring of a monologic authorial center in the stories and claimed that this authorial retreat is one of the important factors that constitute the "meaning" of each story.

Yet for the sake of pure speculation, one may ask what motivated Welty to change her style so radically, since style, no less than content, represents the author's conception of reality. I offer a sociopolitical consideration. The decade of the fifties in Mississippi was a time of suppressed anxiety and unrest, when the meaning of justice, the ideology of democracy, and the accepted standard of morals were being questioned. One sincere way to face such reality would be pluralism, which denounces any monologic principle and admits instead the values of different persuasions equally. A homogeneous conformist society does not, and need not, cultivate such pluralistic thinking. I believe there is a "possibility" that Welty's admission of the sideshadows of life was a gift of the time. She did not write about the actual social scenes of Mississippi at this point; it seems to have taken her a long period of mulling to apply this thinking to concrete sociopolitical events. Welty's "The Demonstrators" (1966), published after a full decade of virtual silence except for the short "Where Is the Voice Coming From?" (1963), is indeed composed of sideshadows of Mississippi history.

CHAPTER 9

❦

Voices and Aphasia in "The Demonstrators"

The Collected Stories of Eudora Welty (1980) reflects not only the author's decisions as to the definitive versions of the stories[1] but also her desire to ensure a more permanent recognition of two of her stories that so far had not been included in collected editions. The two stories, "Where Is the Voice Coming From?" (1963) and "The Demonstrators" (1966), had appeared in the *New Yorker* during the height of the nation's civil rights turmoil, from which both stories' subject matter derived, and had since languished uncompiled among the faded pages of the old numbers of the magazine. Welty's claim for the significance of these stories is well justified, due not only to their explicitly sociopolitical setting, a setting that is rare in her production,[2] but also to their experimental stylistic technique.

Of the two stories, "The Demonstrators" is no doubt the more intricately wrought and the more ambitious; it was awarded a first-place O. Henry Memorial Award in 1968. As early as 1969 Ruth M. Vande Kieft, in her "Demonstrators in a Stricken Land," suggested that the primal theme of the story was not the racial question but a more universal question of the relation between self and society. Her revised monograph on Welty (1987) repeats the main argument of the 1969 essay with a newly added introductory passage in which she assesses "The Demonstrators" as "possibly the greatest story to come out of the civil rights era" (1987, 143). Yet during the preceding two decades critical attention was, quite understandably, directed mostly to the racial and social material in the story[3] until Vande Kieft's 1987 book, in effect, reemphasized the highly metaphysical theme underlying the racial question. Meanwhile, in a 1978 interview, Welty was asked about the choice of her title, something that had puzzled readers from the beginning: why "The

Demonstrators," given that no reference to actual demonstrators appears in the narrative, other than that the protagonist happens to see a photo, in an out-of-town city newspaper, of a solitary demonstrator burning his draft card? Welty answered: "I think every character in it is a demonstrator. In fact, I wanted to suggest that. Even the birds at the end" (Prenshaw 1984, 262).

If the meaning of the title is obscure and challenging (at least until the author responded to queries about it, a response that did not fully clarify the choice of that title), the whole content of the story is equally so. In an attempt to plumb the nature of this obscurity Susan Ferguson's "The 'Assault of Hope': Style's Substance in Welty's 'The Demonstrators'" (1989) advances a sensitive analysis of the style of this story, characterizing it as "the controlled play of cognitive dissonances" (45). This cognitive dissonance is to be observed in diction and imagery, a technique that she notes contrasts with Welty's stories of the thirties and early forties. I believe Welty's propensity for ambiguity became apparent in fact in the fifties, more than a decade earlier than "The Demonstrators." In the preceding chapter I indicated an increased obscurity of meaning of the stories included in *The Bride of the Innisfallen and Other Stories* (1955) over Welty's earlier works and attributed this feature to the author's deliberate blurring of the authorial center. I identified this authorial retreat as actually constituting the "meaning" of each story. I also suggested in the chapter that the sociopolitical debate and unrest in the fifties in Mississippi had contributed to the author's pluralistic admission of different persuasions, resulting in the rejection of a monologic authorial center in fiction. In the trajectory of my analysis of those later stories, it is not surprising to see that "The Demonstrators," the last of her published stories and a story born at the climax of the civil rights turmoil in Mississippi, reveals the intensification of this element of obscurity, first evident in *The Bride*. In this chapter I wish to examine the story from this viewpoint of the time and place of her writing, and observe where, if anywhere, Welty's pluralistic thinking ultimately leads.

"The Demonstrators" is set in the small fictional town of Holden, in the Mississippi Delta, the Mississippi River floodplain in the northwestern part of the state, where antebellum cotton plantations had flourished using slave labor and where even at the time in which the story is set low-paid African Americans labored in the fields, and the cotton gins sustained the area's cotton production. The time is November 1964, the year Mississippi underwent "the second Civil War," the pivot of which was the "Freedom Summer" of that year; it was a time of extreme turmoil, although no specific mention of these events appears in the story. The narrative proceeds from the third-person point of view of the town's only medical doctor, Richard Strickland. It tells of a case of critical injury sustained one night in Holden, for which professional treatment is requested of the doctor. Following this the story simply reproduces a local newspaper article on the crime, which had resulted in two deaths, an article that the doctor reads at home. The kind of complexity and obscurity observed in the stories of *The Bride* has clearly been intensified in "The Demonstrators": at the end of the story, the reader is left still unsure what really happened in the seminal event of the double murder case and of the doctor's thoughts and feeling engendered by it.

Even early on in the story, in contrast to the circumstances of his earlier house call that night on Miss Marcia Pope, an aged, longtime patient of his, Dr. Strickland's unexpected journey and house call at the home of a critically injured African American woman is characterized by disorientation and uncertainty. Richard Strickland does not know his destination, or the young girl who has been sent to summon him, or the injured woman who lies wordless, still dressed in the choir vestment that she must have had on when she was stabbed. Only in the course of treating her wound does the doctor suddenly realize the patient is Ruby Gaddy, the maid who cleans his clinic five days a week, and learn that the assailant was her common-law husband, Dove Collins, a man whom the doctor also realizes he knows well but had not previously associated with Ruby. Gradually from the fragmented speech of the people in the room, the doctor identifies Ruby's baby, then her sister, her brother, and her mother, the latter of whom volunteers the information that she used to be a laundress for the Stricklands when Richard was a baby and that she felt Richard's father was a better doctor than he is. There the doctor also recognizes some familiar chinaware and clothes that apparently had been given to this family by the Stricklands years ago. On his drive home, the unexpected old human relationships he has relived between Ruby's family and his own move him to the verge of tears. But on returning to his office the doctor finds Dove Collins there dying from loss of blood; the only words Dove utters are "Hide me." A few days later, Strickland reads at home the newspaper report of the couple's deaths, and the story ends with the doctor letting the paper drop to the floor and thinking about his severely handicapped daughter who died at thirteen without ever having been able to communicate with anyone throughout her short life.

One of the reasons for the reader's uncertainty comes from the shocking discrepancies between what the doctor saw and did that night, and the newspaper account. Firstly, the newspaper erroneously alters Dove's first name to "Dave." It reports that Dave (that is, Dove) stabbed Ruby in the chest with an ice pick and that Ruby, wresting the weapon from him, stabbed him in the ear or eye in retaliation, leaving unexplained how a woman with such a severe injury could have managed so vigorous a retaliation. Moreover, how the young couple came to such violent blows is not explained at all. It had taken some time for the doctor to reach Ruby's house by car; how could the mortally wounded Dove have *walked* that distance to the clinic to be discovered there by the doctor? The newspaper account locates Dove's mortal wounds in the chest; are these not separate from those Ruby inflicted? It had been Dove's payday, but he was not carrying any money when he was found. Was it not a strange coincidence that the blood-covered ice pick was said to have been discovered by Ruby's own eight-year-old brother on the grounds of a school and not at the scene of the murder? In addition, no part of Dr. Strickland's involvement with the victims or family that night—his having been sent for or having treated Ruby or his discovery of Dove—is mentioned in the article; instead, the doctor is reported to have been at the country club all that evening. There are other details that are by no means clearly explained, but one theme is very clear: that this was a family affair, and no racial conflict was involved. Thus the county sheriff is quoted: "That's one they can't pin the blame on us for. That's how they treat their own kind. Please take note our conscience is clear" (621).

    The kind of uncertainty and obscurity one observes in "The Demonstrators" can be explained, I would like to argue, as deriving from the author's emphasis on what one may call the Bakhtinian heteroglot social situation. In his "Discourse in the Novel," Mikhail Bakhtin presents his unique characterization of the relation between language and society:

> At any given moment of its historical existence, language is heteroglot from top to bottom: it represents the coexistence of social-ideological contradictions between the present and the past, between differing epochs of the past, between different socio-ideological groups in the present, between tendencies, schools, circles and so forth, all given a bodily form. These "languages" of heteroglossia intersect each other in a variety of ways, forming new socially typifying "languages." (291)

The novel, as distinct from the lyric and the epic, extends, in Bakhtin's conception, the arena in which those different languages, often opposing, struggle for ideological legitimacy and authority as truth. Thus, Bakhtin continues, "the decisive and distinctive importance of the novel as a genre: the human being in the novel is first, foremost and always a speaking human being; the novel requires speaking persons bringing with them their own unique ideological discourse, their own language" (332). The speaking persons in the newspaper account that the doctor reads create an ideological discourse that he—and the reader—do not expect of the Ruby-Dove affair. For instance, the place where the weapon was discovered is "the grounds of the new $100,000.00 Negro School" (621); the pastor of a white church is quoted as saying: "Well, I'm surprised didn't more of them get hurt. . . . And yet they expect to be seated in our churches" (621). These examples of ideological discourse embodying the logic of the anti–civil rights whites echo voices expressing such sentiments as, "We [whites] are generous enough to spend as much as a hundred thousand dollars on the Negroes," or "Negroes are so mentally inferior and uncultured that they are constantly using violence against each other and yet are brazen enough to demand admission to our white churches." But the same facts could very well be appropriated to represent the voices of the civil rights advocates: "The whites have built a new school for the blacks to ensure segregation," and "Whites are exploiting the Ruby-Dove case to create groundless contempt for the Negro in general in order to defend racial segregation in white churches." Only, the Holden newspaper adopts as legitimate the anti–civil rights voices and will function as an ideological apparatus to reinforce their authority.

Strickland, however, knows that the civil rights advocates have been employing journalistic tactics just as unfair to force their voices upon the public. The previous June, reading a city newspaper—that is, not the local Holden paper—in which it was reported that a civil rights group had been forced at gunpoint to go into the fields in hundred-degree temperatures and pick cotton, the doctor had protested to the editor, a friend, who had approved the article, that it was a lie: "There isn't any cotton in June" (617). To this the editor friend had responded, "They won't know the difference where the paper is read. . . . It's the way of reaching people. Don't forget—what they *might* have done to us is even worse" (617). The article in the city paper functions to reinforce the pro–civil rights discourse, just as the account of the Ruby-Dove case voices the opposite position. The two rival social groups' intense discursive struggle over legitimacy provided Welty with the material for an effective literary presentation of the heteroglot situation of 1964 in Mississippi.

Yet the heteroglossia presented in "The Demonstrators" is not limited to the sociopolitical voices directly concerning the civil rights struggle. One should keep in mind that Bakhtinian heteroglossia theoretically includes *all* the "languages"—in the Bakhtinian sense, not only linguistically separate languages but *ideologically* separate ones—spoken in the society at any given historical moment and that, more importantly, not all those languages necessarily enjoy equal representation in the narrative: "In a novel . . . the speaking person is not all that is represented, and people themselves need not be represented *only* as speakers" (333). The heteroglot narrative space reflects, among other things, both the inequality of the society's distribution of power among its voices *and* the author's sensitivity or insensitivity toward that inequality. What gives "The Demonstrators" its intellectual and emotional depth is the powerful social *and* literary subtext maintained by Welty's sensitivity toward this inequality.

Welty provides an instance of the social deprivation of voice through an apparently trifling error in one letter in the local newspaper article. The young husband's unusual given name, "Dove," is erroneously altered to the common "Dave." Any given name, since it is "given," is pregnant with the giver's wishes. Welty once said in an interview that while she was very careful about choosing names for her characters, she did not use "anything that couldn't happen, that wouldn't be right for that part of the country or that kind of family" (Prenshaw 1984, 51). Welty's African American characters often have distinctly symbolic names like Phoenix, Narciss, or Missouri, names that, according to Welty, echo African Americans' frequent practice of giving their children as beautiful and meaningful a name as possible when they could hardly give them anything of material value, as so often was the case. The name "Dove" speaks in and of itself of the giver's wishes for that which the bird symbolizes— peace and hope, meekness but also soaring flight. Dove's life had been wishfully prescribed even before he was born, when this name was decided among the family. From the day of his birth up to this day, the name has been spoken by Dove's family, friends, and wife with that feeling special to this name. Changing "Dove" to "Dave" deprives it not only of its African-Americanness and all meaningfulness but the voices of all those who sounded it.

This incident discloses the insensitive carelessness of those who in effect impose what Pierre Bourdieu calls "aphasia" upon a different language group. Bourdieuian aphasia can be considered to exist at the outermost margin of the Bakhtinian heteroglossia. In his *Outline of a Theory of Practice* Bourdieu distinguishes between "the universe of (orthodox or heterodox) discourse and the universe of doxa" (170), the former admitting of the possible coexistence of differing or opposing, thus orthodox or heterodox, persuasions as opposed to the latter's admitting of only the absolute as self-evident. Doxa works in both ways as to what goes without saying and what cannot be said for lack of an available discourse; aphasia is a case of the latter, that is, the plight of "those who are denied access to the instrument of the struggle for the definition of reality" (170). In the newspaper account, "Dove" and the voices of those who had called his name are not even admitted to the pro or con discourse on civil rights; their voices are simply denied existence.

In his *Jarring Witnesses: Modern Fiction and the Representation of History,* Robert Holton provides revealing examples of a kind of authorial deprivation of his characters' voices perpetrated unwittingly by William Faulkner. Holton contends that Welty's fellow Mississippian, trapped within the cultural and epistemological confines of his society, ignorantly and unconsciously imposes what we may call Bourdieuian aphasia upon certain sociolinguistic groups in his fiction, with the result that the reader is unlikely to recognize subjectivity in the members of those groups (128–60). In contrast, "The Demonstrators" is noteworthy for the fact that the reader cannot help but recognize the existence of the aphasia.

Strickland can hear the voices calling the name of Dove behind the aphasia imposed on them by the name printed on the paper, because he has been exposed to this different language group earlier in the story. When the doctor arrives, the patient's house and the whole of its surroundings are shrouded in darkness due to a power failure, and he barely sees a crowd of black persons standing around the house. This setting echoes in mood the disquieting atmosphere in the town caused by the recent racial turmoil and the doctor's uneasy mental state as he steps into an alien African American milieu. Examining the woman's wound under a raised lamp, he feels irritated because the people in the room do not make satisfactory responses to his inquiries, as if they had erected a fence between themselves and him. Yet eventually he realizes they are irritated with *him*, for not recognizing the patient:

> "Don't you know her?" they cried, as if he never was going to hit on the right question.
>
> He let go the girl's arm, and her hand started its way back again to her wound. Sending one glowing look at him, she covered it again. As if she had spoken, he recognized her.
>
> "Why, it's Ruby," he said.
>
> Ruby Gaddy *was* the maid. Five days a week she cleaned up on the second floor of the bank building where he kept his office and consulting rooms.
>
> He said to her, "Ruby, this is Dr. Strickland. What have you been up to?"
>
> "*Nothin'!*" everybody cried for her. (611)

For Strickland up to now, Ruby has existed only as a cleaning maid in white uniform. He has never thought of her as a "speaking person," one having her own private life with her home or church (as her choir vestment suggests), and above all, a passion so strong as to cause her struggle with her husband with a lethal weapon. The accusing question—"Don't you know her?"—is certainly to the point. Ruby belongs to a social and linguistic group whose physical existence the doctor has witnessed but the subjectivity of which he has not recognized. Ruby does not *speak* in a language Strickland knows, but her heatedly "glowing" look and her movement to cover her wound *speak* for her subjectivity. Ruby does not offer an answer to his question, but her people speak on her behalf, although their response—"*Nothin'!*"—denies Strickland permission to share their knowledge and protects her privacy.

Instead of an answer to his question, what the doctor hears is, of all things, the sound of some guinea pigs running about on the floor and the people's "sounds of amusement" (611) in reaction. At the doctor's angry request to remove the guinea pigs, they laugh and finally begin sharing some of their privacy, still in their peculiar language: "'Them guinea pigs ain't been caught since they was born. Let you try.'"

"'Know why? 'Cause they's Dove's. Dove left 'em here when he move out, just to be in the way'" (611). Then a little boy kneels down with a stalk of celery in an effort to catch the animals and the laughter increases. This is a place where the kind of discretion and graveness of manner that Strickland has observed out of respect for a patient in critical condition becomes foreign. Strickland understands the language of Miss Marcia Pope, on whom he had made the house call earlier in the evening. The retired Holden school teacher, who had taught three generations of whites Latin, civics, and English, had eloquently quoted from her bed Shakespeare and Virgil and had not hesitated to ask an embarrassing question of Strickland about his separation from his wife. But the people in Ruby's house exhibit the fluency of a different language, different not only in style but even more so in the cultural and discursive sense.

The doctor's recognition of the differences between the two language groups is further deepened when he tries to find out who the assailant was:

> "All right. I heard you. Is Dove who did it? Go on. Say."
> He heard somebody spit on the stove. Then:
> "It's Dove."
> "Dove."
> "Dove."
> "Dove."
> "You got it right that time."
> While the name went around, passed from one mouth to the other, the doctor drew a deep breath. But the sigh that filled the room was the girl's own, luxuriously uncontained. (611–12)

Due to the soft, placid quality of "Dove," sounding like cooing (especially in contrast to the sound of "Dave"), the repetition of the name creates an almost ritualistic atmosphere. The significance and emotion contained in the speakers' voices and in Ruby's deep sigh upon hearing those voices confirm for Strickland the existence of a linguistic system that has hitherto remained unknown to him.

The awareness of his own alterity among these people in Ruby's house, however, is unexpectedly corrected for Strickland by the series of small incidents that follow. He learns that Ruby's mother used to work for the Stricklands as a laundress, and he notices that some familiar old items of chinaware and clothing, which his mother and sister and wife must have given Ruby's family years ago, are still in full use here. On his way back, Strickland thoroughly appreciates the value of the old connection between Ruby's family and his own: "In that house of murder, comfort had been brought to him at his request. . . . Faintly rocked by the passing train, he sat bent at the wheel of the car, and the feeling of well-being persisted. It increased, until he had come to the point of tears" (616). The reason for this indiscreetly happy feeling in him is that he feels relief, though temporarily, from the burdens of his recent bitter memories—his only daughter's death and the ensuing separation from his wife, who had become absorbed in "an idea" (617), and the various unpleasant experiences caused by the civil rights advocates and opponents, both of whom he feels simplify human relations in their espousal of "an idea." For instance, Strickland had invited a civil rights worker, a student, to dinner because the young man had called his office with a letter of introduction from an old friend of Strickland's. Yet this simple, friendly gesture had provoked threats and vandalism of his home, apparently by the anti–civil rights people. Tonight's reencounter with the old human connections is an affirmation of what he has longed for: "Was it the sensation, now returning, that there was still allowed to everybody on earth a *self*—savage, death-defying, private? The pounding of his heart was like the assault of hope, throwing itself against him without a stop, merciless" (681). Caught between the two linguistic groups with their separate ideologies, Strickland has crossed over to the alien territory, where he has recognized the subjectivity of its people and at the same time been granted affirmation of his own subjectivity, his self.

Although we recognize that Strickland understands the circumstances and effects of the aphasia surrounding the name "Dove" in the newspaper account, there are other, unexplained things, such as why Ruby and Dove fought, the possibility of Dove's having been lynched and robbed, and the lack of mention in the newspaper report of Strickland's involvement that night, all of which the author apparently intends to leave to the reader's imagination. Still, "The Demonstrators" contains an even deeper mystery upon which aphasia, so to speak, has been imposed by the carrier of the story's point of view, Dr. Strickland himself. I believe that the impression of obscurity the reader gets from the story ultimately derives from this mystery that Strickland seems to avoid clarifying. Welty is extremely subtle in presenting this circumstance, and a perfunctory reading would very likely overlook it. It is about Strickland's ability as a medical doctor.

There are several remarks and allusions scattered about in the story that I believe may constitute a subtext telling of the past of the carrier of the point of view: (1) Richard Strickland had succeeded to his father's medical practice, the only one in town; (2) Richard and Irene Strickland's only daughter, Sylvia, had suffered brain damage at birth, depriving her of the ability to move, speak, communicate, or understand; (3) Sylvia had died of pneumonia at the age of thirteen; (4) Ruby's mother says something to the effect that Richard is not as good a doctor as his father was; (5) Following Sylvia's death, Irene had left Richard. From these scattered pieces of information, the reader may be able to construct a rather consistent subtext. As Richard Strickland has been the only doctor in town since his father's death, it must have been he who attended his wife's delivery of Sylvia. Therefore the baby's brain damage may have been caused by malpractice on his part. Besides, one can consider it plain incompetence or negligence for a doctor-father to allow a heavily handicapped child of his own to die of pneumonia. This is the reason his wife left him and why Ruby's mother does not seem to trust his ability as a doctor.

When Ruby's mother says, impulsively giving in to sudden anger, that the doctor is not good like his father because he does not even tie up the injured one, he retorts that it is because the victim is bleeding internally. Strickland becomes aware of Ruby's mother's doubts about his ability, and this time he can refute her accusation with professional confidence. But about his performance with his own daughter at her birth and at her death, Ruby's mother and probably those who know about it must harbor suspicion. Between him and his wife there must have been this kind of blaming and retorting, voiced or unvoiced, many times before they finally separated. Within himself, even now, Strickland may be blaming and defending himself. Did Sylvia's brain damage result from malpractice or from circumstances beyond his control? Even he might not be able to answer with certainty. It is a part of his life upon which he imposes aphasia in his public dealings in order to continue as the only doctor in town. It is a part of his life to which he allows only his "*self*— savage, death-defying, private*" (618) admission.

Why Ruby and Dove had struggled so violently is never explained in the newspaper account or by those present in Ruby's room. Ruby on her deathbed continues attempting to hide the wound from the doctor, and the dying Dove also, when discovered by Strickland, does not offer an explanation nor ask for rescue but only pleads for privacy: "Dove said: 'Hide me'" (619). At the end of the story, another character is remembered as one devoid of speech: Sylvia, who had never communicated with anyone in her short life. But Strickland recalls that when she was placed to look out on the garden her eyes would follow the flight of birds, and he is fairly sure Sylvia sensed the birds were there. In contrast, Miss Marcia Pope, whom Strickland also recalls at the end of the story, is a person whose clear voice resolutely resounds for all, despite her advanced age and bedridden condition. At the close of "The Demonstrators," Strickland knows that he hears many voices—political, apolitical, domestic, angry, peaceful, inquisitive voices—but he also knows that many other voices are left unheard either by others or by the possessors of the voices themselves. Earlier, I quoted Welty's words concerning the title of this story that every character in the story is a demonstrator. I believe that "every character" certainly includes those whose voices go unheard and that the author wishes to express the weight of the self, the subjectivity of those whose voices are silenced either by others or by themselves—at a time when ideological and political voices were being heard so loudly in the streets of America and in the national media.

In 1965, the year prior to the publication of "The Demonstrators," Welty contributed to the *Atlantic Monthly* an essay, "Must the Novelist Crusade?" It can be considered her response to criticism of her silence as a Mississippi writer when national censure poured out upon the state for such ignominious incidents as the assassinations of Medgar Evers (1963) and of three civil rights workers (1964), shocking even among the many other tragedies and atrocities of racial hatred. Having been exhorted to become a "speaking person," Welty speaks out in this essay not about her specific political convictions but about the distinction between the writer and the crusader:

> The crusader's voice is the voice of the crowd and must rise louder all the time, for there is, of course, the other side to be drowned out. . . . Writing fiction is an interior affair. Novels and stories always will be put down little by little out of personal feeling and personal beliefs arrived at alone and at firsthand over a period of time as time is needed. To go outside and beat the drum is only to interrupt, interrupt, and so finally to forget and to lose. Fiction has, and must keep, a private address. For life is *lived* in a private place; where it means anything is inside the mind and heart. Fiction has always shown life where it is lived, and good fiction, or so I have faith, will continue to do this. (153)

"The Demonstrators" is a genuine example of Welty's putting into practice that stated conviction. It is an expression of the complex private feeling of a conscientious white Mississippian who is compelled by conviction to denounce racial discrimination and support the goals of the civil rights movement and yet cannot simplify the problem as neatly as do the "crusaders" of either side.

In the open racial strife of the day, Welty saw that people viewed all human relations as quite simply divided between good and evil. But having lived all her life in that society, Welty had realized, "There are relationships of the blood, of the passions and the affections, of thought and spirit and deed. There is the relationship between the races. How can one kind of relationship be set apart from the others?" (1978, 155). In "The Demonstrators" the author retreats into a heteroglot narrative space where each person has his or her special complex mesh of interlocked relationships, which in effect constitutes his or her self, and which utters his or her voice. In her heteroglot narrative space, where ideologically laden voices are resolutely loud, Welty's story reaches out to include the outermost margin of the society's heteroglossia, where aphasia is imposed upon voices. Welty's greatest insight is that aphasia is imposed on one not only by others but by oneself, since life is after all a private thing. This is where Welty's admission of the pluralism of the society's heteroglossia has led, and in this silenced periphery Welty discovers the fiction writer's ultimate voice.

CHAPTER 10

The Authorial Retreat
in *Losing Battles* and
The Optimist's Daughter

Welty's *Losing Battles* (1970) appeared sixteen years after the publication of *The Bride of the Innisfallen and Other Stories*, during which period two short stories on the civil rights turmoil in Mississippi and a story for children were her only published fictions. The book attracted great public and critical attention not only because it was a full-fledged novel—by far the longest she had done—after long years of virtual silence, but also because of its unique style.[1]

Welty described her intention with regard to the novel's style in more or less the same wording in several interviews: that by "translating every thought and feeling into action and speech," she had "tried to see if [she] could make everything shown, brought forth, without benefit of the author's telling any more about what was going on inside the characters' minds and hearts" (Prenshaw 1984, 76–77), or that "[t]he thought, the feeling that is *internal* is *shown* as external" (Prenshaw 1984, 46). Karl-Heinz Westarp maintains that this kind of remark cannot be interpreted "in any other way than as a clear authorial statement that the surface, the story, 'manners' are not all, that we have to look for something 'beyond'" (59). What he sees as the thing "beyond" is an allusion to Bunyan's *Pilgrim's Progress* and ultimately the Christian moral of forgiveness. Westarp's contention that the reader is expected to look for something "beyond" the action and speech in this novel is certainly well taken; the abundance of varied interpretations of the novel testifies to the critics' efforts to seek that "beyond."[2] Yet does any serious work of literature not invite the reader to read "beyond" what is written? I am interested specifically in what is particular about the author's heightened expectation for interpretation placed upon the reader in *Losing Battles*, an expectation that is observable in the notable exclusion of character interiority descriptions.

Welty expounded on the kind of effects she counted on the reader to sense in the novel's dialogues in an interview: "I needed to make a speech do three or four or five things at once—reveal what the character said but also what he thought he said, what he hid, what others were going to think he meant, and what they misunderstood, and so forth—all in his single speech" (Prenshaw 1984, 77). From her earliest collection of stories and throughout her career, Welty has demonstrated the skill to produce somewhat similar effects in her dramatic monologues such as "Why I live at the P.O.," "Shower of Gold," *The Ponder Heart*, or "Where Is the Voice Coming From?" In these monologues what the author expects of the reader is to read what the speaker does *not* say, namely, the version of the story he or she consciously or unconsciously conceals or is blind to, the unspoken word that reveals more about the speaker than about what happened. The dialogue in *Losing Battles*, as Welty elucidates above, is intended to bring about a dialogization, so to speak, of what would be the effects of numerous such dramatic monologues. Welty's dramatic monologues were intended to affect directly the listener/reader, while the assumed effects of the dialogues in *Losing Battles* are, though similar in nature, interwoven far more complexly. In *Losing Battles* the reader is given only what each character says and is expected to intuit "what he thought he said, what he hid, what others were going to think he meant, and what they misunderstood, and so forth." What is remarkable about this style is that it invites a significant transmutation of authorship. The author not only directs the reader to seek some implicit theme or moral for the whole novel, as authors have traditionally done, but also inspires the reader to produce every stage of the novel out of the dialogized effects of the characters' voices.

As discussed in the preceding chapter, the deliberate blurring of the authorial center is already seen clearly in Welty's fictions of the early fifties collected in *The Bride of the Innisfallen and Other Stories* and is indeed intensified in "The Demonstrators" of the mid-sixties. Welty's thinking behind this feature is, I have argued, a pluralistic grasp of the world and human beings and the awareness of the self existing in a complex mesh of human relationships and personal experiences. Welty's technique in that period to represent such a situation is to enumerate physical details of the situation as the protagonist perceives them, including the other characters' speeches and actions, or to enumerate the details of the protagonist's inner being, that is, his or her passing feelings and fragmentary thoughts. This technique caused these fictions often to become too ambiguous in plot and theme for the less heedful reader, and as a result they never gained the broad public acceptance that her earlier fictions enjoyed. Welty's later estimation that she had been "writing too much by way of description, of introspection on the part of [her] characters" (Prenshaw 1984, 76–77), can be considered her own criticism of this kind of style. Although the style of *Losing Battles* appears drastically changed from that of the preceding fictions, the ultimate effect Welty hopes for has not changed; rather, this new style derives from an effort from the opposite direction, to achieve the same kind of authorial retreat to an intensified degree. If one adopts Roland Barthes's concept of the "Text," the space for the creative process of the reader, as distinguished from the "work," the author's finished product, proposed in his "From Work to Text," *Losing Battles* is something that the author *purposely* produced as a "Text," each thread of which is left for the reader to weave into the long textile of a story. Equally significantly, as will be shown in this chapter, *Losing Battles* unfolds consistent subtexts on this unique relation between the author and the text, a relation that is self-reflexively embodied in the novel.

Although action and speech fill most of its pages, *Losing Battles* includes some purely descriptive passages that create either physical frames for some of the parts or temporal frames in the course of events. In these passages, quite unlike the rest of the novel, Welty's language is highly figurative, incorporating numerous similes and allusive expressions. The novel's opening section, especially the first several paragraphs, is so rich in allusion and technique that critics often find it an effective example with which to substantiate their respective arguments. For instance, Douglas Messerli points to the presence of a prominent feature of Welty's similes in this passage wherein "the nonvisible is made visible (for example, heat is 'solid as a hickory stick') and all the visible is brought into action into a world that the family mentally knows and spiritually feels safe in" (359); he connects this feature with the family's use of language for the protection of its presentism. Richard Gray, discussing the role of language in the characters' lives, sees in this passage what Welty's own language achieves: "a shifting, evanescent place that nevertheless seems to have been caught for a while and composed" (52). Ruth D. Weston sees in this passage Welty's modernist experiment of merging the characteristics of the three classic genres—the epic, the lyric, and the drama—indicating that "the birth of the day" is described "as if it were the beginning of time" and submitting that it also suggests "the classical or Shakespearean dramatic prologue" (33). To these I would add that this opening section of the novel (3–6) also sets up the preliminary stage from which develops the unique relation between the author and the text in this novel.

Weston points out the epic modality of comparing a mundane daybreak to "the beginning of time." The passage, in effect, makes a definite

allusion to Judeo-Christian Genesis. Just as God, after creating the heavens
and the earth, created light over the void and darkness by naming them,
in *Losing Battles* the first motion in the sky is of a thin cloud "drawing
itself out like *a name being called*" (3, emphasis added). Then the air transforms itself, with the warmth rising from the river below the hills in darkness, hills that are later described as shrouded in "mists, voids" (4). Just
as "out of the ground the Lord God formed every beast of the field"
(Genesis 2:19), a dog leaps up "from where he'd lain like a stone" (3).
A naked baby bolts out of the house, "monkey-climbed" (evolutionism
included!) down the steps and runs into the yard "open-armed" (3), as
if to receive whatever comes her way on the earth. When the baby pushes
over a crate and lets "a stream of white Plymouth Rocks loose on the
world" (3), the biblical beginning of time and life is localized and
historicized as America's beginning through this reference to the sym-
bolically named breed of chickens. Under the pecan tree stands "familiar
in shape as Noah's Ark—a school bus" (4). Finally, when the whole shape
of the house is revealed, "for the length of a breath, everything [stays]
shadowless, as *under a lifting hand*" (4, emphasis added). The whole
course of the daybreak is paralleled, with a slight comical touch, to the
First Book of Moses.

The allusion to Genesis, however, applies not only to the beginning
of the day but to other matters that will unfold in the novel now begun.
When God formed the beasts and fowls, He let Adam name them:
"[W]hatsoever Adam called every living creature, that was the name
thereof" (Genesis 2:19). Thus God, in effect, granted to Adam the power
of naming, the same power by which He brought the world into existence. One may consider that at this point the original entity of God's act,
which equated naming with creating, was split into two distinct acts of
forming and naming, the latter being entrusted to Adam. Naming is an
act of distinguishing one creature from another, establishing the relationship of the signifier and the signified, thus endowing each creature with
meaning. It is by being named, being given meaning, thus being distinguished from other creatures, that a creature becomes a whole being,
occupying an autonomous place between the heavens and the earth. The
power of naming, which is nothing but the primal power of language,
has often been the basis for Western thinking about the physical and
metaphysical existence of the human being through history. Indeed, despite all the malecentrism involved in the parable of Adam's acquisition
of this power, most of us agree that what makes humans human is language. The human use of language, the main "action" of *Losing Battles,*
is thus a natural outcome of the allusion of the novel's beginning to the
biblical beginning of humans' life on earth. The evocation of Noah's Ark

by the familiar shape of the school bus parked by the yard suggests that language learning, in school or in the family, is closely related to the survival and continuation of the human species. This is the human state the Creator's "lifting hand" has sanctioned.

When the Renfro family members enter the scene to start the reunion day in the latter half of the novel's opening section, further outcomes of the divinely sanctioned human state are represented in their actions, actions that seem to foreshadow what is to happen in the novel. One such action is the telling of lies. The first speech that Granny Vaughn, the family's spiritual mainstay, makes to her great-grandchildren contains the lie that she is one hundred on this day, this day actually being her ninetieth birthday. Yet despite the senior's obvious mendacity, Beulah tells her children: "Don't contradict her" (5). Granny's and Beulah's manipulation of language and the children's acceptance of what is said veil the truth and create a new "reality," even if it is valid only within the family, and if only for a while. Then follows the listing of numerous names of flowers blooming in the yard, certainly exhibiting the human power of naming. It is as if these flowers came into being through the act of being named, since there is no necessity in these particular flowers, and not others that would grow just as well, being there. Other actions that follow are violence and killing, actions that both also occur in Genesis. The twelve-year-old Vaughn Renfro finishes the chore that his elder brother, if he were home, would do—that is, "catching and killing the escaped rooster and his whole escaped flock" (6) with a hatchet. With the rag he has used for washing, Vaughn swabs the dust off the mirror, which becomes streaked with "a color delicate as watermelon juice on a clean plate" (6). On the mirror, the face of the youth who has performed the man's work for the family is seen behind the streaks of the diluted blood of the creatures he has just killed.[3]

Such being the preliminary modality of the novel, the actual setting of the novel is the 1930s in the fictional hamlet of Banner in Mississippi's northeastern hill country, the poorest area of the nation's poorest state. To the Renfro house beneath the biblical dawn at the novel's opening come people from the wife Beulah's Beecham side and from the husband Ralph's Renfro side, to gather with their spouses and children in celebration of the ninetieth birthday of Beulah's grandmother, "Granny" Elvira Jordan Vaughn, who, together with her husband, had raised their seven orphaned grandchildren after the parents' untimely deaths. The talk at the reunion is apparently motivated by the desire to introduce the Vaughn-Beecham-Renfro circle's family tales to Noah Webster Beecham's new wife Cleo. Their first topic is why and how Jack Renfro, Beulah and Ralph's eldest son and the reunion members' star of hope, was sent to the state penitentiary after an unfair trial; he is expected finally to return home today. Their talking continues, and various other people within and related to the family become a topic of their conversations, each speaker more or less contributing his or her story in turn. Although the reunion members' ostensible motive for talking about these individuals is to initiate Cleo into the reunion, it soon becomes clear that they speak out of a need to reassure themselves of what and how they are. Gray, in his "Needing to Talk: Language and Being in *Losing Battles*," characterizes the speeches of the reunion as "a web of words that constitutes their identity, their moment in space and time" (43). He identifies their speaking with their sense of being: "that, in human terms, to say is to be: that it is through speech that people enter into consciousness of self and community" (47). His interpretation of the family's act of speaking in terms of the Bakhtinian concept of language and dialogism is a convincing argument, but possibly as an extension of that, I believe that a further consideration of the content of their speeches, not simply their speeches as actions, will reveal another important aspect of this novel.

The contents of their speeches, in Gray's frame of argument, are the materials for "their identity." But it is noteworthy that although the reunion members speak their knowledge and views, what their words constitute as their own or someone else's "identity" is often suspect, at best incomplete. This is one of the reasons why Louis Rubin, as early as 1970, argued that part of the reason they talk is "to dissemble, to mask, to hide" (196) and why Noel Polk maintains that "all their fine talk [is] a ritualistic paean to a unity that in fact does not otherwise exist" (1989, 157). While the reunion members laugh at Julia Mortimer for having had her own self-willed "designs on everybody" (235), they themselves strive to *make up* their own self-willed "identities" for everybody, whenever there is a chance, so that they can identify the person within their perspective. Thus actually the "identities" they make up are *stories*.

Gloria Short Renfro is the foremost target of this practice. Since, for a living person's identity, origins—parentage and time and place of birth—are crucial, trying to determine her origins occupies a large portion of their talking about her. She is at first "a little nobody from out of nowhere" (60), as one of the reunion members calls her; she is an orphan who has no clue as to her parentage. In the course of their talking, Granny Vaughn produces out of her Bible a postcard written by Sam Dale, one of Jack's uncles, long deceased, to Rachel Sojourner, who had sojourned with the family as a sewing woman, expressing his love to his "wife," Rachel, and for the coming baby. Along with the circumstances of Gloria's having been found abandoned newly born and Rachel's having died despite Julia Mortimer's attempts to rescue her, and also considering Gloria's having recalled how Julia cautioned her not to marry Jack for fear that her child might be "deaf and dumb" (317), the possibility that Gloria is Jack's first cousin turns up. The reunion members grab onto this story as proof that Gloria is truly a family member. They force her to admit this discovery and say "Beecham" by cramming watermelon chunks into her mouth, in one of the most violent scenes in all of Welty's fictions, though Judge Moody says that "there's not a particle of it [he]'d accept as evidence" (315). Later, Uncle Nathan's confession discloses an even more complicated, gruesome circumstance: Sam Dale had chosen to marry Rachel to save her reputation, she having been made pregnant by someone else, probably Dearman, whom Nathan had killed for Sam's sake and for which he had let an innocent black man be hanged. Faced with all these disclosures Judge Moody cannot offer anything but groans; he knows that the lack of evidence is compounded by the facts that the state of Mississippi does not have birth certificates and that all local official registers have been lost in a courthouse fire. Yet although the Vaughn-Beecham-Renfro reunion seems to strive to find the truth surrounding Gloria's origins and embraces the story constituted out of the disclosures, the reader cannot help noticing some things the reunion has kept hidden. Julia's intimacy with Dearman—"She didn't discourage him enough" (304)—for instance, and Uncle Nathan's association with Julia until her death suggest that Nathan's murder of Dearman might not have been wholly motivated by his love for his brother Sam Dale but also by his own passion and jealousy. For indeed Julia must have understood Nathan's feeling toward her when he confessed the murder only to her, unknowingly being overheard by Beulah. Or, if it was Dearman who had impregnated Rachel—a real possibility—then it turns out that Nathan had killed Gloria's father, a fact that would cause the family union to crumble. If Julia had really loved Dearman—also a very strong possibility, since he seemed the only civilized and enterprising man in the area who could match her intellectually at that time—then her grief on hearing Nathan's confession must have been truly profound. All these possibilities are not spoken of at the reunion; the reader is left to notice them.

Another story that the reunion is determined to *make up* concerns Mama and Papa Beecham. The focus of the reunion's talk about the Beechams is Clyde Comfort's selfish choice to catch a "big fat frog" in the river rather than holler to their parents in the buggy about the hole in the bridge they were about to cross. Why Mama and Papa Beecham left home by themselves in the middle of the night without being noticed is never probed by the members of the reunion, but Uncle Noah Webster maintains that they were deserting their children and parents for a better life elsewhere. The reunion naturally excludes such a possibility from their story and says "that part of the story's been lost to time" (218). The reunion makes up Mama and Papa Beecham's "identity" with their romantic love story and pretty wedding, neither of which they ever actually witnessed.

The reunion also belittles, almost ignores, the monstrosity of Lexie's abuse of the aged and powerless Julia Mortimer and ridicules Julia's lifelong devotion to enlightening the ignorant people of the area. When Lexie tells about the difficulties she has had as a live-in nurse for Julia, the reunion accepts them as valid proof of Julia's stubbornness and officiousness, even insanity. Unbeknown to the others, Lexie in fact has been stealing from Julia's pantry, withholding her books unless she can cite the exact titles, tying her to the bed, taking her pencil away and leaving her to write only with a wetted finger on her sheets, not giving her her mail. Now Lexie, to come to the reunion, has left Julia to die, in the care of a useless seven-year-old boy. The complacent reunion hears her stories understandingly, and when Julia's last letter to Judge Moody, filled with the truly insightful, moving words of a dedicated educator, is read to the reunion, Beulah's comment represents the reunion's reaction: "Now I know she's a crazy" (299).

The episode of Lexie and Julia is just one of numerous stories the reunion tells, by which it makes up "identities" of themselves and others around them; indeed, even the very names of people, places, and institutions are often self-congratulatory *stories*. Polk points out the local people's "smug, insular, self-righteousness" expressed in such place names as Peerless, Wisdom, Upright, Morning Star, Harmony, Deepstep, and Banner, in contrast to "the values of true community" implied in the name Alliance, where Julia Mortimer taught her school (1989, 157). In a similar vein, the mentality behind a name such as Defeated Creek Church, apparently commemorating a victory over the Creek Indians, coincides with the petty rivalry among the Christian denominations often expressed at the reunion. Regarding personal names, Beulah says of how she named her children: "I named all mine a pretty name. . . . Give 'em a pretty name, say I, for it may be the only thing you *can* give 'em" (255). Beulah's statement seemingly expresses a heartwarming attitude, one that we can apply to the place names listed above, but in either case it is only an *attempt* to create a permanent reality through simple naming; usually such naming remains a *story*, and the reality is something different. Making up *stories* by prevaricating and concealing occurs because *stories* "may be the only thing" people can give to themselves to be proud of.

An episode regarding the old family photograph shown by Beulah suggests the vanity of the reunion members' conception of family identity. The occasion for this, the "only picture that ever was made of [Beulah's] whole family" (327), was taken by an itinerant photographer at Beulah and Ralph's wedding twenty-five years earlier. In the picture are all the Vaughn-Beecham-Renfro family members, including Sam Dale as well as the people the reunion has been talking about—Julia Mortimer, Rachel, and even Dearman. It is a moment in the past made permanent to testify to the fact that the family was thus then. Yet this very testimony in photographic form deceives itself and discloses the fictionality of the moment's permanence. For Sam Dale is seen twice in the picture: "Evidently by racing the crank of the camera and running behind backs, Sam Dale had got in on both ends of the panorama, putting his face smack and smack again into the face of oblivion" (328). What his two faces unmask is that even in this apparently frozen moment time was passing and the family portrait changing; indeed, we are at once witness to a further reality beyond the surface of the photograph and the surface of the story.

From all the talk at the reunion, the reader realizes that on the surface *Losing Battles* is about the battles between Julia Mortimer the educator and the ignorant backwoods people, represented by the Vaughn-Beecham-Renfro reunion, who reject learning and progress. Donaldson terms the battles as those between "two opposing modes of discourse" (32), namely, between the discourse held by the reunion, "defined by devotion to kinship, tradition, community, and oral storytelling," and the one held by Julia, Judge Moody, and Gloria, who are "associated with writing, solitude, and change" (33). On a more abstract level, Messerli sees the battles as those between two uses of language: one adopted by Julia, Judge Moody, and Gloria, who, by writing, adhere to historicism; and the other, adopted by the reunion, who, by speaking, adhere to presentism (362–63). Critics agree that whatever battles are waged and whatever victory is won, either by the reunion or by Julia, the battles are losing battles in the end for both sides against the passage of time and the coming of death. It is thus appropriate that the novel ends at the scene of the cemetery, carrying the definite suggestion that each of the living characters in the novel will eventually be buried there. Even the passages leading to the cemetery scene are permeated with connotations of mortality, including the old and the new election posters along the road to the cemetery, with the faces of "losers and winners, the forgotten and the remembered . . . looking like members of the same family" (404), the candidates' words of qualifications printed "like a poem on a tombstone" (405). Is it the novel's ultimate message that all human efforts through language for survival and continuation result in defeat at the language user's physical death? I believe what the novel says to us is otherwise. *Losing Battles* presents the language user's victory in two distinct manifestations.

Before entering into a discussion on these manifestations, it should be noted that the cemetery scene, saturated with the reminders of death, also suggests, paradoxically, the continuation of life, when one reads it in relation to the novel's opening scene. Corresponding to the comparison of the school bus to Noah's Ark in the novel's opening passage, the image of the reunion as carried on the flowing water, isolated from the rest of the world, is maintained through the novel, as in the following descriptive passage:

> As they sang, the tree over them, Billy Vaughn's Switch, with its ever-spinning leaves all light-points at this hour, looked bright as a river, and the tables might have been a little train of barges it was carrying with it, moving slowly downstream. Brother Bethune's gun, still resting against the trunk, was travelling too, and nothing at all was unmovable, or empowered to hold the scene still fixed or stake the reunion there. (223)

Or again later:

> Suddenly the moonlit world was doused; lights hard as pick-axe blows drove down from every ceiling and the roof of the passage, cutting the house and all in it away, leaving them an island now on black earth, afloat in night, and nowhere, with only each other. In that first moment every face, white-lit but with its caves of mouth and eyes opened wide, black with the lonesomeness and hilarity of survival, showed its kinship to Uncle Nathan's, the face that floated over theirs. (312)

Retaining the imagery of Noah's Ark, the reunion night closes with a biblical rainfall: "Then thunder moved in and out of the house freely, like the voice of Uncle Noah Webster come back to say once more, 'Goodnight, blessed sweethearts.' / Then the new roof resounded with all the noise of battle" (367–68).

The next morning, before the sun comes out, in the landscape around the cemetery the river presents "the color of steeping tea," and "a long colorless tree" lies crosswise to the current holding "white and green leaves" (431). But when the sun appears "as if *for good*" (433, emphasis added), the landscape takes on the primary colors; it presents "a red world" of heat, sycamore trees "tinged on top with yellow," and a gas pump "like a little old lady in a blue sunbonnet who had nowhere to go" (433–34). Even "the shadow of the bridge on the river floor" (433) takes on a rainbow-like appearance. If the rainbow of colors is "the token of the covenant" between God and mankind and every living creature for "perpetual generations," what, then, is confirmed by the rainbow seen in the Banner cemetery?

As one manifestation of the language user's victory, the primary out-come of the "covenant" must be the cycle of life, represented in the baby Lady May. The cyclic view of life is not new in Welty; it is a theme of such fictions as "The Wide Net" and *The Golden Apples*. Early on in *Losing Battles*, Aunt Nanny, seeing Lady May running about the porch, asks, "Who you hunting?" (64), but the baby cannot yet speak. All through the reunion's garrulous talking, Lady May's inability to talk, at least not yet, seems to cast a muffled anxiety on the more sensitive people, such as Gloria and Beulah, especially after the possibility that Lady May's parents are first cousins is raised. But at night, while running about the house to close up the windows against sudden torrential rain, Beulah hears Lady May's first words:

> Hearing what sounded like great treads going over her head, the baby opened her eyes. She put her voice into the fray, and spoke to it the first sentence of her life: "What you huntin', man?"
> Miss Beulah ran out onto the porch, snatched up the baby, and ran with her back to her own bed, as if a life had been saved. (368)

Here Jack and Gloria's child and Beulah's grandchild has become a le-gitimate member of the speaking family, that is, of the language-using species. The family's continuation is assured, as this new speaking life is rescued from drowning in the flood. That the baby speaks virtually the same words that were spoken to her at the same spot earlier this day emphasizes the cyclic nature of the incident. The question of what one is seeking points to the reunion's search for their "identity" and also echoes Julia Mortimer's deathbed question: "What was the trip for?" (241). The next morning in the cemetery, the familial union of Jack, Gloria, and Lady May is confirmed by the young couple. But Gloria, at this point, is yet to learn that unless their union is backed by the pros-pect of "a string of other little chaps to come along behind [Lady May]" (435), as Jack hopes, the happy privacy of the core family cannot avoid ending in the privacy of the grave.

The biological cycle of life, however, is only one aspect of the cyclic paradigm that is featured in this novel. *Losing Battles* contains another, more subtle cyclic view of moral and spiritual continuity. In this connec-tion, one should recall an incident at the end of part 5, in which Granny Vaughn invites the young Vaughn Renfro, who has come in from a late night ride, to share her bed. In an interview in 1993, objecting to some critics' observations alluding to "the dark side of humanity" in this scene, Gretlund holds that "the old woman sees the outline of Grandpa Vaughn's hat on the boy and in her exhaustion believes she is addressing her late husband" (268). To this, Welty's response is affirmative, albeit rather indefinite: "She was thinking of Grandpa, or. . . . She was able to take care of anybody's problem, no matter what" (268). Welty's avoidance of a clear-cut answer is perfectly understandable, for such an act of interpretation is totally antithetical to her scheme of authorial retreat in this novel. Welty's ambiguity notwithstanding, however, I believe Gretlund's interpretation of the incident to be the most reasonable. In fact, Granny Vaughn behaves in the same way in an earlier incident. When Jack catches and saves her from falling while dancing during the reunion, Granny Vaughn at first mistakes him for Sam Dale, deceased for more than two decades, and cries out: "But you're not Sam Dale!" (308). Told by Uncle Noah Webster fondly, "Granny, you just slipped back a generation there for a little," Granny's mind still hovers for a while in the past, and all she can say to Jack is, "Who are you?" (308). Thus it is quite plausible that she should later take the silhouette of Vaughn Renfro in her husband's hat for that of her recently deceased husband.

Yet I see in this incident another significance that implies moral and spiritual continuity to ensure some kind of victory over death. Granny Vaughn and Vaughn Renfro are the only major characters who have *not* earnestly participated in the talk of the reunion, keeping distant from the "smug, insular, self-righteous" garrulity. It is they, not Gloria, who see the true nature of the reunion. Thus Granny, at the end of the reunion, breaks her silence and casually, as if in unmeaning rant, declares the true identity of the reunion: "Thieves, murderers, come back" (357). Vaughn, during the night ride, remembers the reunion's voices as those of "bragging, lying, singing, pretending, protesting, swearing everything into being, swearing everything away" (363). Despite their familial affection toward the reunion, Granny and Vaughn understand the falsehood of it all. This continuation of insight into the truth, three generations apart, is assurance that some values do not die out with physical death: the young Vaughn is Granny Vaughn's spiritual namesake. Moreover, Vaughn Renfro's passionate yearning for learning, revealed in this section of the novel, proves that he is also entitled to be the namesake of Grandpa Vaughn, who founded Banner School. The "pretty name" Beulah and Ralph gave their youngest son, since it was "the only thing [they *could*] give" him, has produced a reality that exceeded their vision.

Another manifestation of the language user's victory, ironically, is inherent in the reunion's use of language, namely, the *making up* of *stories*. Uncle Noah Webster Beecham, as the legitimate namesake of the builder of the Ark and the compiler of *An American Dictionary of the English Language,* drops a memorable remark to Gloria at the end of the reunion: "Gloria, this has been a story on us all that never will be allowed to be forgotten. . . . Long after you're an old lady without much further stretch to go, sitting back in the same rocking chair Granny's got her little self in now, you'll be hearing it told to Lady May and all her hovering brood" (354). He even adds without reserve his presentiment that this will be Granny's "last celebration" (354). In his mind it is clear that at future reunions when the story of today's reunion is told, with Gloria occupying the chair in which Granny is now seated, most of the members of today's reunion will have been long dead. Yet the stories about them will remain and be told over and over. Vaughn Renfro's recognition of the reunion's "swearing everything into being, swearing everything away" means that what the reunion members have brought into being is not their physical beings or their true identities but their stories, made up freely out of words, in the form of their "swearing." It is solely because in their made-up stories they are not living, breathing beings but rather static, made-up characters that the reunion members will live on in these stories, unaltered and unaffected by time, into an indefinite future. Just as Mama and Papa Beecham have been living on in the stories of their "pretty wedding" and of their "mysterious" deaths with nobody present but Granny Vaughn, she having been a partial witness, Jack Renfro will live on in the story of his heroic retrieval of Judge and Mrs. Moody's car. So will Uncle Nathan live on as having murdered Dearman out of his devotion for his brother Sam Dale, his passion for Julia probably dropping from his story.

At the cemetery, remembering her mentor, Gloria says: "Miss Julia Mortimer didn't want anybody left in the dark, not about anything. She wanted everything brought out in the wide open, to see and be known. She wanted people to spread out their minds and their hearts to other people, so they could be read like books. . . . No, people don't want to be read like books" (432). Here Gloria unwittingly touches upon the secret of what people do to create the kind of "identity" they wish of themselves and of others as well. People, however talkative, do not want every part of their being to be known to other people; there are some things, often many things, about themselves and others that they want to keep hidden, to which end they remake their and others' "identities." Language enables them to do this. Rather than let themselves be read like books, people write their own books of *stories* in their own ways, to be read by others and by posterity. In such a use of language, whether language is spoken or written is irrelevant. The stories told at the reunion about Julia Mortimer and Julia's last letter to Judge Moody are each an "identity" of Julia as the reunion and as Julia herself, respectively, wish to be remembered and to live on.

It is noteworthy that not only do these unreal people in their stories live on but that they can be treated and responded to by living people, just as if they were living people as well. Thus, although Jack Renfro "never laid eyes on [Julia Mortimer]," he says, "I reckon I even love her. . . . *I heard her story*" (361, emphasis added). Writing can affect the reader in the same way, as, after reading Julia's last letter, Judge Moody says, "I don't care quite the same about living as I did this morning" (307). It is this interaction between the living and the dead, who exist only in the spoken and written stories, that grants the dead eternal lives. The stories are no longer the possessions of their authors—neither the speakers nor the writers—but "Texts," which are heard and read by living others in their own ways, and thus are given new lives over and over again. Messerli makes a distinction between writing and speaking in *Losing Battles:* "All three [Miss Julia, Judge Moody, and Gloria] put their experience down on paper and thus into something in space, something dead. The family, on the other hand, by speaking can live their experiences over and over again" (363). Messerli's distinction between the existence of those who write and those who speak is well taken. Yet at another level of analysis we must recognize the common element of fiction that constructs the realities of all the characters, both writers and speakers, who are not living their real experience but are simply lending life to their pasts, pasts that are fictional, not even real.

The relation between mortality and fiction has been a long-term interest of Welty's, as witnessed by the fact that it appeared early on as one of the themes of her 1949 story "Circe." It is clear that her linking of mortality and storytelling expressed in *Losing Battles* is the subsequent deepening of a continuous concern. Further, the same frame of linkage underlies *The Optimist's Daughter,* the composition of which apparently coincided with the completion of *Losing Battles.* When *The Optimist's Daughter* was published in 1972—its shorter, story version had been published in the *New Yorker* of 15 March 1969—Welty's readers were amazed by the stylistic versatility demonstrated in her production, in a short span of time, of such dissimilar fictions. Although *Losing Battles* became an overnight success, it did receive some adverse criticism. Kreyling calls Welty's feat of publishing the vastly distinct latter novel "the best 'revenge' on critics, such as Jonathan Yardley and Joyce Carol Oates . . . , who had pronounced Welty and her métier 'extinct' with the appearance of *Losing Battles*" (1999, 210). *The Optimist's Daughter,* which garnered a Pulitzer Prize, seems to have firmly reinstated Welty as a first-rank author. Despite these indications of apparent divergence, however, within our trajectory of metafictionality and authorship, the two novels are very similar.

My contention of similarity in the two novels is related to the site of authorial intelligence in each. With its literary value unquestionably established since publication, *The Optimist's Daughter* still leaves one old question open to speculation by its readers. That question relates to how one is to interpret the character of Fay, the young second wife of Judge Clinton McKelva and stepmother of the novel's protagonist, Laurel McKelva Hand. As Fay is the antagonist of Laurel, the question is whether the author has intended Fay to be taken as morally inferior to Laurel. This leads to another question, whether Laurel's "new understanding," as critics call it, reached at the time of the confrontation with Fay toward the end of the novel, is meant to be any kind of victory earned by the daughter over Fay. The reason why such crucial points, on which the basic meaning of the novel seems to depend, are still open to speculation is that the reader encounters quite a few instances in which Fay's behavior and speech may be taken as reasonable and even salubrious. At the same time, the reader may feel that to understand the author's intention, one is expected to accept the narrator's moral attitude unquestioningly and start from there. In view of the unresolved issues surrounding *The Optimist's Daughter*, I would like to suggest that a rigorous distinction between author and narrator may be a more effective starting point for analysis.

Reynolds Price in "The Onlooker, Smiling: An Early Reading of *The Optimist's Daughter*" (1969)—actually a review of the earlier, story version in the *New Yorker*—emphasizes the consistency of Laurel's third-person point of view throughout the story: "It is essentially seen and told by Laurel herself" (79). Yet he also confirms, "I take Laurel's understanding [at the end of the story] to be also the author's and ours; there can be no second meaning, no resort to attempt to discredit Laurel's vision" (88). In other words, Price's interpretation is that despite the *limited* and by definition *subjective* third-person point of view of Laurel, which is maintained throughout the story, the final understanding she reaches can be appreciated as universal by the reader as well as the author.

Through the years since the publication of the book version, critics have offered their respective interpretations of the character of Fay, and these have been greatly affected by how the critics conceive of the relationship between author and narrator (or protagonist). Those who accept the character of Fay simply from Laurel's perspective seem to have ignored or made light of the importance of this authorial-narratorial distinction.[4] On the other hand, those critics who recognize this distinction tend to see in Fay a certain asset of "sexuality" and "vitality," qualities that Laurel unconsciously ignores.[5] Gretlund emphasizes Laurel's "limited" point of view (198) and states that Fay offers, in addition to sex appeal, vitality, and spontaneity, "the desire to live fully in the moment" (197), a quality he maintains Laurel ultimately learns to acquire: "Instead of being a load on her mind, the past should enable her to treasure her memory without a sense of guilt, so she can live fully in the present" (204). From a different viewpoint, adhering to a rigorous distinction between author and narrator (or protagonist) in reading *The Optimist's Daughter* leads to a self-reflexive revelation of the roles of the author and the reader in this fiction.

In my discussion on *Losing Battles* above, I argued that the dialogue is intended to bring about in the reader the dialogization, so to speak, of what otherwise would be the effects of numerous dramatic monologues. The reader is given only what each character says, without his or her feelings or thoughts, and is expected to imagine of that character, as Welty explains, "what he thought he said, what he hid, what others were going to think he meant, and what they misunderstand, and so forth," and ultimately to construct a comprehensive story involving the interiority of all the characters. In contrast, *The Optimist's Daughter* is narrated from the limited, single perspective of Laurel as a third person, with her feelings and thoughts extensively reported, together with her and other characters' speech and behavior, but only as Laurel hears and sees them. Hans H. Skei aptly characterizes this style as "monologic": "Perhaps the monologic narrative is modified and finally questioned by the implied author we can establish in this text, . . . who is not necessarily in agreement with the narrator" (124).

To apply the framework I have used to describe the style of *Losing Battles*, *The Optimist's Daughter* presents *a particular version* of the story of Laurel by a narrator who shares Laurel's consciousness, propensities, feelings, and thoughts. Thus the effect of the narrative of *The Optimist's Daughter* is not far from that of a dramatic monologue or a "fallible" narrator, in which the author expects the reader to discover, under the surface story, the subtext of what the narrator consciously or unconsciously conceals as well as reveals or what the narrator's biased eye is blind to, as well as particularly sharpened to. If we call this kind of narrative "monologic," the role of the reader becomes one of *understanding it dialogically,* by noting signs and hints scattered in the characters' speeches and behaviors and in descriptive passages; the author retreats from that eminence where she would exert her authoritative dialogizing power. In this sense, *Losing Battles* and *The Optimist's Daughter,* so unlike at first sight, are actually twin texts, born of the same authorial stance toward fiction.

As early as on the first page of *The Optimist's Daughter,* the narrator's subjectivity is already expressed. Contrasting Laurel's clothes with Fay's, the narrator describes Laurel's suit as "of an interesting cut and texture" (3) and Fay's dress simply as "with the gold buttons" (3), implying that Fay's dress is *not* of any "interesting" quality. Having no way to know how and why the cut and texture of Laurel's suit is "interesting," one is obliged to accept the narrator's evaluation of Laurel's aesthetic sophistication over Fay's gaudy taste. Throughout her stay in New Orleans and the train ride with Fay back to Mount Salus accompanying Judge McKelva's body, the narrator follows the consciousness of Laurel, who cannot but face Fay's (in Laurel's perception) objectionable, insensitive speech and behavior, and these compound her grief over her father's death.

Back in Mount Salus, not only the matters related to Fay and her family but many remarks made by the McKelvas's longtime friends contradict Laurel's expectations. For instance, Major Bullock's eulogy for Judge McKelva, declaring that he, standing before the courthouse all by himself, fearlessly confronted Klansmen who came to free a white murderer, is grossly contrary to Laurel's memory of her father. Laurel keeps on saying in a low voice that this was very unlike her father, to which Major Bullock retorts that she was away in Chicago, whereas he was here in Mount Salus. Laurel is also annoyed that the people at the funeral called her father a "humorist," a "crusader," an "angel on the face of the earth"; she insists, "The least anybody can do for him is *remember* right" (82–83). Even casual remarks by her "bridesmaids" and old acquaintances seem to Laurel to disgrace her father's memory. It is only during her last night at Mount Salus that she reminisces fully about her father and her mother, Becky, and finally about her deceased husband, Phil, without being disturbed by others' versions.

But the next morning Laurel meets Fay, now back from her old home in Texas, and a direct confrontation commences. Laurel's explosion of anger is triggered by the sight of Becky's cherished old breadboard, made for her by Phil years ago, abused and neglected by Fay. Laurel capitalizes on the breadboard to accuse Fay of desecrating Laurel's family's past—her father's, mother's, husband's, and her own—and of having physically abused her father in the New Orleans hospital and thus causing his untimely death. To Laurel's recollection of how Phil carefully made the breadboard and how Becky appreciated the labor and treasured the piece, Fay sneeringly responds that it is "just an old board" (173) and that Becky was not here to make the bread but "died a crazy" (174). Again, in response to the accusation of her having struck Judge McKelva in the hospital bed, Fay shouts back, "I was trying to scare him into living! . . . I was going to make him live if I had to drag him! . . . It's more than anybody else was doing. . . . I was being a wife to him!" (175). To Laurel's condemnation of Fay's inability to see in the breadboard "the whole story[,] . . . the whole solid past" (178), Fay retorts, "Whose story? Whose past? Not mine. . . . The past isn't a thing to me. I belong to the future, didn't you know that?" (178–79). Although some of Fay's earlier remarks and actions might have aroused in the reader some sympathy, it is in this final exchange between Laurel and Fay that the reader gets a first clear glimpse of the legitimacy of Fay's discourse on its own terms. Within the context of the novel, it is also through this exchange that Laurel herself reaches a "new understanding" of the nature of memory:

> The past is no more open to help or hurt than was Father in his coffin. The past is like him, impervious, and can never be awakened. It is memory that is the somnambulist. It will come back in its wounds from across the world, like Phil, calling us by our names and demanding its rightful tears. It will never be impervious. The memory can be hurt, time and again—but in that may lie its final mercy. As long as it's vulnerable to the living moment, it lives for us, and while it lives, and while we are able, we can give it up its due. (179)

At this point Laurel resolves her dismay and anger through an understanding that memory is something one creates by imbuing the past with one's own meanings, namely, that memory is a fiction, what she unwittingly called "the whole story." With this new understanding, Laurel no longer has a reason to feel that her memories have been betrayed and contaminated by Major Bullock, her "bridesmaids," Mr. Cheek, or even Fay.

Yet we should not take Laurel's understanding as the happy denouement of the novel before we have applied it to the memories of Laurel herself. Throughout *The Optimist's Daughter*, the narrator has presented Laurel's consciousness and memories as the novel's truthful and unchangeable center, with any remark or behavior contradicting them treated as untruth or deceit. But now Laurel's own understanding of the vulnerability of human memory nullifies this assumption and exposes the narrator as potentially fallible. Just as the others' memories of Laurel's loved ones are their own creations out of what amounts to the past, so Laurel's memories are no more than fictions assigning her own particular meanings to the past. The reader, dialogizing the narrative, recognizes the weight of this irony, an irony the author intends as the ultimate message of the novel.

One of the titles Welty originally considered for what was to become "The Optimist's Daughter" (the 1969 *New Yorker* version) was "Poor Eyes" (Kreyling 1991, 204). What this discarded title implies may be exactly this irony, that when the protagonist finally sees a truth, the truth serves only to show that one can never see an absolute reality but rather one's version of the reality, one's own fiction. Laurel is the daughter of Judge McKelva and Becky, both of whom suffered from "poor eyes" and died blind under the humiliation of misunderstanding and in "exile"—

he in New Orleans, she far away from her West Virginia mountains. Such therefore will Laurel's own life and death be, she being their faithful daughter; with her "poor eyes" she is destined to see nothing but *her* story and will die in exile in Chicago without even "father, mother, brother, sister, husband, chick nor child" (69) to keep her alive in memory. Yet are not we all, the novel implies, ultimately the children of Judge McKelva and Becky, who will live with only our particular story to see and die blind in the lonely knowledge that nobody else really knows our particular story? Whether this implied message is an expression of pessimism or optimism is again left to the reader to answer. One thing is clear, that memory is understood here to be a fiction capable of suspending the mortality of the person. Those past stories endure in the minds of the living long after the "authors" who lived those stories are dead, because the living, in "reading" the past, appropriate the past in the form of their own stories— memory—to construct their present lives.

This relationship between author and reader is no different from that aimed at in the relationship between the author and the reader of *Losing Battles*. By setting before the reader almost exclusively the actions and speeches of the characters, Welty obliges the reader to fill in the characters' interior and create meaning in *Losing Battles*. The text of *Losing Battles* is similar to the creatures God formed in Genesis, alluded to at the very beginning of the novel, those life forms that He allows Adam to name and thereby endow with meaning, thus passing to him the task of rendering the creatures whole beings. Welty allows each reader to lend meaning to the characters' actions and speeches, thus to complete the wholeness of their beings, with their interiors imagined from the words describing their exteriors.

The kind of authorship that Welty chose to assume in *Losing Battles* and *The Optimist's Daughter* brings to mind a short piece by Jorge Louis Borges. Borges's protagonist in "Everything and Nothing" is a playwright who has formed his characters—Richard, Antony, Macbeth, and the others—so well that the spectators can pour their own meanings into them and interact with them as though they were living like themselves. The playwright, one presumes, should be happy over his achievement, but he has one regret, which he shares with the Author who formed *him:*

> History adds that before or after dying he found himself in the presence of God and told Him: "I who have been so many men in vain want to be one and myself." The voice of the Lord answered from a whirlwind: "Neither am I anyone; I have dreamt the world as you dreamt your work, my Shakespeare, and among the forms in my dream are you, who like myself are many and no one." (249)

Conclusion

Each of Welty's fictions I have discussed in this book embodies a certain aspect of the role and status of fiction and fiction writing. Most of these fictions do not manifestly draw the reader's attention to their own metafictionality. Rather, the metafictional quality one identifies in these fictions is for the most part a subtext—a literary or social subtext, or a combination of the two. Those subtexts are like a foundation fabric fortuitously glimpsed beneath the textile woven from the various elements of the fiction, including the plot, the characters, and the setting. Yet that foundation may be considered all the more intrinsic to the existence of each fiction, because it is something that each of the fictions inherently possesses in order to become what it is.

In the essay "Some Notes on Time in Fiction" (1973), Welty reiterates and expounds on one of the themes in her story "Circe" (1949), an explicitly metafictional theme—rare in her work—and the one from which the title of the present book is taken. By 1973 all her fictions had been published, including the two later novels *The Optimist's Daughter* and *Losing Battles*. The essay suggests that for a quarter-century Welty's focus regarding the role and status of fiction had not changed, or if it had by chance taken another course, it had returned to that expressed in "Circe."

In the essay, as in "Circe," Welty emphasizes the relationship between the nature of fiction and the human condition: "The novel's progress is one of causality, and with that comes suspense. Suspense is a necessity in a novel because it is a main condition of our existence. Suspense is known only to mortals, and its agent and messenger is time. . . . The novelist can never do otherwise than work with time, and nothing in his novel can escape it" (165). Welty's advocacy of the unique significance of "place" in fiction has been widely appreciated, and for good reasons, but it should not be forgotten that Welty understood to the core that the fiction writer's primary and inescapable confrontation is with time, probably the greatest concern of modernism. Since time defines the human condition as mortal, humans are all, Welty is aware, wanderers, seafarers, stargazers (as some of Welty's characters are literally), for they have no sure knowledge of the course of their journey. This lack of knowledge of the future results in the journey being filled with suspense and surprises. Yet it is for this reason that time compels humans to seek ways to overcome and outwit its tyranny. In "Circe," the immortal protagonist laughs at, but at the same time envies, mortals' illusion of controlling time within a fictional time frame of the past, in which suspense and surprise are created by the teller and enjoyed by the listener. This is a "felicity," as Circe calls it, a thing that can be appreciated because of one's being mortal, of not being able to know in real life the effects of time a moment later. As a more realistic realization of the felicity of fiction writing, Welty recognizes in the modernist "stream of consciousness" novels an attempt to humanize, so to speak, rather than overcome, time's tyranny; in it "fiction penetrates chronological time to reach our deepest version of time that's given to us by the way we think and feel" (168). In her own practice, rather than the "stream of consciousness," Welty cultivated what can be called "sideshadowing," a pluralistic perception of the world, demonstrated in the stories collected in *The Bride of the Innisfallen and Other Stories* and "The Demonstrators."

The 1973 essay also recapitulates another aspect of the relationship between human mortality and fiction as represented by Welty in *Losing Battles* and *The Optimist's Daughter*, the idea that I have argued in chapter 10 to be the further deepening of the theme in "Circe." It is about fiction's role of perpetuating the present, ephemeral moment as eternal:

> We are mortal: this is time's deepest meaning in the novel as it is to us alive. Fiction shows us the past as well as the present moment in mortal light; it is an art served by the indelibility of our memory, and one empowered by a sharp and prophetic awareness of what is ephemeral. It is by the ephemeral that our feeling is so strongly aroused for what endures, or strives to endure. One time compellingly calls up the other. Thus the ephemeral, being alive only in the present moment, must be made to live in the novel as *now*, while it transpires, in the transpiring. (168)

The ephemeral, which the fiction writer transforms to the eternal *"now,"* exists not only for the writer but, more importantly, for any reader in the future. An ephemeral moment of the present remains in the text eternally present. Thus the family members at the reunion in *Losing Battles* tell the stories of their past as they *now* think and feel about the events and the people of the past, and they respond to the stories with their mind and heart as they are *now*. The stories take on different meanings depending upon the teller and when they are told, and still different meanings are extracted by each reader and listener. The ephemeral, given a new life by each writer and each reader, lives on. The vulnerability of a story's meaning to each reader's interpretation at each living moment is the inevitable condition for the story's longevity. In *The Optimist's Daughter*, the same concept is applied to memory. The protagonist Laurel believes at the end that memories may be hurt—contaminated and transformed—constantly by the people who remember them, but that due to their vulnerability to the power of the living moment, memories live on for those people. *The Ponder Heart* can be considered Welty's glorification of the vulnerability of mortals' verbal constructs, as they rejuvenate themselves by being destroyed. The essay "Some Notes on Time in Fiction" thus confirms and justifies what Welty has done through the years as a fiction writer.

In her essays and interviews Welty often voiced her views about the difference between the novel and the story. This was a question that she had seriously to address in her creative activity if she was to establish herself as a successfully marketable writer. Knowing her own inclination for the story and recognizing it as her forte, she made it one of her constant efforts throughout her career to reconcile her personal preference for the aesthetic tightness of the story with the mass market's demand for the novel, on which her career after all depended. *Delta Wedding* is a straightforward attempt to develop a story into a novel by spatially juxtaposing, as Kreyling contends, the consciousness of the major characters and by vertically layering social subtexts, as I have shown, in order to achieve the sheer substance of a novel in length and content. In contrast, *The Golden Apples* never abandons the tightly strung unity of the short story and yet secures the attributes Welty supposes concomitant only with the novel, and actually something more. In this sense *The Golden Apples* is truly metafictional, since this new structure informs the meaning of what I believe to be the main theme of the work.

Another point of interest I have indicated is the fact that Welty's fictions often deal with the fact that they are "lies," or illusions. A practical application of this aspect of fiction exemplified in her fictions is to involve the reader in the "play" the author devises. With the full knowledge of its fictionality, its unreality, the reader become complicit in the made-up situations. Some of Welty's fictions reveal her ideas as to why we allow ourselves to be deceived in such a way or what sort of effects this aspect of fiction can produce in the reader. In my view, "Old Mr. Marblehall,"

The Robber Bridegroom, and "The Wide Net" address the first question, that of our willingness to be deceived, from the psychological and metaphysical viewpoints in their respective ways. As for the other question, that of what sort of effects, "Powerhouse" and *Delta Wedding* solidly demonstrate how a playful or the beautiful surface story of unreality can be presented only to waken the reader to the social and institutional immorality and unhappiness in the real world. The camouflaged fictive settings self-reflexively disclose the illusory quality of what is presented in these fictions and point to the reality beneath the illusion.

Finally, I should like to maintain two points, points that are not necessarily related to the metafictional aspect of Welty's fictions but have emerged from this study. One is that although Welty no doubt exhibits some fundamental characteristics of the modernist writer and apparently adheres to the New Critical aesthetic ideals for the most part, some of her fictions—such as *The Ponder Heart*, the stories in *The Bride of the Innisfallen and Other Stories*, and *Losing Battles*—reveal features that can be very well categorized as postmodernist. As my discussions have shown, certain aspects of these fictions echo some of the aesthetic qualities of postmodernism, such as those listed by Ihab Hassan, namely, "Play," "Chance," "Decreation/Deconstruction," "Text/Intertext," or "Indeterminacy" (84–96)* These postmodernistic elements may simply show that a writer never wholly *belongs* to an ism but jumps back and forth, staggering and swaying in literary history in his or her own way, or, more positively, *transforms* the ism to which he or she is supposed to belong. Welty's case could be a testimony to the kind of contention that holds postmodernism as nothing more than "the periodic style- and fashion-change determined by an older high-modernist imperative of stylistic innovation" (Jameson 2). But we can at least say that some of Welty's fictions reveal tendencies and features that we may now identify as poststructuralist or postmodernist and that for Welty modernism and postmodernism are often coexistent within a work.

The second point to note is that Welty has never been the apolitical, socially disengaged writer that still lingers in the minds of such critics as Claudia Roth Pierpont. Although an author is by no means obliged to produce socially and politically conscious works, Welty's oeuvre, if read as literary texts and without bias, shows she has been a politically and

---

*I am using the qualifier "aesthetic" here to distinguish earlier theories of the postmodern by such scholars as Hassan and Leslie Fiedler, whose main concern did not extend to economics and politics, from later more comprehensive conceptions by scholars like Fredric Jameson, who grasps postmodernism as a "cultural dominant" of late capitalism on a world scale.

socially engaged writer. Even one of her earliest stories from the 1930s, "Powerhouse," should be seen as an expression of sympathy for African American entertainers and audiences and indignation at the racism not only of the South but indeed present throughout the United States. My chapter on *Delta Wedding* demonstrates that this novel is nothing less than an indictment of the racist, basically patriarchal (despite some strongly matriarchal elements), and insular aspects of the South. Not many critics would call "The Demonstrators" a work of protest, but as Vande Kieft points out, it is one of the most moving portrayals we have of the complexity of the human relations, including the racial relations, at the time of the civil rights turmoil in Mississippi. Welty's treatment of African American characters in other works that I have discussed in this book— *The Ponder Heart, The Golden Apples, The Optimist's Daughter*—shares among them the author's keen awareness of the kind of complexity in racial relations that characterizes *Delta Wedding* and "The Demonstrators." Not only the African Americans but the underprivileged whites as well are given voice by her pen. *Losing Battles* depicts the reality of the Mississippi poor whites in the 1930s, with their smug insularity and indomitable optimism.

The recognition of these two points comes as a by-product, as it were, of the main subject of my study in this book. Yet if my discussion of the metafictional quality of Welty's fictions has brought to the fore her ideas about the ahistorical question of the "strange felicity" of writing and reading fiction, the postmodernist quality and the political and social criticism observed in her fictions locate this author in a more specific social and historical context. We should not ignore these two features as we undertake to determine Welty's position in the history of American literature.

Notes

INTRODUCTION

1. "Metafiction" seems to have been adopted as a term first by the American novelist and critic William H. Gass in his *Fiction and Figures of Life* (1970) (Waugh 2, 151); it was soon discussed extensively by Robert Scholes in "Metafiction" (1970). The fictions Scholes discusses in his essay as examples of metafiction are John Barth's *Lost in the Funhouse*, Donald Barthelme's *City Life*, Robert Coover's *Pricksongs and Descants*, and W.H. Gass's *In the Heart of the Heart of the Country*. Scholes's selection shows that for him "metafiction" is a product of writers roughly grouped as postmodernist writers who have attempted "to assault or transcend the laws of fiction—an undertaking that can only be achieved from within fictional form" (107). Patricia Waugh's definition given in the text below appears in her *Metafiction: The Theory and Practice of Self-Conscious Fiction* (1984). Jerome Klinkowitz's "Metafiction" (1998) offers an extremely narrow definition, probably having Waugh's definition in mind. He further qualifies the application of the term: "Most properly, the term designates fiction writing that not only draws attention to the author's act of composition but makes that act the work's subject matter" (836).

2. See note 1.

CHAPTER 1

1. The former group of critics includes Chester E. Eisenger in his "Traditionalism and Modernism in Eudora Welty" and Michael Kreyling in his "Modernism in Welty's *A Curtain of Green and Other Stories*." In the latter group, Cheryll Burgess in "From Metaphor to Manifestation: The Artist in Eudora Welty's *A Curtain of Green*" maintains that "Powerhouse" is about storytelling and

storytellers; Benjamin W. Griffith's "'Powerhouse' as a Showcase of Eudora Welty's Methods and Themes" focuses on the mythic allusions and the protagonist's role as both a lover and an artist; Harriet Pollack's "Words between Strangers: On Welty, Her Style, and Her Audience" reveals Welty's conception of the relation between the artist and the audience expressed in "Powerhouse"; Ray B. West, Jr.'s "Three Methods of Modern Fiction: Ernest Hemingway, Thomas Mann, Eudora Welty," one of the earliest criticisms on this story, takes interest in these writers' musical themes; Smith Kirkpatrick's "The Anointed Powerhouse" makes a convincing archetypal approach to the story; William B. Stone focuses on the story's water imagery; Loretta M. Lampkin's "Musical Movement and Harmony in Eudora Welty's 'Powerhouse'" on pagan-Christian motifs in relation to black music. Diana R. Pingatore's *A Reader's Guide to the Short Stories of Eudora Welty* (1996) offers the most comprehensive overview of the criticisms on "Powerhouse" to date.

2. Such essays as "From the Prehistory of Novelistic Discourse" and "Forms of Time and of the Chronotope" discuss the role and potential of laughter in "folkloric structures."

3. Gary Saul Morson and Caryl Emerson in their collaborated work *Mikhail Bakhtin* (1990) sum up the difference in the concept of "carnival" in the revised Dostoevsky book from that in the earlier Rabelais book: "Carnival is now described not as a pure force of antinomian destruction [as in the Rabelais book], but as a clearing away of dogma *so that* new creation can take place. It allows potential to be realized. Laughter, too, is recharacterized in more positive and creative terms" (95).

4. We now know that being "apolitical" was then, as now, nothing but "political." Paul A. Bové's "Agriculture and Academe: America's Southern Question" shows that the American New Criticism grew out of highly specific political contexts in the South, which led to Southern academe's avoidance of social involvement for years to come.

CHAPTER 2

1. Diana Trilling, "Fiction in Review," *Nation*, 11 May 1946, 578, and Isaac Rosenfeld, "Double Standard," *New Republic*, 29 April 1946, 633–34, criticize the work for the lack of social awareness, while "*Delta Wedding*, a Novel," *Christian Century* 63 (22 May 1946), 657–58, complains of the weakness of the plot.

2. "Women's World, Man's Place: The Fiction of Eudora Welty" (1979); "Cultural Patterns in Eudora Welty's *Delta Wedding* and 'The Demonstrators'" (1970).

3. In "Fairchild as Composite Protagonist in *Delta Wedding*," M.E. Bradford maintains that the motif of the game "Go in and out the window" is reflected on the characters' escaping from and rejoining the Fairchild family circle, which constitutes the main action of the novel.

CHAPTER 3

1. One of the most comical and yet bitterly miserable descriptions of Clement's hallucinosis appears when he does battle all night with a willow tree which he takes for a monster or a spirit (105–6). Clement's sweeping vision of the historical process of the New World, which he gains in the stone circle in the woods (141–44), is a thematically important hallucination beyond the power of normal human vision.

2. This kind of reaction is often expressed by critics who emphasize the modal differences in characterization between *The Robber Bridegroom* and its alleged source stories. Barbara Harrell Carson states: "We end up feeling strangely ambivalent even about Salome, whose defiance of all in heaven or on earth demands a kind of admiration as well as scorn" (59); Deborah Wilson, pointing out that "[Salome's] participation in the 'heroic' pioneer expedition destroys all but the greed that motivated the journey all along," maintains that Salome's true heroism is shown toward the end of the novella when "she exerts the only real power she has: this time she *chooses* to be a victim" (65).

CHAPTER 4

1. A similar image is used for Phil Hand in Welty's *The Optimist's Daughter* (1972), who had died an untimely death in the war. He appears in the protagonist Laurel's imagination: "He looked at her out of eyes wild with the craving for his unlived life, with mouth open like a funnel's" (154).

CHAPTER 5

1. Brenda G. Cornell's "Ambiguous Necessity: A Study of *The Ponder Heart*" presents a good discussion of the degree and nature of Joseph Fields and Jerome Chodorov's "rewriting," along with the indications of Welty's uneasiness over their stage adaptation.

CHAPTER 6

1. In his *Eudora Welty's Chronicle: A Story of Mississippi Life*, Albert J. Devlin points out that the dual life of Mr. Marblehall/Mr. Bird reflects the dual character of the city of Natchez: "High on the bluffs, [where the Marblehall mansion stands,] elegant homes and gardens displayed the hopes of Mississippi's direct native aristocracy. Natchez-under-the Hill, [where the Bird home stands,] attracted thieves, gamblers, prostitutes, and all the hardy adventurers who traveled river and Trace in the first quarter of the nineteenth century" (18).

2. The criticisms focusing on the identity of the narrator and the relationship between the narrator and Mr. Marblehall may be categorized into four kinds of views: (1) As seen in Vande Kieft's *Eudora Welty*, the narrator and Mr. Marblehall

are taken as separate individuals, accepting the surface meaning of the story at least regarding this point; (2) represented by Howard's *The Rhetoric of Eudora Welty's Short Stories*, the double life of Mr. Marblehall is considered to be the narrator's fantasy created by his jealousy of the complacent life of Mr. Marblehall; (3) in Pitavy-Souques's "A Blazing Butterfly: The Modernity of Eudora Welty" and Polk's "Welty, Hawthorne, and Poe: Men of the Crowd and the Landscape of Alienation," Mr. Marblehall and the narrator are viewed as the same individual whose double life is purely fictitious and simply the projection of his desire; (4) in Schmidt's *The Heart of the Story: Eudora Welty's Short Fiction* "Old Mr. Marblehall" is considered to be more a story about Mrs. Marblehall and Mrs. Bird, whose lives are suppressed, with the story's narrator seen as a group of women of the city.

CHAPTER 7

1. A rare but major exception to this critical attitude is seen in Patricia S. Yaeger's essay "'Because a Fire Was in My Head': Eudora Welty and the Dialogic Imagination." Drawing on Bakhtin's theory of the novel, Yaeger proceeds to call the work a novel as in the phrase "the last story of Welty's novel" (152).

2. Pitavy-Souques's "Technique as Myth: The Structure of *The Golden Apples*" (1979) observes Welty's use of the Perseus myth as the central theme of "the artist in all roles, Perseus, Medusa and the mirror shield" (262). Recent feminist criticisms include Yeager's 1987 essay, which sees in Welty's treatment of myths a unity of "dialogic" relationship with Yeats's poems, and Rebecca Mark's *The Dragon's Blood: Feminist Intertextuality in Eudora Welty's "The Golden Apples,"* the exhaustive feminist intertextual annotations of which supplement well McHaney's 1973 essay, attempts to testify to Welty's revolutionary rereading of those materials throughout *The Golden Apples*.

3. Later this idea of "organic unity" was expounded by Cleanth Brooks in various ways in his *The Well Wrought Urn* (1947), such as "the 'beauty' of the poem considered as a whole" (194), or "the unification of attitudes into a hierarchy subordinated to a total and governing attitude" (207).

4. In her essay "Writing and Analyzing a Story" (1955), Welty states, "The source of the short story is usually lyrical" (*Eye*, 108).

5. Gary Saul Morson and Caryl Emerson in their *Mikhail Bakhtin: Creation of a Prosaics* argue that Bakhtin is "interested in two distinct views of language and the world, two form-shaping ideologies that have found expression in a large number of novels and a large number of lyric poems. . . . His concern, in other words, is with novel*ness* and lyric*ness*" (319–20).

CHAPTER 8

1. The story first appeared in *Accent* 10 under the title "Put Me in the Sky!"

2. Michael Kreyling's *Eudora Welty's Achievement of Order* (1980) is one of the earliest of the kind (125–26), while other early critics such as D. James Neault

(1978), Ruth M. Vande Kieft (1962, 1987), and Elizabeth Evans (1981) do not incorporate a feminist interpretation of this story. More recent critical works by Ann Romines (1989) and Peter Schmidt (1991), referred to below, treat the story from feminist viewpoints.

3. Kreyling (1980) cites early reviewers' outspoken puzzlement (118–19). Vande Kieft (1962) speaks for the casual reader in saying, "What is any story 'about'?" (152) and even in her later book (1987) uses the words "obscure" and "vagueness" (127). Evans (1981) states that the book "remains a difficult volume, the stories complex, their meanings somewhat elusive" (113).

4. Danièle Pitavy-Souques's "Of Suffering and Joy: Aspects of Storytelling in Welty's Short Fiction" and Noel Polk's "Going to Naples and Other Places in Eudora Welty's Fiction" offer excellent metaphysical critiques of some of the stories.

5. The reference to Bakhtin is not arbitrary. Morson's idea of sideshadowing draws heavily on Bahktin and Isaiah Berlin.

CHAPTER 9

1. For *The Collected Stories* Welty corrected expressions that had become racially inappropriate by that time and also made other textual changes, including some radical deletions in the stories of *The Golden Apples*.

2. The only other works by Welty that explicitly treat current social subjects are, in my opinion, "Flowers for Marjorie" (1937) and "The Whistle" (1938), both of which belong to her earliest collection.

3. For example, from Hardy (1968), immediately after the publication of the story, until Devlin (1983), critics focused on the aspect of the author's response to the actual racial strife, or, like Romines (1979), who interpreted it as a kind of initiation story, had discussed the story's relation to Welty's other works. Prenshaw (1970) indicates the accuracy of Welty's representation of the cultural and social peculiarities of the South and of her depth of thought, which universalizes the peculiarities.

CHAPTER 10

1. The book became an overnight best-seller (and has been in print ever since). All the major journals and newspapers ran a review on it: the *New York Times Book Review, Newsweek, Atlantic Monthly, Saturday Review, New Republic, Washington Post, New Yorker, New York Times, Washington Post Book World,* etc. Concise summaries of the early reviews are given in Kreyling's *Eudora Welty's Achievement of Order* (140–43) and Waldron's *Eudora: A Writer's Life* (294–96). The novel's magnitude, attained through sheer length and the multiplicity of voices of its people despite the short time span of its plot, was compared to the work of Shakespeare, Tolstoy, Mark Twain, or Thomas Mann. Yet this magnitude was also taken cynically by some critics as "endless talk" and "pointless activity" (*New York Times,* quoted in Waldron, 297) and "tiring" (*Newsday,* 2 June 1970). *Time*

listed *Losing Battles* as one of the top ten novels of 1970. It was one of ten nomi-
nees for the National Book Award and one of three finalists for the Pulitzer. Luis
D. Rubin, Jr., one of the first reviewers of the book, declared that Welty was "a
major author, one of the three or four most important writers to come out of
twentieth-century America" (197).

   2. Of the great number of criticisms on *Losing Battles*, the variety of inter-
pretations may be classified as follows. Bridget Smith Pieschel's "From Jerusalem to Jericho: Good Samaritans in *Losing Battles*" and Jan Nordby Gretlund's
Eudora Welty's Aesthetics of Place are representative of discussions that maintain
Welty's admiring, affirmative stand, based on her agrarianism, toward the
Vaughn-Beecham-Renfro reunion. Noel Polk's "Going to Naples and Other
Places in Eudora Welty's Fiction" presents an opposite view, regarding the novel
as "a devastating critique of Welty's native 'place'" (158). As for the kind of
"battles," critical focuses vary a great deal. Michael Kreyling as early as 1980
distinguishes the battles between the mythical and the historical as represented
by the reunion and Julia Mortimer, respectively; Ruth D. Weston in "Eudora
Welty as Lyric Novelist: The Long and the Short of It" sees in the novel "the
eternal human battles against ignorance, poverty, and change" (35) and the individual battles among the characters; Sally Wolff in "'Foes well matched or
sweetheart come together': The Love Story in *Losing Battles*" characterizes the
battle as one between "loyalty to the family and the need for privacy" (86); other
views by Susan V. Donaldson and Douglas Messerli are introduced later in this
text. The novel is also interpreted from the ritualistic, celebratory function of
the reunion by such critics as Seymour Gross in "A Long Day's Living: The
Angelic Ingenuities of *Losing Battles*" and Louise Y. Gossett in "*Losing Battles*:
Festival and Celebration"—"the human genius of inventing meaning through
form" (350). The importance of Welty's view of language in relation to human
existence is the focus of Gray's and Messerli's essays, which are referred to in
the course of my argument. The novel is also interpreted from its epic aspects
in Mary Anne Ferguson's "*Losing Battles* as a Comic Epic in Prose" and in
Darlene Unrue's "*Losing Battles* and Katherine Anne Porter's *Ship of Fools*: The
Commonality of Modernist Vision and Homeric Analogue." Women's roles in
Welty's fictions, including *Losing Battles,* are discussed in Margaret Jones
Bolsterli's "Woman's Vision: The World's of Women in *Delta Wedding, Losing
Battles* and *The Optimist's Daughter*" and Peggy Whitman Prenshaw's "Woman's
World, Man's Place: The Fiction of Eudora Welty," "The Harmonies of *Losing
Battles,*" and "The Construction of Confluence: The Female South and Eudora
Welty's Art." An ingenious comparison of *Losing Battles* with Virginia Woolf's
The Waves is offered by Suzan Harrison in her *Eudora Welty and Virginia Woolf:
Gender, Genre, and Influence.*

   3. The association of watermelon juice with blood also occurs later in the
novel when the reunion members force Gloria down to the ground and, as if in
rape, cram "the flesh of the melon with its blood heat" (269) into her mouth,
forcing her to say she is a Beecham.

   4. Especially some of the earlier criticisms have this tendency. Thomas Daniel
Young's "Social Form and Social Order: An Examination of *The Optimist's*

Daughter" (1979) considers the narrator as "omniscient" (369), and apparently as representing the author; it seems to assume neither Laurel nor the author admits any positive value in Fay's behavior. A similar assumption is seen in such otherwise perceptive explications of the novel as Cleanth Brooks's "The Past Reexamined: *The Optimist's* Daughter" (1972), Vande Kieft's *Eudora Welty* (1987), or Elizabeth Evans's *Eudora Welty* (1981), and also in some more recent essays, such as Mary Ann Wimsatt's "Region, Time, and Memory: *The Optimist's Daughter* as Southern Renaissance Fiction" (1998).

5. Kreyling in his earliest book (1980) compares the *New Yorker* story version and the novel version, observing in the novel the "negative aspects of sex as a weapon" exhibited by Fay, against which Laurel is powerless. His discussion on the novel in his recent book *Understanding Eudora Welty* (1999) focuses on "Fay's surplus" of sexuality, which Laurel lacks and unconsciously forces herself to ignore. He adds, "Since Fay is the future and the future is life, Laurel's 'triumph' might be in name only" (233). Fay's sex appeal and vitality and Laurel's conscious or unconscious ignoring her own defeat in this matter have been pointed out by several other critics. John Edward Hardy's "Marrying Down in Eudora Welty's Novels" (1979), Ruth Weston's "The Feminine and Feminist Texts of Eudora Welty's *The Optimist's Daughter*" (1987), and Suzan Harrison's *Eudora Welty and Virginia Woolf: Gender, Genre, and Influence* (1997) are good examples.

Works Cited

Adams, Timothy Dow. "A Curtain of Black: White and Black Jazz Styles in 'Powerhouse.'" *Notes on Mississippi Writers* 10 (Winter 1977): 57–61.

Albert, Richard M. "Eudora Welty's Fats Waller: 'Powerhouse.'" *Notes on Mississippi Writers* 19, no. 2 (1987): 63–71.

Appel, Alfred, Jr. "Powerhouse Blues." *Studies in Short Fiction* 2 (Spring 1965): 193–203.

Arnold, Marilyn. "The Strategy of Edna Earle Ponder." In *Eudora Welty: Eye of the Storyteller*. Ed. Dawn Trouard. Kent, Ohio: Kent State University Press, 1989. 69–77.

Bakhtin, M.M. "Discourse in the Novel." In *The Dialogic Imagination: Four Essays by M.M. Bakhtin*. Ed. Michael Holquist. Trans. Caryl Emerson and Michael Holquist. Austin: University of Texas Press, 1981. 259–422.

———."Epic and Novel." In *The Dialogic Imagination: Four Essays by M.M. Bakhtin*. Ed. Michael Holquist. Trans. Caryl Emerson and Michael Holquist. Austin: University of Texas Press, 1981. 3–40.

———."Forms of Time and of the Chronotope in the Novel." In *The Dialogic Imagination*. Ed. Michael Holquist. Trans. Caryl Emerson and Michael Holquist. Austin: University of Texas Press, 1981. 84–258.

———. "From the Prehistory of Novelistic Discourse." In *The Dialogic Imagination*. Ed. Michael Holquist. Trans. Caryl Emerson and Michael Holquist. Austin: University of Texas Press, 1981. 41–83.

——— (Bakhtin, Mikhail). *Problems of Dostoevsky's Poetics*. Ed. and trans. Caryl Emerson. Minneapolis: University of Minnesota Press, 1984.

———. *Rabelais and His World*. Trans. Hélène Iswolsky. Bloomington: Indiana University Press, 1984.

Balibar, Etienne, and Pierre Macherey. "On Literature as an Ideological Form." In *Marxist Literary Theory*. Ed. Terry Eagleton and Drew Milne. Oxford: Blackwell Publishers, 1996. 275–95.

Barthes, Roland. "From Work to Text." In *Image-Music-Text*. Trans. Stephen Heath. New York: Hill and Wang, 1977. 155–64.

Bloom, Harold. *Shakespeare: The Invention of the Human*. New York: Riverhead Books, 1998.

———. *The Western Canon: The Books and School of the Ages*. New York: Harcourt Brace, 1994.

Bolsterli, Margaret Jones. "Woman's Vision: The Worlds of Women in *Delta Wedding*, *Losing Battles* and *The Optimist's Daughter*." In *Eudora Welty: Critical Essays*. Ed. Peggy Whitman Prenshaw. Jackson: University Press of Mississippi, 1979. 149–56.

Borges, Jorge Luis. "Everything and Nothing." In *Labyrinths: Selected Stories and Other Writings*. Ed. Donald A. Yates and James E. Irby. New York: New Directions, 1964.

Bourdieu, Pierre. *Outline of a Theory of Practice*. Trans. Richard Nice. Cambridge: Cambridge University Press, 1977.

Bové, Paul A. "Agriculture and Academe: America's Southern Question." In *Mastering Discourse: The Politics of Intellectual Culture*. Durham, N.C.: Duke University Press, 1992. 113–42.

Bradford, M.E. "Fairchild as Composite Protagonist in *Delta Wedding*." In *Eudora Welty: Critical Essays*. Ed. Peggy Whitman Prenshaw. Jackson: University Press of Mississippi, 1979. 201–207.

Brooks, Cleanth. "The Past Reexamined: *The Optimist's Daughter*." *Mississippi Quarterly* 26 (Fall 1973). Reprint in *The Critical Response to Eudora Welty's Fiction*. Ed. Laurie Champion. Westport, Conn.: Greenwood Press, 1994. 226–34.

———. *The Well Wrought Urn: Studies in the Structure of Poetry*. New York: Harcourt, Brace and World, 1947.

Brooks, Peter. *Reading for the Plot: Design and Intention in Narrative*. Cambridge, Mass.: Harvard University Press, 1984.

Burgess, Cheryll. "From Metaphor to Manifestation: The Artists in Eudora Welty's *A Curtain of Green*." In *The Eye of the Storyteller*. Ed. Dawn Trouard. Kent, Ohio: Kent State University Press, 1989. 133–41.

Carson, Barbara Harrel. "Eudora Welty's Dance with Darkness: *The Robber Bridegroom*." *Southern Literary Journal* 22, no. 2 (Spring 1988): 51–68.

———. "In the Heart of Clay: Eudora Welty's *The Ponder Heart*." *American Literature: A Journal of Literary History, Criticism, and Bibliography* 59 (December 1987): 609–25.

Cohn, Alan M. "Welty, Waller, and 'Hold Tight': A Footnote." *Notes on Mississippi Writers* 20, no. 2 (1988): 75–77.

Cohn, David L. "The Deep South: An Editorial." *Saturday Review of Literature* (19 September 1942): 3.

Cornell, Brenda G. "Ambiguous Necessity: A Study of *The Ponder Heart*." In *Eudora Welty: Critical Essays*. Ed. Peggy Whitman Prenshaw. Jackson: University Press of Mississippi, 1979. 208–19.

"*Delta Wedding*, a Novel." *Christian Century* 63 (22 May 1946): 657–58.

Dentith, Simon. *Bakhtinian Thought: An Introductory Reader.* London: Routledge, 1995.

Derrida, Jacques. "Before the Law." In *Acts of Literature.* Ed. Derek Attridge. New York: Routledge, 1992. 181–220.

———. "From Restricted to General Economy: A Hegelianism without Reserve." In *Writing and Difference.* Trans. Alan Bass. Chicago: University of Chicago Press, 1978. 251–77.

Devlin, Albert J. *Eudora Welty's Chronicle: A Story of Mississippi Life.* Jackson: University Press of Mississippi, 1983.

Donaldson, Susan V. "'Contradictors, Interferers, Prevaricators': Opposing Modes of Discourse in Eudora Welty's *Losing Battles.*" In *Eye of the Storyteller.* Kent, Ohio: Kent State University Press, 1989. 32–43.

———. "Recovering Otherness in *The Golden Apples.*" *American Literature* 63 (September 1991): 489–506.

Eagleton, Terry. *Literary Theory: An Introduction.* Oxford: Blackwell, 1983.

Eisinger, Chester E. "Traditionalism and Modernism in Eudora Welty's Fiction." In *Eudora Welty: Critical Essays.* Ed. Peggy Prenshaw. Jackson: University Press of Mississippi, 1979. 3–25.

Evans, Elizabeth. *Eudora Welty.* New York: Frederick Ungar, 1981.

Faulkner, William. "Mississippi." In *Essays, Speeches and Public Letters by William Faulkner.* Ed. James B. Meriwether. New York: Random House, 1954.

Federman, Raymond. "Self-Reflexive Fiction." In *Columbia Literary History of the United States.* Ed. Emory Elliott et al. New York: Columbia University Press, 1988. 1142–57.

Ferguson, Mary Anne. "*Losing Battles* as a Comic Epic in Prose." In *Eudora Welty: Critical Essays.* Ed. Peggy Whitman Prenshaw. Jackson: University Press of Mississippi, 1979. 305–24.

Ferguson, Susan. "The 'Assault of Hope': Style's Substance in Welty's 'The Demonstrators.'" *The Eye of the Storyteller.* Ed. Dawn Trouard. Kent, Ohio: Kent State University Press, 1989. 44–54.

Forster, E.M. *Aspects of the Novel.* 1927. Harcourt, Brace and World, 1954.

French, Warren. "'All Things Are Double': Eudora Welty as a Civilized Writer." In *Eudora Welty: Critical Essays.* Ed. Peggy Whitman Prenshaw. Jackson: University Press of Mississippi, 1979. 179–88.

Freud, Sigmund. *Beyond the Pleasure Principle* [*Jenseits des Lustprinzips*] (1920) *The Complete Standard Edition of the Complete Psychological Works of Sigmund Freud.* Ed. James Strachery. London: Hogarth Press, 1953–74. Vol. 18.

Gass, William H. *Fiction and the Figures of Life.* New York: Knopf, 1970.

Godden, Richard. *Fictions of Labor: William Faulkner and the South's Long Revolution.* Cambridge: Cambridge University Press, 1997.

Gossett, Louise Y. "*Losing Battles*: Festival and Celebration." In *Eudora Welty: Critical Essays.* Ed. Peggy Whitman Prenshaw. Jackson: University Press of Mississippi, 1979. 341–50.

Gray, Richard. "Needing to Talk: Language and Being in *Losing Battles*." In *The Late Novels of Eudora Welty*. Ed. Jan Nordby Gretlund and Karl-Heinz Westarp. Columbia: University of South Carolina Press, 1998. 41–55.

Gretlund, Jan Nordby. *Eudora Welty's Aesthetics of Place*. 1994. Columbia: University of South Carolina Press, 1997.

Griffith, Benjamin W. "'Powerhouse' as a Showcase of Eudora Welty's Methods and Themes." *Mississippi Quarterly* 19 (Spring 1966): 79–84.

Gross, Seymour. "A Long Day's Living: The Angelic Ingenuities of *Losing Battles*." In *Eudora Welty: Critical Essays*. Ed. Peggy Whitman Prenshaw. Jackson: University Press of Mississippi, 1979. 325–40.

Hardy, John Edward. "The Achievement of Eudora Welty." *Southern Humanities Review* 2 (Summer 1968): 269–78.

———. "Marrying Down in Eudora Welty's Novels." In *Eudora Welty: Critical Essays*. Ed. Peggy Whitman Prenshaw. Jackson: University Press of Mississippi, 1979. 93–119.

Harrison, Suzan. *Eudora Welty and Virginia Woolf: Gender, Genre, and Influence*. Baton Rouge: Louisiana State University Press, 1997.

Hassan, Ihab. *The Postmodern Turn*. Columbus, Ohio: Ohio State University Press, 1987.

Holton, Robert. *Jarring Witnesses: Modern Fiction and the Representation of History*. New York: Harvester Wheatsheaf, 1994.

Howard, Zelma Turner. *The Rhetoric of Eudora Welty's Short Stories*. Jackson: University and College Press of Mississippi, 1973.

Humphries, Jefferson, ed. *Conversations with Reynolds Price*. Jackson: University Press of Mississippi, 1991.

Idol, John L., Jr. "Edna Earle Ponder's Good Country People." *Southern Quarterly: A Journal of the Arts in the South* 20, no. 3 (Spring 1982): 66–75.

Jameson, Fredric. *Postmodernism, or, The Cultural Logic of Late Capitalism*. Durham: Duke University Press, 1991.

Keppler, Carl F. *The Literature of the Second Self*. Tucson: University of Arizona Press, 1972.

Kirkpatrick, Smith. "The Anointed Powerhouse." *Sewanee Review* 77 (January–March 1969): 94–108.

Klinkowitz, Jerome. "Metafiction." In *Encyclopedia of the Novel*. Vol. 2. Ed. Paul Schellinger. Chicago: Fitzroy Dearborn, 1998. 836–38.

Kreyling, Michael. *Author and Agent: Eudora Welty and Diarmuid Russell*. New York: Farrar Straus Giroux, 1991.

———. *Eudora Welty's Achievement of Order*. Baton Rouge: Louisiana State University Press, 1980.

———. "Eudora Welty as Novelist: A Historical Approach." In *The Late Novels of Eudora Welty*. Ed. Jan Nordby Gretlund and Karl-Heinz Westarp. Columbia: University of South Carolina Press, 1998. 3–17.

———. "Modernism in Welty's *A Curtain of Green and Other Stories*." *Southern Quarterly* 20 (Summer 1982): 40–53.

———. *Understanding Eudora Welty*. Columbia: University of South Carolina Press, 1999.

Lampkin, Loretta M. "Musical Movement and Harmony in Eudora Welty's 'Powerhouse.'" *CEA Critic* 45 (November 1982): 24–28.

Manning, Carol S. *With Ears Opening Like Morning Glories: Eudora Welty and the Love of Storytelling.* Westport, Conn.: Greenwood Press, 1985.

Mark, Rebecca. *The Dragon's Blood: Feminist Intertextuality in Eudora Welty's* The Golden Apples. Jackson: University Press of Mississippi, 1994.

McDonald, W.U., Jr. "A Checklist of Revisions in Welty *Collected Stories.*" *Eudora Welty Newsletter* 7, no. 1 (1983): 6–10.

McHaney, Thomas L. "Eudora Welty and the Multitudinous Golden Apples." *Mississippi Quarterly* 26 (Fall 1973): 589–624.

———. "Falling into Cycles: *The Golden Apples.*" In *Eudora Welty: Eye of the Storyteller.* Ed. Dawn Trouard. Kent, Ohio: Kent State University Press, 1989. 173–89.

Messerli, Douglas. "'A Battle with Both Sides Using the Same Tactics': The Language of Time in *Losing Battles.*" In *Eudora Welty: Critical Essays.* Ed. Peggy Whitman Prenshaw. Jackson: University Press of Mississippi, 1979. 351–66.

Miller, J. Hillis. "Narrative." In *Critical Terms for Literary Study.* Ed. Frank Lentricchia and Thomas McLaughlin. 2nd ed. Chicago: University of Chicago Press, 1995. 66–79.

Morson, Gary Saul. *Narrative and Freedom: The Shadows of Time.* New Haven: Yale University Press, 1994.

Morson, Gary Saul, and Caryl Emerson. *Mikhail Bakhtin: Creation of a Prosaics.* Stanford, Calif.: Stanford University Press, 1990.

Neault, D. James. "Time in the Fiction of Eudora Welty." In *A Still Moment: Essays on the Art of Eudora Welty.* Ed. John F. Desmond. Metuchen, N.J.: Scarecrow Press, 1978. 35–50.

Peden, William. "The Incomparable Welty." *Saturday Review* 9 (April 1955): 18.

Pierpont, Claudia Roth. "A Critic at Large—A Perfect Lady: How a Shrewd Storyteller Became the Patron Saint of Mississippi." *New Yorker* (5 October 1998): 94–104.

Pieschel, Bridget Smith. "From Jerusalem to Jericho: Good Samaritans in *Losing Battles.*" In *The Late Novels of Eudora Welty.* Ed. Jan Nordby Gretlund and Karl-Heinz Westarp. Columbia: University of South Carolina Press, 1998. 67–83.

Pingatore, Diana R. *A Reader's Guide to the Short Stories of Eudora Welty.* New York: G.K. Hall, 1996.

Pitavy-Souques, Danièle. "A Blazing Butterfly: The Modernity of Eudora Welty." In *Welty: A Life in Literature.* Ed. Albert J. Devlin. Jackson: University Press of Mississippi, 1987.

———. "Of Suffering and Joy: Aspects of Storytelling in Welty's Short Fiction." In *Eudora Welty: Eye of the Storyteller.* Ed. Dawn Trouard. Kent, Ohio: Kent State University Press, 1989. 142–50.

———. "Technique as Myth: The Structure of *The Golden Apples.*" In *Eudora Welty: Critical Essays.* Ed. Peggy Whitman Prenshaw. Jackson: University Press of Mississippi, 1979. 258–68.

Polk, Noel. "Going to Naples and Other Places in Eudora Welty's Fiction." In
    Eudora Welty: Eye of the Storyteller. Ed. Dawn Trouard. Kent, Ohio: Kent
    State University Press, 1989. 153–64.
———. "Welty, Hawthorne, and Poe: Men of the Crowd and the Landscape of
    Alienation." *Literatur in Wissenschaft und Unterricht* 29, no. 4 (1996):
    261–70.
Pollack, Harriet. "Words between Strangers: On Welty, Her Style, and Her
    Audience." In *Welty: A Life in Literature*. Ed. Albert J. Devlin. Jackson:
    University Press of Mississippi, 1987. 54–81.
Porter, Katherine Anne. "Introduction." In Eudora Welty, *A Curtain of Green
    and Other Stories*. Garden City, N.Y.: Doubleday, Doran, 1941.
Prenshaw, Peggy Whitman. "The Construction of Confluence: The Female South
    and Eudora Welty's Art." In *The Late Novels of Eudora Welty*. Ed. Jan
    Nordby Gretlund and Karl-Heiz Westarp. Columbia: University of South
    Carolina Press, 1998. 176–94.
———. "Cultural Patterns in Eudora Welty's *Delta Wedding* and 'The Demon-
    strators.'" *Notes on Mississippi Writers* 3 (Fall 1970): 51–71.
———. "The Harmonies of *Losing Battles*." In *Modern American Fiction: Form
    and Function*. Ed. Thomas Daniel Young. Baton Rouge: Louisiana State
    University Press, 1989.
———. "Sex and Wreckage in the Parlor: Welty's 'Bye-Bye Brevoort.'" *South-
    ern Quarterly* 33 (Winter–Spring 1995): 107–16.
———. "Woman's World, Man's Place: The Fiction of Eudora Welty." In *Eudora
    Welty: A Form of Thanks*. Ed. Louis Dollarhide and Ann J. Abadie. Jack-
    son: University Press of Mississippi, 1979. 46–77.
———, ed. *Conversations with Eudora Welty*. Jackson: University Press of Mis-
    sissippi, 1984.
———, ed. *More Conversations with Eudora Welty*. Jackson: University Press of
    Mississippi, 1996.
Price, Reynolds. "The Onlooker, Smiling: An Early Reading of *The Optimist
    Daughter*." *Shenandoah* 20 (Spring 1969). Reprinted in *Eudora Welty*. Ed.
    Harold Bloom. New York: Chelsea House, 1986. 75–88.
Randisi, Jennifer Lynn. *A Tissue of Lies: Eudora Welty and the Southern Romance*.
    Washington, D.C.: University Press of America, 1982.
Richards, I.A. *Practical Criticism: A Study of Literary Judgment*. New York:
    Harcourt Brace, 1929.
———. *Principles of Literary Criticism*. New York: Harcourt, Brace and World,
    1924.
Rogers, Robert A. *A Psychoanalytic Study of the Double in Literature*. Detroit:
    Wayne State University Press, 1970.
Romines, Ann. "How Not to Tell a Story: Eudora Welty's First-Person Tales."
    In *Eudora Welty: Eye of the Storyteller*. Ed. Dawn Trouard. Kent, Ohio:
    Kent State University Press, 1989. 94–104.
———. "The Powers of the Lamp: Domestic Ritual in Two Stories by Eudora
    Welty." *Notes on Mississippi Writers* 12 (Summer 1979): 1–16.

Rosenfeld, Isaac. "Double Standard." *New Republic* (29 April 1946): 633–34.

Rubin, Louis D., Jr. "Everything Brought Out in the Open: Eudora Welty's *Losing Battles*." In *The Critical Response to Eudora Welty's Fiction*. Ed. Laurie Champion. Westport, Conn.: Greenwood Press, 1994. 196–204.

Schmidt, Peter. *The Heart of the Story: Eudora Welty's Short Fiction*. Jackson: University Press of Mississippi, 1991.

Scholes, Robert. "Metafiction." *Iowa Review* 1 (Fall 1970): 100–115.

Seaman, Gerda, and Ellen L. Walker. "'It's All in a Way of Speaking': A Discussion of *The Ponder Heart*." *Southern Literary Journal* 23, no. 2 (Spring 1991): 65–76.

Skei, Hans H. "The Last Rose of Mount Salus: A Study of Narrative Strategies in *The Optimist's Daughter*." In *The Late Novels of Eudora Welty*. Ed. Jan Nordby Gretlund and Karl-Heinz Westarp. Columbia: University of South Carolina Press, 1998. 122–33.

Snyder, Lynn. "Rhetoric in *The Ponder Heart*." *Southern Literary Journal* 21, no. 2 (Spring 1989): 17–26.

Sterns, Marshall W. *The Story of Jazz*. New York: New American Library, 1958.

Stone, William B. "Eudora Welty's Hydrodynamic 'Powerhouse.'" *Studies in Short Fiction* 11 (Winter 1974): 93–96.

Trilling, Diana. "Fiction in Review." *Nation* 162 (11 May 1946): 578.

Tymms, Ralph. *Doubles in Literary Psychology*. Cambridge: Cambridge University Press, 1949.

Unrue, Darlene. "*Losing Battles* and Katherine Anne Porter's *Ship of Fools*: The Commonality of Modernist Vision and Homeric Analogue." In *The Late Novels of Eudora Welty*. Ed. Jan Nordby Gretlund and Karl-Heinz Westarp. Columbia: University of South Carolina Press, 1998. 94–104.

Vande Kieft, Ruth M. "Demonstrators in a Stricken Land." In *The Process of Fiction*. Ed. Barbara McKenzie. New York: Harcourt, Brace, 1969. 342–49.

———. *Eudora Welty*. Boston: Twayne, 1962.

———. *Eudora Welty*. Revised Edition. Boston: Twayne, 1987.

Waldon, Ann. *Eudora: A Writer's Life*. New York: Doubleday, 1998.

Walker, Ellen L., and Gerda Seaman. "*The Robber Bridegroom* as a Capitalist Fable." *Southern Quarterly* 26, no. 4 (Summer 1988): 57–68.

Waugh, Patricia. *Metafiction: The Theory and Practice of Self-Conscious Fiction*. London: Routledge, 1984.

Weiner, Rachel V. "Eudora Welty's *The Ponder Heart*: The Judgment of Art." *Southern Studies: An Interdisciplinary Journal of the South* 19 (1980): 261–73.

Welty, Eudora. "The Bride of the Innisfallen." In *The Bride of the Innisfallen and Other Stories*. New York: Harcourt Brace Jovanovich, 1955. 47–83.

———. "Circe." In *The Bride of the Innisfallen and Other Stories*. New York: Harcourt Brace Jovanovich, 1955. 102–11.

———. *Delta Wedding*. New York: Harcourt Brace Jovanovich, 1974.

———. "The Demonstrators." In *The Collected Stories of Eudora Welty*. New York: Harcourt Brace, 1980. 608–22.

———. *Eudora Welty Photographs.* Jackson: University Press of Mississippi, 1989.
———. "Fairy Tale of the Natchez Trace." In *The Eye of the Story: Selected Essays and Reviews.* New York: Random House, 1978. 300–314.
———. "Going to Naples." In *The Bride of the Innisfallen and Other Stories.* New York: Harcourt Brace Jovanovich, 1955. 156–207.
———. *The Golden Apples.* 1947. New York: Harcourt Brace Jovanovich, 1977.
———. "Ladies in Spring." In *The Bride of the Innisfallen and Other Stories.* New York: Harcourt Brace Jovanovich, 1955. 84–101.
———. "Looking at Short Stories." In *The Eye of the Story: Selected Essays and Reviews.* New York: Random House, 1978. 85–106.
———. *Losing Battles.* New York: Random House, 1970.
———. "Must the Novelist Crusade?" *The Eye of the Story: Selected Essays and Reviews.* New York: Random House, 1978. 146–58.
———. "No Place for You, My Love." In *The Bride of the Innisfallen and Other Stories.* New York: Harcourt Brace Jovanovich, 1955. 3–27.
———. "Old Mr. Marblehall." In *The Collected Stories of Eudora Welty.* New York: Harcourt Brace Jovanovich, 1980. 91–97.
———. *One Writer's Beginnings.* Cambridge, Mass.: Harvard University Press. 1984.
———. *The Optimist's Daughter.* New York: Random House, 1969.
———. *The Ponder Heart.* New York: Harcourt Brace Jovanovich, 1954.
———. "Powerhouse." In *The Collected Stories of Eudora Welty.* New York: Harcourt Brace Jovanovich, 1980. 131–41.
———. *The Robber Bridegroom.* 1942. New York: Harcourt Brace Jovanovich, 1970.
———. "Some Notes on River Country." In *The Eye of the Story: Selected Essays and Reviews.* New York: Random House, 1978. 286–99.
———. "Some Notes on Time in Fiction." In *The Eye of the Story: Selected Essays and Reviews.* New York: Random House, 1978. 163–73.
———. "The Wide Net." In *The Collected Stories of Eudora Welty.* New York: Harcourt Brace Jovanovich, 1980. 169–88.
———. "Writing and Analyzing a Story." In *The Eye of the Story: Selected Essays and Reviews.* New York: Random House, 1978. 107–15.
West, Ray B. "Three Methods of Modern Fiction: Ernest Hemingway, Thomas Mann, Eudora Welty." *College English* 12 (January 1951): 193–203.
Westarp, Karl-Heinz. "Beyond Loss: Eudora Welty's *Losing Battles.*" In *The Late Novels of Eudora Welty.* Ed. Jan Nordby Gretlund and Karl-Heinz Westarp. Columbia: University of South Carolina Press, 1998. 56–66.
Weston, Ruth D. "Eudora Welty as Lyric Novelist: The Long and the Short of It." In *The Late Novels of Eudora Welty.* Ed. Jan Nordby Gretlund and Karl-Heinz Westarp. Columbia: University of South Carolina Press, 1998. 29–40.
———. "The Feminine and Feminist Texts of Eudora Welty's *The Optimist's Daughter.*" *South Central Review* 4 (1987): 74–91.
White, Hayden. "The Value of Narrativity in the Representation of Reality." In *The Content of the Form: Narrative Discourse and Historical Representation.* Baltimore: Johns Hopkins University Press, 1987.

Wilson, Deborah. "The Altering/Alterity of History in Eudora Welty's *The Robber Bridegroom.*" *Southern Quarterly* 32, no. 1 (Fall 1993): 62–71.

Wimsatt, Mary Ann. "Region, Time, and Memory: *The Optimist's Daughter* as Southern Renaissance Fiction." In *The Late Novels of Eudora Welty.* Ed. Jan Nordby Gretlund and Karl-Heinz Westarp. Columbia: University of South Carolina Press, 1998. 134–44.

Wolff, Sally. "'Foes Well Matched or Sweethearts Come Together': The Love Story in *Losing Battles.*" In *The Late Novels of Eudora Welty.* Ed. Jan Nordby Gretlund and Karl-Heinz Westarp. Columbia: University of South Carolina Press, 1998. 84–93.

Woolf, Virginia. *A Room of One's Own.* 1929. London: Hogarth Press, 1967.

Yaeger, Patricia S. "'Because a Fire Was in My Head': Eudora Welty and the Dialogic Imagination." In *Welty: A Life in Literature.* Ed. Albert J. Devlin. Jackson: University Press of Mississippi, 1987. 139–67.

——— (Yaeger, Patricia). *Dirt and Desire: Reconstructing Southern Women's Writing, 1930–1990.* Chicago: University of Chicago Press, 2000.

Young, Thomas Daniel. "Social Form and Social Order: An Examination of *The Optimist's Daughter.*" In *Eudora Welty: Critical Essays.* Ed. Peggy Whitman Prenshaw. Jackson: University Press of Mississippi, 1979. 367–85.

Index

About the Author

NAOKO FUWA THORNTON is a Professor of English and Comparative Literature at Japan Women's University in Tokyo. She has published Japanese translations of Welty's *The Golden Apples* and *The Ponder Heart*.